REFLECTIVE PRACTICE TO IMPROVE SCHOOLS

SECOND EDITION

To Barb Vallejo and Jane Stevenson, who continue to be our extraordinary reflective practice partners. Thanks for all the learning!

REFLECTIVE PRACTICE TO IMPROVE SCHOOLS

An Action Guide for Educators

Foreword by
Arthur L. Costa

Jennifer York-Barr
William A. Sommers
Gail S. Ghere
Jo Montie

SECOND EDITION

CORWIN PRESS
A SAGE Publications Company
Thousand Oaks, California

For information:

Corwin Press
A Sage Publications Company
2455 Teller Road
Thousand Oaks, California 91320
www.corwinpress.com
SAGE Publications Ltd

1 Oliver's Yard
55 City Road
London EC1Y 1SP
United Kingdom

Sage Publications India Pvt. Ltd.
B-42, Panchsheel Enclave
Post Box 4109
New Delhi 110 017 India

Printed in the United States of America

Library of Congress Cataloging-in-Publication Data

Reflective practice to improve schools : an action guide
for educators / Jennifer York-Barr . . . [et al.].—2nd ed.
    p. cm.
Includes bibliographical references and index.
ISBN 1-4129-1756-5 (cloth) — ISBN 1-4129-1757-3 (pbk.)
    1. Learning, Psychology of. 2. Self-knowledge, Theory of.
3. School improvement programs. I. York-Barr, Jennifer, 1958-
LB1060.R395 2006
370.15'23—dc22

                                        2005021740

This book is printed on acid-free paper.

        06 07 08 09 10 9 8 7 6 5 4 3 2

Acquisitions Editor:	Rachel Livsey
Editorial Assistant:	Phyllis Cappello
Production Editor:	Kristen Gibson
Typesetter:	C&M Digitals (P) Ltd.
Indexer:	Sheila Bodell
Proofreader:	Doris Hus
Cover Designer:	Rose Storey

Contents

List of Tables and Figures

Tables

Figures

Foreword

Meaning making is not a spectator sport. It is an engagement of the mind that transforms the mind. The brain's capacity and desire to find patterns of meaning are keys of brain-based learning. Human beings are active, dynamic, self-organizing systems integrating the mind, body, and spirit. Their natural tendency is to organize experiences into greater levels of complexity and diversity. We never really understand something until we can create a model or metaphor derived from our unique personal world. The reality we perceive, feel, see, and hear is influenced by the constructivist processes of reflection. Humans don't get ideas, they make ideas.

Furthermore, meaning making is not just an individual operation. The individual interacts with others to construct shared knowledge. There is a cycle of internalization of what is socially constructed as shared meaning. Constructive learning, therefore, is viewed as a reciprocal process in that the individual influences the group, and the group influences the individual.

Children come fully equipped with an insatiable drive to explore, to experiment, and to inquire. Toddlers are in a constant state of exploring everything they can lay their hands, eyes, and lips on. They live in a state of continuous discovery: dismayed by anomaly, attracted to novelty, compelled to mastery, intrigued by mystery, curious about discrepancy. They derive personal and concrete feedback from their tactile and kinesthetic adventures. Their brains are actually being transformed with each new experience.

Unfortunately, the educational process often is oriented toward controlling rather than learning, rewarding individuals for performing for others rather than cultivating their natural curiosity and impulse to learn. Our fragmented curriculum teaches us, from an early age, competitiveness and reactiveness. We are trained to believe that deep learning means knowing accepted truths rather than developing capacities for effective and thoughtful action; acquiring knowledge is for passing tests rather than accumulating wisdom and personal meaning. We are taught to value certainty rather than doubt, to give quick answers rather than to inquire, and to know which choice is correct rather than to reflect on alternatives.

Learning is perceived to have little or no relevant application beyond the school to everyday living, further inquiry, or knowledge production.

Schools and classrooms today are busy, active places in which students and teachers are pressured with high-stakes testing to learn more, to learn faster, and to be held accountable for demonstrating to others their achievement of specified standards and mastery of content. For that reason, classrooms are much more present- and future-oriented than they are past-oriented, and it is often easier to discard what has happened and simply move on. Thus children, whose natural tendency is to create personal meaning, are gradually habituated to think they are incapable of reflecting on and constructing meaning on their own. Eventually, students become convinced that knowledge is accumulated bits of information and that learning has little to do with their capacity for effective action, their sense of self, and how they exist in their world. Later, as they mature, they may confront learning opportunities with fear rather than mystery and wonder. They seem to feel better when they know rather than when they learn. They defend their biases, beliefs, and storehouses of knowledge rather than inviting the unknown, the creative, and the inspirational. Being certain and closed provides comfort, whereas being doubtful and open causes fear. Life experiences and actions are viewed as separate, unrelated, and isolated events rather than as opportunities for continuous learning. Psychologists refer to this syndrome as an *episodic grasp of reality.*

Schools' and districts' improvement efforts may also signal an episodic approach. Proudly striving to keep abreast of educational improvement practices, some schools adopt an array of innovations (block scheduling, cross-grade groupings, multiple intelligences, interdisciplinary instruction, technology, mentoring, national standards, and so forth). Whereas a great deal of time may be spent in planning, limited time is spent in reflecting. As a result, teachers and administrators soon become impervious to integrating all the disparate pieces. In such an intellectually barren school climate, some teachers and administrators understandably grow depressed. Their vivid imagination, altruism, creativity, and intellectual prowess soon succumb to the humdrum, daily routines of unruly students, irrelevant curriculum, impersonal surroundings, and equally disillusioned coworkers. In such an environment, the likelihood that staff members would value reflectivity would be marginal.

The authors of this richly documented and valuable book provide a brighter vision. They believe that the organization that does not take time to reflect does not have time to improve and that reflective organizations view school improvement from a broader perspective, as a process of revealing and emancipating human and organizational resourcefulness. They make a strong case for the less-is-more principle and believe that to take the time, to set the tone, and to provide the opportunities for reflection prove beneficial not only for students but also for entire faculties. The time and effort invested in reflection yield a harvest of greater student learning, higher teacher morale, enhanced feelings of efficacy, and a more collaborative professional community.

They propose that a major but often overlooked goal of education should be habitual reflection on one's actions so as to maximize the autonomous, continual, and lifelong construction of meaning from those experiences. They offer compelling evidence that

Reflecting on one's own work enhances meaning

Constructing meaning from experiences enhances the applicability of that knowledge beyond the situation in which it was learned

Insights and complex learning result from reflecting on one's experiences

Reflecting on experiences is amplified when done with partners and in group settings

Reflection by individuals is signaled and encouraged when reflection is implicit in the organization's values, policies, and practices

Maximizing meaning from life's experiences requires enhancing and amplifying the human capacities for reflection. To be reflective means to mentally wander through where you have been and try to make some sense out of it. Reflection involves such habits or dispositions as:

Metacognition: Thinking about thinking and conducting an internal dialogue before, during, and after an event

Connecting information to previous learning

Drawing forth cognitive and emotional information from several sources: visual, auditory, kinesthetic, tactile

Acting on and processing the information—synthesizing, evaluating

Applying insights to contexts beyond the one in which they were learned

As individuals, staffs, and organizations reflect on their learning, they gain important information about how they perceive the efficacy of their planning, experimenting, data gathering, assessment, and self-modification. These experiences provide opportunities to practice the habit of continuous growth through reflection. The authors refer to this as the *Reflective Practice Spiral.* Seizing opportunities to reflect individually, in partnerships, and in group situations within an atmosphere of trust, individuals, groups, and schools begin to learn how to become a continuously growing and learning professional community.

Reflection is not just kid stuff. The authors make a strong case for habitual reflection throughout the learning community—in students, teachers, administrators, and parents—as well as for integrating reflectivity in organizational practices. Because imitation is the most basic form of learning, impressionable students often need to see adults—parents, teachers, and administrators—reflect on their practice. Adults are not only facilitators of meaning making but also models of reflection. Their role is to help learners approach an event in a thoughtful and strategic way, to help monitor their progress during the experience, and to construct meaning from the content learned as well as from the process of learning it—and then to modify one's actions and apply those learnings to other contexts and settings. Educators in reflective schools and classrooms seek to ensure that all the inhabitants are fully engaged in the making of meaning, organizing experiences and activities so that stakeholders are the producers of knowledge rather than just the consumers of knowledge.

If the goal is to engage in deep reflection on one's work so as to make life experiences meaningful and to acquire the humility of continuous learning, then potent strategies must be employed in all quarters of the organization, for students, teachers, and administrators, as well as at all levels of the school community, in the classroom, in the school, in the school district, and in the community. Developing habits of continuous growth requires not only the capacity to be self-reflective; time also must be regularly scheduled to reflect on learning. Opportunities must be seized; strategies must be experimented with and evaluated for their productivity. And that is what this book so abundantly furnishes: clear directions for engaging in reflection individually, with partners, and in small and large groups; creative techniques for engaging in meaning making, clever ways to find the time, and practical strategies for deliberately setting an organizational tone of reflectivity.

We must vow to serve and maintain this natural tendency of humans to inquire and experience and, then, through reflection, find pattern, integrate meaning, and seek additional opportunities to satisfy the human propensity for learning. A goal of education, therefore, should be to recapture, sustain, and liberate the natural, self-organizing, learning tendencies inherent in all human beings: curiosity and wonderment, mystery and adventure, humor and playfulness, connection finding, inventiveness and creativity, continual inquiry, and insatiable learning through reflection.

The school that commits its resources of time, energy, and talent to reflection makes a clear statement of its valuing of the continuous intellectual growth for all its inhabitants and its desire to make the world a more thoughtful place.

—Arthur L. Costa, EdD
Granite Bay, California

Preface

Reflective Practice to Improve Schools: An Action Guide for Educators is about tapping internal hopes and desires that inspire continuous learning by educators who, in turn, inspire and nurture continuous learning by today's young people in schools. As with the first edition, we are drawn to images of nature, nurture, and growth and bristle from images of fixing inadequacies or remediating deficiencies. Authentic and lasting change is motivated internally. We are compelled by the thoughts of John Goodlad, who distinguishes between conceptions of *reform* and *renewal* in the context of education. He explains,

> [Reform suggests] somebody is trying to do something to somebody else who is thought to be wrong and who will be reformed if he or she follows these directions. By contrast, in renewal, [insiders] want to change and to do so in the light of knowledge, in the light of inquiry into what is needed. It's the difference between digging up a garden to replace all the plants with something else and nurturing the garden. (Ferrace, 2002, p. 31)

This is a book about renewal and renewing of individuals and schools. In the five years since our first edition was published, there has been an increasing stream of literature on the topic of reflective practice. Still dominant is literature about reflection in preservice teacher education. Adding to this core is literature from the fields of nursing, adult education, and professional or ongoing development for practicing educators. Emergent emphases include use of technology to support reflection, engaging students in reflective practice, and using reflection to foster cultural proficiency. Further, there are even more accounts of meaningful, ongoing, and collaborative reflective practice among educators in the context of instructional teams and also schoolwide. Importantly, there is a sharper focus on reflection as a means for advancing teaching and learning practices with the explicit intent of increasing student achievement. We view the expanding literature base on reflective practice, including research on its effectiveness, as a sign of hope and encouragement that more reflection and learning is and can be happening in the lives of educators, to the ultimate benefit of students.

We believe that, at its core, reflective practice is about tapping into things deeply human: the desire to learn, to grow, to be in community with others, to contribute, to serve, and to make sense of our time on earth. We believe the vast majority of educators have chosen this most noble of professions in hopes of making a positive difference in the lives and development of young people and, in so doing, making a difference in societal life for years to come. We believe this work is enormously challenging given complex contexts of practice, the wide variety of individuals and communities with whom educators engage, and the unrelenting pressure to perform and be accountable. We believe that effective teaching involves both the hard focus on standards, instruction, and outcomes and the softer focus on relationships, intuition, and emotion. Students remind us that both caring and competence are necessary teacher attributes. Without care, there is no connection to the competence. Without competence, there is no respect.

We are concerned about the prevalence of structures and cultures in schools that disallow or, at least, impede our natural tendencies to learn, to connect, to create, and to contribute. Working in schools can feel like living in a container, with limited space, time, and access to nutrients. Plants in such environments eventually wither and die. They are cut off from essential nutrients. Their growth is constrained, then deformed, and eventually terminated. The human corollary is alarmingly clear. When teachers stop learning, stop connecting, stop caring, stop showing up, we believe, as Edward Deming asserted many years ago, much of the reason lies in the culture and the structure of the environment. Fortunately, much has been learned about how to initiate and sustain the process of re-creating culture, structure, expectations, and support such that educators are renewed in their development work with children.

Reflective practice is at the root of renewed life and energy in schools. Trust is at the root of collaborative cultures that sustain growth. Reflective practice is the vital and largely untapped resource for significant and sustained effectiveness. Experience by itself is not enough. Reflection on experience with subsequent action is the pathway to renewal and continuous improvement. Reflection is a means for examining beliefs, assumptions, and practices. It can lead to encouraging insights about instructional effectiveness. It can also result in the discovery of incongruities between espoused beliefs and actual actions. Either way, the self-awareness gained through reflection can motivate individuals to initiate changes in practice to enhance student learning. Effective implementation of reflective practice requires continuous development of both individual and organizational learning capacities. The hectic pace and rigid structures in many of today's schools make it difficult to take time out to reflect and learn. The learning demands, however, continue to escalate for both students and staff.

The desired outcomes for readers of this book are to understand the potential, if not the necessity, of reflective practice to improve teaching and learning in schools; to initiate or extend individual commitments to reflective practice as a way to continuously learn and improve educational practice; and to support implementation of individual and collaborative reflective practices within schools. Implied is the assumption that in order for students to learn well in school, so, too, must the community of educators who encircle them. In the words of Art Costa, who wrote the foreword for both the first and second editions of this book and who is renowned for his work in cognitive coaching, "If we don't provide intellectually stimulating environments for teachers, why do we think they will provide that for students?"

This book offers a framework and strategies for thinking and acting as reflective educators. It is organized into seven chapters. In Chapter 1, we define reflective practice, provide a rationale for its potential to improve schools, describe characteristics of reflective educators, and present the Reflective Practice Spiral as the organizing framework for the book. This framework asserts that the place to begin implementation of reflective practices is with oneself. From that base, reflective practice can expand to include colleagues throughout the school and organization. In Chapter 2, we identify and describe fundamental considerations for the design and development of reflective practices, including principles of adult learning, personal capacities for promoting trust and thinking, designs to promote staff learning, and meaningful topics or emphases for reflection. In Chapters 3 through 6, we work through the levels of the Reflective Practice Spiral to provide examples of individual reflective practice (Chapter 3), partner reflective practice (Chapter 4), reflective practice in small groups or teams (Chapter 5), and reflective practices that extend schoolwide (Chapter 6). Finally, in Chapter 7, we share lessons learned from our experiences working with educators and schools to implement reflective practices. We also offer ideas and strategies for remaining hopeful about possibilities in our work. At the end of every chapter, we include a reflection page for you to write down your own reflection with an aim toward application. New to this second edition are greater attention to reflection for fostering equity and cultural competence. There are more strategies for individual reflection as a means of continually clarifying, grounding, and refining both purpose and practice. There are new examples from practice, including more administrator and schoolwide examples. We also included, at the end of the book, a Resources section of reflection protocols that can be copied and used to guide reflective practice.

As with the first edition, the primary audiences for this book are teacher leaders, staff-development specialists, program coordinators, site administrators, and other educators who assume responsibility for renewal, improvement, and staff development in their school communities. Faculty involved in preservice, in-service, and ongoing service in the development of teachers and administrators may also find this book to be a useful resource, as it offers foundations, strategies, and examples for continuous learning and development of the professional educator. To this original list we add "positive deviants" as an intended audience. Since the first edition, the concept of positive deviance, grounded in the work of Jerry Sternin, an international development specialist for Save Our Children, has taken root in some educational circles (described more fully in Chapter 2). Briefly, positive deviants are individuals who thrive in situations that others do not and would not necessarily be expected to. In the context of education, positive deviants are those individuals who just continue along doing good works and inspiring others to do the same. They are the seemingly innate reflective practitioners. They continue to think and learn and grow and do, despite what seem to be constraining forces and conditions around them. We intend this book for the positive deviants among us, who we hope will feel affirmed and supported in extending their enviable and attainable propensity for growth and renewal. Maybe this book can serve as a lifeline to those who know it can be different and who continue to see possibilities and align their actions with these positive future visions. We believe that now more than ever before, educators must continuously and meaningfully reflect on their practice—by themselves and with their colleagues. We look forward to more learning about reflective practice and its results for years to come. We are convinced of the extraordinary talent, good intentions, and steadfast commitments demonstrated by the vast majority of practicing educators in K–12 schools. We are equally convinced that without significant advances in the capacity of individuals and schools to foster continuous renewal and improvement, the demands on educators will exceed their capacity to promote high levels of learning for all students. We offer this book as encouragement and reference for individual and collective efforts to create schools in which both students and adults continually learn. A commitment to reflective practice is a journey toward realizing our potential as educators and human *beings,* not only human doings.

ACKNOWLEDGMENTS

This book represents a collective effort not only among the four authors but also of a larger community of educators who dedicate themselves to creating schools that promote high levels of learning for students and staff. Specifically, we extend our heartfelt thanks and deepest respect to Barb Vallejo, Jane Stevenson, Nancy Nutting and Cindy Stevenson, Jim Roussin, Diane Zimmerman, David Schumaker, Roanne Elliott, Scott McLeod, Gary Aylward, Andrea Forcier, and Sarah Holm for your contributions to the field-based examples of reflective practice. Your persistence and creativity are an inspiration!

We are grateful to Dr. Art Costa for his review of this second manuscript and the gift of the foreword for this book. Over the years, your wisdom and insights about reflection, learning, and unleashing the enormous capacity within people have been a source of great inspiration and intellectual intrigue.

We express sincere appreciation to Dana Setterholm, who assisted with searching the library for updated literature on reflective practice. We also acknowledge Rachel Livsey and the team at Corwin Press for their patience and enthusiasm during the revision and for their expert preparation in the final stages of development.

Finally, and most important, we are particularly blessed by the love, patience, understanding, and encouragement expressed by our partners, Dean, Liz, Dave, and Carl, and by our children, Jason, Justin, Sam, Temple, Perry, Erin, Aaron, Chris, Shannon, Emma, and Amelia. You are our inner circle of support. You ground us as we attempt to "walk our talk" in living a life of service to children, educators, and the field of education. Our parents, too, Jim and Barbara, Bill and Frances, Howard and Kathy, and Len and Carol, are gratefully acknowledged for the many seeds they planted and nurtured from which we grew into grown-ups who care deeply about education and about the children who are our future. We love and appreciate you, beyond what words can express.

Thank you *all!*

Corwin Press gratefully acknowledges the contributions of the following reviewers:

Michele R. Dean
Principal, Montalvo Elementary School
Ventura Unified School District
Ventura, CA

Janet Crews
Teacher
Wydown Middle School
Clayton, MO

Kate Gillan
Director of Social Studies K–8
East Irondequoit Central Schools
Rochester, NY

About the Authors

Jennifer York-Barr is associate professor in the Department of Educational Policy and Administration at the University of Minnesota–Minneapolis. She received her PhD from the University of Wisconsin–Madison. Her work focuses on how educators work together to support student learning, particularly students with various exceptionalities. She is energized by learning with (and from) practicing PreK–12 colleagues through teaching and school-based research and development activities. She serves as faculty coordinator for graduate programs in educational administration, teacher leadership, and staff development. Jennifer has been honored with two distinguished teaching awards. She has authored more than 100 publications, most of which are focused on instructional collaboration, inclusive schooling, teacher leadership, and professional learning.

William A. Sommers, Ph.D., is currently a program manager for SEDL, Southwest Educational Development Laboratory in Austin, Texas, and a Senior Fellow at the University of Minnesota in the Urban Leadership Academy. Before retiring in June 2005, he had been the principal of Chaska High School in Chaska, Minnesota. He has been in K–12 education for thirty-five years as a teacher, assistant principal, and principal in urban, suburban, and rural schools. He has been an adjunct faculty member at Hamline University, the University of St. Thomas, and St. Mary's University. Bill has written five books on school leadership, professional development, and reflective practice. He consults and trains in the areas of cognitive coaching, conflict management, organizational development, understanding poverty, group-dynamics facilitation, thinking skills, and brain research. As part of his doctoral program, his dissertation researched teaching and modeling reflective practice and how this affected students in the classroom. With a minor in industrial relations, he reads books and articles constantly in the area of business management and leadership in addition to educational literature. He sees that solutions in the future for our complex problems will be a combination of education and business communities. Learning is his main personal goal, but he worries about the continual separation of the haves and have-nots. Learning is about freedom, and education gives people the freedom to make good choices.

Gail S. Ghere is an education and program evaluation consultant. She received her doctorate in educational policy and administration with an emphasis in program evaluation from the University of Minnesota. She has more than twenty-five years of experience working in rural, suburban, and urban public schools. Currently, she divides her time between the Saint Paul Public Schools facilitating special education–general education collaboration and program development, and program evaluation consultation in K–12 and higher education. Gail is the coauthor of several publications focused on collaboration, program evaluation, and paraprofessional development. Her belief in creating inclusive learning opportunities for all students has continually led her to be involved in collaborative projects where reflection is an integral part of adult learning.

Jo Montie is a learner, teacher, and gardener of inclusive community. Jo is also an adjunct faculty member at the University of St. Thomas School of Education, where she works with teachers and student teachers who teach students with disabilities. She holds an MA in educational psychology from the University of Minnesota, and her professional work of over seventeen years has included serving as a special education teacher, conflict resolution and inclusive education consultant, and project coordinator with inclusive education initiatives. The children and adults in her life teach Jo about the importance of living in the present moment, developing our reflective capacities, and being surrounded by a web of loving relationships.

1

Reflective Practice for Continuous Learning

The ultimate guardians of excellence are not external forces, but internal professional responsibilities.

—Paul Ramsden (1992, p. 221),
Learning to Teach in Higher Education

Learning is the foundation of individual and organizational improvement (Argyris, 1977; Argyris & Schon, 1974; Senge, 1990; Starkey, 1996; Wheatley, 1992). Learning requires reflection. From an individual perspective, "It can be argued that reflective practice . . . is the process which underlies all forms of high professional competence" (Bright, 1996, p. 166). From an organizational perspective, reflective practice is a powerful norm that is required for continuous improvement of teaching and learning practices that results in high levels of student achievement (DuFour & Eaker, 1998; Garet, Porter, Desimone, Birman, & Yoon, 2001; Hawley & Valli, 2000; Ingvarson, Meiers, & Beavis, 2005; Kruse, Louis, & Bryk, 1995; Osterman & Kottkamp, 2004; Senge et al., 2000). Reflective practice is the means by which learning, renewal, and growth continue throughout the development of career educators (Steffy, Wolfe, Pasch, & Enz, 2000). Sparks-Langer and Colton (1991) explain the emergence of reflective practice in schools:

> The shift toward an interest in reflective thinking has come about partly as a reaction to the overly technical and simplistic view of teaching that dominated the 1980s. Gradually, however, experts in supervision, staff development, and teacher education have begun to recognize that teaching is a complex, situation-specific dilemma ridden endeavor. . . . Today, professional knowledge is seen as coming both from sources outside the teacher and from the teachers' [sic] own interpretations of everyday experience. (p. 37)

Most educators—both teachers and administrators—experience a continuously hectic pace in their daily professional lives. Such a pace is not conducive to reflection and learning. The dominant culture in many schools is one of doing, with little or no time for reflection and learning. The context of teaching has, in fact, been referred to as *hot action*, meaning that "educators must develop habits and routines in order to cope; and [that] self-awareness is difficult as there is little opportunity to notice or think about what one is doing" (Eraut, 1985, p. 128). It is not unusual for teachers to put aside carefully constructed lessons because of unanticipated events, circumstances, or responses. It is also not unusual for those same lessons to become fragmented as a result of the comings and goings of students and staff in classrooms. Educators routinely juggle multiple tasks, process information on many levels, manage a continual stream of interruptions, and make on-the-spot decisions to meet the changing needs and demands in the teaching environment. All of us continually make midcourse corrections based on feedback, monitoring others, and self-referencing our own speed and actions.

In the 1950s, studies conducted by Harvey (1967) revealed that air traffic controllers manage the greatest number of mental tasks and that teachers are number two in this regard. Jackson (1968) says teachers make more than three thousand decisions each day. And we wonder why teachers are tired? The intensity of work for both teachers and administrators does, indeed, compare well with that experienced by air traffic controllers. Teachers keep an eye on the big picture and simultaneously oversee the nuance and details of daily practice. Glickman (1988) describes an inherent dilemma for the teaching profession as having "knowledge but not certainty" (p. 63). Within each specific teaching context lie multiple and unpredictable circumstances that require spontaneous and unique responses. The demand for accountability and the steady flow of curricular and instructional initiatives add to the pressured context of teaching. The critical balance between pressure and support for improvement (Fullan, 2001b) is almost always tilted toward the side of pressure. To change our practices, to change our beliefs, and to alter our own theories of change, we must slow down and have reflective conversations that allow us to think through possible changes. As Kagan (1969) writes, reflection reduces error rates. Shifting from a culture of doing to a culture of learning and doing, however, is not easily accomplished.

Given these challenging context variables, why is it reasonable to assume that significant improvements in educational practice are possible? What changes in school culture are necessary to support continuous learning by educators? Where does an individual educator start? A primary purpose of this book is to support practicing teachers and principals in the development of capacities within themselves and within their schools to continuously learn and improve by embedding norms of reflective practice into their work. A major premise is captured by the Chinese proverb "Sometimes you must go slow to go fast." Reflective practice cannot be done in the fast lane. Although much of educational practice occurs in the fast lane, educators must locate a rest area to reflect on past practices and to determine adjustments for future practice.

This chapter begins with a brief review of historical and theoretical contributions to reflective practice. Then, multiple perspectives on the meaning of reflective practice are considered. Next, a rationale for the potential of reflective practice to improve schools is articulated and characteristics of reflective educators are described. Presented last is the *Reflective Practice Spiral*, which serves as the organizing framework for this book. This framework suggests that the seeds of reflective practice begin first within individuals and then, with continuous nurturing, spread and take root in the broader educational community.

WHERE DID REFLECTIVE PRACTICE COME FROM?

> A tree has a growth spurt, but it is grounded by the depth of its roots.
>
> —Natalie Goldberg (1993),
> *Long, Quiet Highway: Waking Up in America*

Understanding some of the historical and theoretical roots of reflective practice may support and even inspire educators already committed to strengthening their reflective capacities. For others, learning more about the origins and theory may address some healthy skepticism surrounding reflective practice: Is reflective practice new, or even New Age? As one of the latest educational buzzwords, is reflective practice an initiative soon to fade away and be replaced by another initiative claiming to be a panacea for educational problems? Should we simply hold our breath because "this, too, shall pass"? Although reasons abound for educators to be cautious of blindly embracing any new initiative, reflective practice has deep roots and is firmly planted historically. Its knowledge base has continued to expand, and we believe it holds much promise for meaningful educator development and school renewal that benefits students.

Thought about reflection and reflective practice has evolved over many decades, if not centuries, through carefully constructed theory and research applications. Numerous philosophers, theorists, teacher educators, and researchers have contributed to this body of knowledge. John Dewey is frequently recognized as the eminent 20th-century influence on reflection in education (Fendler, 2003; Rodgers, 2002; Sparks-Langer & Colton, 1991; Zeichner & Liston, 1996). His work, however, drew from much earlier Eastern and Western philosophers and educators, including Buddha, Plato, and Lao-tzu. More recently, the work of Donald Schon (1983, 1987) has inspired a resurgence of interest in reflective practice in the field of education.

The collective literature on reflective thinking (see Table 1.1) reveals numerous common themes. Reflective thinking's origins reach back centuries to early philosophical works. Reflection is viewed as an active thought process aimed at understanding and subsequent improvement. Both personal and contextual variables influence reflective processes and outcomes. Reflection occurs in different ways and for different purposes, yielding different results (Haefner, 2004; Perry & Power, 2004; Pultorak, 1996; Reiman, 1999; Risko, Vukelich, & Roskos, 2002). Reflection that considers social, moral, and ethical perspectives has the potential to affect community values and action.

Most of the perspectives shared in Table 1.1 appear reasonably aligned. There are, however, distinctions of particular interest. In education literature, John Dewey and Donald Schon are two of the most cited contributors to foundational concepts of reflective practice. Careful examination of their views reveals significant differences. Dewey, whose views emerged during the Progressive Era, when scientific advances were shaping education and social science, emphasized not just rigor but specific consideration of scientific knowledge. In contrast, Schon, nearly half a century later, emphasized context and experiential knowledge. His work held strong appeal for educators in the 1980s, when validation of knowledge gained from professional practice served to support efforts aimed at professionalizing teaching. Fendler (2003) observes, "These days the meaning of reflective practice is riddled with tensions between Schon's notion of practitioner-based intuition, on the one hand, and Dewey's notion of rational and scientific thinking on the other hand" (p. 19).

Considered in context, the views of Dewey and Schon and the embracing of those views by educators make good sense. Evident in current practice is an integration of these perspectives such that both research-based and experiential, context-based knowledge are viewed as important

Table 1.1   Significant Contributions to Thought About Reflective Practice

Buddha, 624 BC (Nhat Hanh, 1993; Suzuki, 1982)

- A core teaching involves awareness of impermanence and the teaching of transience or change. Because change is always occurring, an emphasis is placed on being fully aware and *mindful* of the present moment.
- Buddhism emphasizes the direct experience of reality. "Direct practice-realization, not intellectual research, brings about insight. Our own life is the instrument through which we experiment with truth" (Nhat Hanh, 1993, p. 8).
- Deep listening and compassionate responses are a part of Buddha's teachings. Encourages an open, nonjudgmental mind, "a mind that is free of defilement and distortion" (Goldstein & Kornfeld, 1987, p. 78).

Socrates (who was born sometime between 471 BC and 469 BC)

- Known for his famous phrase "The unexamined life isn't worth living," as quoted by Plato in *Apology*, suggesting that behind every experience there is room for interpretation of the meaning of that experience. It is through our interpretation of what our life is amounting to that our life becomes worth living (Robinson, 1997).
- The Socratic method has led to a theory of education grounded in skepticism and a "dialectic" approach of questioning and answering with the goal to build more "consistent thinking with a view to consistent action" as a goal ("The Socratic Method and Doctrine," 2002, retrieved March 21, 2005, from http://www.2020site.org/. Click on "The Life of Socrates," under "History").

John Dewey, 1933; 1938

- Views the purpose of education as promoting intellectual, social, and moral growth of the individual in order to create a strong democratic society.
- Interested in how people think when faced with real and relevant problems.
- Views learning as a reflective process on a continual series of experiences (described as interactions between an individual and his or her surrounding context) from which continuity of meaning occurs over time.
- Reflective thinking involves a systematic, scientific process of describing experience, articulating questions that arise from experience, generating hypotheses which include considering sources outside oneself, and taking intelligent action to test hypotheses.

Max van Manen, 1977; 2002

- Suggests three levels of reflectivity to describe various aims of reflection: *technical reflection*, which examines the skills, strategies, and methods used to reach predetermined goals (e.g., Are the techniques applied, and are they effective in accomplishing the goal?); *practical reflection*, which considers the underlying assumptions of methods used to reach goals, as well as the effect or outcome for students, and also reexamines the goals themselves

(Continued)

Table 1.1 (Continued)

(e.g., What are the assumptions and beliefs underlying practices? What are the outcomes for students? Is this a worthy goal to strive for?); and *critical reflection*, which focuses on inquiry about the moral, ethical, and equity aspects of practice (e.g., Does this promote equity, and for whom?).

- Includes significance of "pathic" elements (e.g., relational, affective, perceptual, contextual, noncognitive) of teacher practice that influence effectiveness.

Kenneth Zeichner and Daniel Liston, 1987; Kenneth Zeichner, 1993

- Argues the essential role of critical reflection in education, emphasizing that educators must critically examine how instructional and other school practices contribute to social equity and to the establishment of a just and humane society.
- Challenges the assumption that education will necessarily be better if teachers reflect, because reflection can validate and justify current practices that are harmful to students.

Donald Schon, 1983; 1987

- Describes a "crisis in professional knowledge," referring to the gap between professional knowledge and actual competencies required for practicing teachers.
- Emphasizes practitioner-generated, intuitive knowledge derived from experience.
- Uses the terms *the swamp* to connote the ambiguity, uncertainty, complexity, and oftentimes conflicting values that define the daily teaching context, and *swamp knowledge* to describe the tacit knowledge teachers develop from construction and reconstruction of their swamp experiences. (Contrasts *swamp* knowledge with *high hard ground* knowledge of researchers who may observe but are removed from practice.)
- Differentiates between *reflection-in-action*, referring to the process of observing our thinking and action as they are occurring, in order to make adjustments in the moment; and *reflection-on-action*, referring to the process of looking back on and learning from experience or action in order to affect future action. Killion and Todnem (1991) expanded Schon's reflection-in-action and reflection-on-action typology to include *reflection-for-action*.

David Smyth, 1989

- Suggests four forms of action that can guide reflection on practice: describe (e.g., What do I do?), inform (e.g., What does this mean?), confront (e.g., How did I come to think or act like this?), and reconstruct (e.g., How might I do things differently?).

Karen Osterman and Robert Kottkamp, 1993; 2004

- "Emphasizes thought and action as integral processes but extends beyond to consider how context and culture shape both thought and action . . .

respects the autonomy of the learner but recognizes the value of incorporating lessons drawn from theory, research, and practice" (p. xi).

- Contrasts traditional and reflective practice models of professional development: knowledge acquisition versus understanding and competence; transmission of knowledge versus constructed learning; and practitioner as passive versus practitioner as action researcher.
- Brings attention to consideration of the theories or views that individuals talk about (i.e., espoused theories) versus the theories or views that are evident in watching individuals behave (i.e., theories in use); suggest reflective practices as a way to examine and uncover underlying theories and views that affect action.
- Defines reflective practice as an experiential learning cycle, including problem identification, observation and analysis, abstract reconceptualization, and active experimentation; emphasizes data gathering as the keystone of reflective practice.

Georgea Sparks-Langer and Amy Colton, 1991; Langer and Colton, 1994

- Identifies multiple influences on the knowledge construction involved in reflective practice: experiential knowledge, professional knowledge, feelings, the surrounding collegial environment, and personal characteristics or attributes.
- Introduces a cyclical process, referred to as the *Framework for Developing Teacher Reflection*, that includes these steps: gather information about an experience or event; conduct analysis by considering multiple influencing variables; form hypotheses; and then test hypotheses through implementation.

Linda Valli, 1997

- Presents typology for reflection in teacher preparation based on literature and review of teacher preparation programs.
- Includes *technical reflection*, which focuses on general instruction and management practices based on research; *reflection-in and on-action*, which focuses on one's own teaching performance and making decisions based on one's own unique situation; *deliberative reflection*, which can focus on a wide array of teaching related practices and concerns but involves intentional consideration of assumptions, different perspectives, and research findings; *personalistic reflection*, which focuses on one's own growth and relationships with students and involves learning to listen to one's own inner voice, as well as the voices of others; *critical reflection*, which focuses on social, moral, and political dimensions of education and involves making judgments based on ethical criteria (p. 75).

dimensions of reflective processes. As is often the case, the answer is not "either/or" of Dewey and Schon but "both/and." We need all the internal and external resources we can tap to make the best decisions. As you read the next section, in which a variety of definitions and examples of reflective practice are offered, search for examples of both/and thinking.

WHAT IS REFLECTIVE PRACTICE?

Reflective practice is as much a state of mind as it is a set of activities.

—J. C. Vaughan (1990, p. ix), foreword in
Clift, Houston, & Pugach (Eds.), *Encouraging Reflective Practice in Education: An Analysis of Issues and Programs*

There is no universally accepted definition of reflective practice but a multitude of perspectives. In reading definitions of reflective practice, consider your own way of defining reflective practice so that this can become an organizer for your own thinking and learning. What key words or processes stand out in your mind? What kind of thinking is prompted when you engage around a problem, event, or puzzle of practice? Reflective practice can be considered

- "A genuinely critical, questioning orientation and a deep commitment to the discovery and analysis of positive and negative information concerning the quality and status of a professional's designed action" (Bright, 1996, p. 165)
- "The practice or act of analyzing our actions, decisions, or products by focusing on our process of achieving them" (Killion & Todnem, 1991, p. 15)
- "Deliberate thinking about action, with a view to its improvement" (Hatton & Smith, 1995, p. 40)
- "The ability to frame and reframe the practice setting, to develop and respond to this framing through action so that the practitioner's wisdom-in-action is enhanced and . . . articulation of professional knowledge is encouraged" (Loughran, 2002, p. 42)
- "The practice of periodically stepping back to ponder the meaning of what has recently transpired . . . [Reflective practice] privileges the process of inquiry . . . probing to a deeper level than trial and error experience" (Raelin, 2002, p. 66)

It can also be clarifying to articulate what reflection is *not.* It is not "mindless following of unexamined practices or principles" (Sparks-Langer & Colton, 1991, p. 37). It is not "pointless reflection of one's navel as symbolized by Rodin's 'The Thinker'" (Bright, 1996, p. 166). It is not just talking about work or thinking self-validating thoughts about how to teach or lead.

Drawing on the perspectives offered above and on our own practice, we identify the following elements of a Theory of Action for Reflective

Figure 1.1   Theory of Action for Reflective Practice

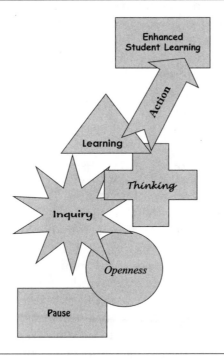

Practice that maps the linkages between thinking, action, and student learning (see Figure 1.1). Each element is described briefly here. (A copy of the Theory of Action for Reflective Practice is available as Resource 1.A.)

Reflective practice requires a *pause*. Sometimes the pause is intentional—a purposeful slowing down to create a space in which presence and openness can emerge. Sometimes the pause happens unexpectedly in response to a crisis or dilemma. As we move through our daily routines, we are often not aware. The concept of "hot action" and the metaphor of educational practice occurring in the fast lane express the familiar, often intense pace of the environment that educators navigate on a daily basis. There is a need to find, create, and intentionally choose opportunities to pause in today's teaching environments; simply waiting for this pause to happen or waiting for someone else to "hand you" space to pause is unlikely. Kahn (1992) describes the importance of psychological presence as a requisite for individual learning and high-quality performance. Covey (1989) emphasizes the pause between a stimulus and a response in which options for action can be considered. Frankl (1959), the renowned physician survivor of the Holocaust, developed an approach for helping people overcome various debilitating conditions. Referred to as Logotherapy, this approach is grounded in the belief that human beings have the capacity to choose their responses to life's experiences even in dire, extreme, and life-threatening situations. An intentional pause is precursor to conscious deliberative thought, response, and action.

Openness—an open perspective and open heart—is an important dimension of our reflective practice framework. Open perspective or open-mindedness (Dewey, 1933; Ross, 1990; Zeichner & Liston, 1996) means recognizing that there are multiple ways to view particular circumstances or events. It means consideration of changing viewpoints and letting go of the need to be right or the desire to win (Webb, 1995). Do we have the ability to see or hear an honest assessment of reality? Openness to other perspectives requires a mindful and flexible orientation. Mindful people are awake (Nhat Hanh, 1993), conscious of thought and action. Being awake includes having an awareness of others and extending learning beyond the immediate sphere. In education, awareness is layered, ranging from immediate instructional circumstances to caring about democratic foundations and encouraging socially responsible actions (Littky & Grabelle, 2004; Sparks-Langer & Colton, 1991). *Open heart* is a term for acknowledging the constant role of care and connection in the life of an educator. Both openness in thought and openness in relationships are important qualities in reflective practice.

Openness creates the possibility for *inquiry,* the state in which questions about practice are invited and genuinely engaged. Inquiry can be prompted by a dilemma, puzzle, surprise, or feeling. Doubt, perplexity, and tentativeness are part of an inquiry cycle (Dewey, 1933; Langer & Colton, 1994), as is humility. By pausing to see what is happening in a given moment or context and by assuming a curious disposition (openness), questions are allowed to emerge. As Albert Einstein put it, "The important thing is to not stop questioning."

Questions prompt further *thinking*—the active, deliberate, and conscious processing of thoughts for examining goals, beliefs, and practices. *Goals* encompass desired aims, outcomes, or intentions. They can be general or specific. A goal could focus on creating a classroom community in which respect, support, and learning are held as values. A goal could address teaching children how to learn effectively in groups. *Beliefs* encompass people's values, visions, biases, and paradigms. Beliefs stem largely from experience and significantly influence listening, thinking. and behaving. Beliefs undergird assumptions which are often unconscious and unexamined. *Practice* refers to one's repertoire of dispositions, knowledge, and skills across a range of performance domains, such as instructional design, assessment, student interactions, relationships with families, or collaboration with colleagues and administrators. Embedded in practice are a multitude of daily "in-action" decisions that influence others. Our Theory of Action involves thinking about goals, thinking about beliefs, and thinking about practice.

Creative and critical thinking processes support deliberative thinking. Metacognition, analysis, integration, and synthesis also may be used in a reflective process. Reflection, for example, may take the form of self-observation (Bergsgaard & Ellis, 2002) to gain insight about the reasons for one's own thinking and one's actions and their consequences. It may involve group members being aware of their thoughts during a decision-making process (Hatton & Smith, 1995). Higher-level thinking processes provide the means to move beyond a focus on isolated facts, events, or data to perceive a broader context for understanding and decision making.

The intended outgrowth of deliberative thinking is *learning* by the reflecting person. Practitioners gain new or deeper insights that lead to actions aimed at improving teaching and learning processes to benefit students. Understanding provides the basis for considering new forms of action. Awareness and understanding are critical elements for initiating and sustaining changes in practice. New understandings without changes in practice, however, will not make differences in the lives of students. Application of knowledge—*action*—is essential in the reflective practice cycle (Dewey, 1933; Smyth, 1989). Reflective practice leads to improvement only when deepened understandings lead to action.

The ultimate desired outcome of reflective practice is, of course, *enhanced student learning.* Learning is broadly defined to include students' capacities to think, their motivations to learn, and their effectiveness in engaging constructively with others and contributing to the world around them, along with more traditionally defined measures of student learning. In our push toward measurable forms of accountability, we must not make the fatal flaw of ignoring the broader and less easily measured array of dispositions, knowledge, and skills required for future life in an even more complex and diverse world than today.

In sum, reflective practice is an active process. "Rather than reflective practice being seen as impractical, passive, or irrelevant to action, it can be regarded as centrally important and relevant to the understanding of ongoing action" (Bright, 1996, p. 167). It serves as the foundation for continuous learning and more effective action in educational practice so that children are successful in school and in life. It is a complex process that requires high levels of conscious thought and commitments to change practice based on new understandings.

It is our hope that our Theory of Action for Reflective Practice (Figure 1.1) assists educators in engaging with the complexity of reflective practice by considering these manageable, concrete elements. The Theory of Action is included in the Resources.

WHY REFLECTIVE PRACTICE? AND WHAT IS ITS POTENTIAL TO IMPROVE SCHOOLS?

Increasing evidence suggests what common sense has always told us: student learning is linked with staff learning (Garet et al., 2001; Ingavarson, Meiers, & Beavis, 2005; Lambert, 2003). By engaging in reflective practices, educators can increase their learning and improve their practices. Bright explains (1996), "The main objective of reflective practice is to ensure a more accurate and relevant understanding of a situation such that professionally designed action in that situation is more likely to produce effective, relevant action which will facilitate the occurrence of more desired and effective outcomes" (p. 177). High levels of student learning require high levels of staff competence.

Described below (and listed in Table 1.2) are numerous benefits that can be realized when reflective practices are well implemented in schools:

• *Guidance for new career teachers or educators in new roles.* Aleman (2003) likens the early teacher career period of "waiting to teach" to the pre-parenting period of "waiting to parent." Regardless of how well teachers are prepared in preservice programs, until teachers begin the actual practice of teaching, they cannot know what it means to teach, they cannot know what they need to know, and they cannot fully comprehend the central place that continuous learning must take in their careers in order to be successful. Before teaching or parenting actually starts, one can be prepared through a variety of means: reading, studying, conversing, observing, even practicing with someone else's children or students. Before actually assuming the role, however, it is all just background knowledge, not knowledge in action. This is also true with administrators. The importance of structuring reflection to support educators as they assume new roles also has been well substantiated (Perry & Power, 2004; Pultorak, 1996; Reiman, 1999; Risko et al., 2002).

• *Continuous learning through integration of teaching dimensions.* For experienced educators, reflective practice serves as the catalyst for continuous learning about educational practice. If educators do not reflect on and learn from their practice, they are likely to continue doing what they have been doing. Recall the old adage "If you always do what you've always done, you'll always get what you've always gotten." Further, reflective practice is aptly considered the hub of a teaching excellence wheel, the means of integrating the subject-knowledge, teaching-skills, interpersonal-relationship, research, and personality dimensions of teaching (Kane, Sandretto, & Heath, 2004).

• *Bridges between theory and practice.* As educators consider externally generated theory and knowledge from the research community and then determine appropriate, customized applications to their specific contexts of practice, they bridge the gaps between research, theory, and practice. In doing so, they contribute to the overall knowledge base of the profession. Reflective practices can also bridge gaps between what we say (our espoused theory) and what we do. Bridging this gap is at the heart of integrity and authenticity.

- *Consideration of multiple perspectives.* Collaborative reflective practices engage a greater variety of perspectives for addressing the many challenging and complex dilemmas of practice. Consideration of different perspectives and different knowledge bases, including experiential, sociopolitical, and empirical ones (Kinchloe, 2004), can result in more effective solutions that are more solidly grounded and more broadly understood, accepted, and implemented. (See p. 18–19 for further discussion of Kinchloe's work.)

- *More productive engagement of conflict.* At the core of conflict is difference. Reflective thinking offers a way to understand differences and to support productive engagement of conflict (Valiga, 2003). Understanding can result in decreased judgment and recognition of different values, experiences, and priorities. It can also reveal points of agreement that often serve as common ground for moving forward.

- *New context knowledge for immediate application.* New understandings that have immediate application in practice are created when experience leverages thinking. Knowledge constructed within "hot action" (Eraut, 1985) contexts of practice is needed to effectively teach the increasing variety of school-age students. By sharing newly constructed knowledge among colleagues, the impact on effectiveness can be multiplied.

- *Embedded means of formative assessment.* When teacher reflection is specifically focused on evidence and indicators of student learning, it serves as a primary means of formative assessment of instructional effectiveness. Such ongoing, embedded assessment results in immediate and relevant instructional accommodations aimed at increasing student learning today. It has also been suggested that formative assessment yields the information needed for educators to determine what Vygotsky refers to as the "zone of proximal development," the area in which appropriate amounts of challenge and support exist to foster learning and growth of individual students (Ash & Levitt, 2003).

- *Growth in cultural awareness and competence.* Given appropriate guidance in the reflection process, "introspective behavior could lead teachers to better understand and relate to their students of color because they better understand themselves as racial beings . . . Because many White teachers do not see themselves as racial beings and often (idealistically) dismiss notions of race explicitly in their work, the idea of race reflection in cultural contexts could prove effective as they grapple with ways to better meet the need of diverse learners" (Milner, 2003, p. 179). As we become a nation with an increasingly culturally diverse student population, in combination with a current majority of Caucasian educators, the call for increased cultural awareness and competence becomes urgent if public schools in the United States are to educate all children well (Delpit, 1995; Robins, Lindsey, Lindsey, & Terrell, 2002).

• *Deepened understanding of role and identity.* That the roles and responsibilities of today's educators are increasingly complex is apparent to even the most doubting of education outsiders. Such role expansion necessitates reflection as a way to articulate and understand the many competing demands and opportunities, to set priorities for focusing action, and to clarify and keep present one's identity and purpose as contributor to the development of today's young people. Such reflection has the potential to support growth of individual professionals and growth of the profession (Wesley & Buysse, 2001).

• *Individual and collective sense of efficacy. Efficacy* refers to the belief that one can make a difference in the lives of students. Efficacy increases as educators see positive effects of their actions. As the internal capacities of teachers to learn and make a positive difference are recognized and harnessed, a collective sense of efficacy and empowerment emerges. Teacher empowerment is recognized as a key dimension in school renewal efforts aimed at changes in classroom practice (Marks & Louis, 1997, 1999).

• *Strengthened relationships and connections among staff.* As continuous learning and improvement become a shared goal when reflection becomes embedded in the practice repertoire of educators, isolation is reduced and relationships strengthened. This lays the foundation for schoolwide improvement, because as educators come to know one another, their network of resources for students expands and the coherence of schoolwide practices increases.

• *Greater professionalism and voice.* As reflective practices build capacity for individual and organizational learning, educators grow in their responsibility, competence, and confidence for improvement. Their professionalism increases, which can give rise to greater participation and advocacy in policy decisions that impact education. Too often, the voices of teachers are missing from policy debates and decisions (Kinchloe, 2004).

• *Reduction of external mandates.* Arguably, a history of external mandates in education has diminished internal capacity and fostered a cycle of dependence on such external directives to leverage change (Butler, 1996). As educators noticeably assume a lead role in school renewal policy and practice, it is conceivable that a reduction in the scope and rapidity of external mandates could ultimately result.

Table 1.2   Potential Benefits of Reflective Practice

- Guidance for new teachers, or educators in new roles
- Continuous learning for experienced educators
- Bridges theory and practice
- Consideration of multiple perspectives
- Productive engagement of conflict
- Knowledge for immediate action
- Embedded formative assessment
- Growth in cultural competence
- Understanding of role and identity
- Individual and collective efficacy
- Strengthened connections among staff
- Greater professionalism and voice
- Reduced external mandates

Reflective practice has the potential to significantly improve education if its foundations, assumptions, and rigorous processes are honored. If the integrity of reflective practice is not upheld, its use will be superficial and its results insubstantial. In reviewing Table 1.2, which of the potential benefits of reflective practice seem most compelling in your teaching context?

WHAT DOES IT MEAN TO BE A REFLECTIVE EDUCATOR?

What do reflective educators look like? How do they behave? How would you know a reflective educator if you met one? Before reading on, pause and generate your own list of reflective-educator qualities. One of the distinguishing characteristics of reflective educators is a high level of commitment to their own professional development (Zeichner & Liston, 1996). They have a sustained interest in learning. Inquiry, questioning, and discovery are norms embedded in their ways of thinking and practice (Bright, 1996; Zeichner & Liston, 1996). Their inquiry focuses not only on the effectiveness of their instruction or leadership but also on the underlying assumptions, biases, and values that they bring to the educational process. Reflective educators consider issues of justice, equity, and morality as they design and reflect on their practice. Their interest in learning is continually sparked by triggers of curiosity about some aspect of practice (Clarke, 1995). Instead of blindly accepting or rejecting new information or ideas, they carefully examine, analyze, and reframe them in terms of specific context variables, previous experiences, and alignment with desired educational goals (Clarke, 1995; Costa & Garmston, 2000; Zeichner & Liston, 1996). Reflective educators are decision makers who develop thoughtful plans to move new understandings into action so that meaningful improvements result for students (Clarke, 1995; Costa & Garmston, 2002).

Reflective educators recognize that much of the knowledge about effective practice is tacit, meaning that it is learned from experience within the practice context. To learn in and from dynamic, unpredictable, and sometimes ambiguous contexts, reflective educators are keenly aware of their surrounding context, are open to and seek feedback, and can effectively distill the information that should be considered in a reflective process (Bright, 1996). We offer the profile of a reflective educator as one who

- Stays focused on education's central purpose: student learning and development
- Is committed to continuous improvement of practice
- Assumes responsibility for his or her own learning—now and lifelong
- Demonstrates awareness of self, others, and the surrounding context
- Develops the thinking skills for effective inquiry
- Takes action that aligns with new understandings
- Holds great leadership potential within a school community
- Seeks to understand different types of knowledge, internally and externally generated

The last two items on the list, leadership potential and different types of knowledge, warrant further explanation. We begin with a discussion of leadership, including a positive reframing of the term *deviant*. Reflective educators often serve as leaders, formal and informal, who attract others. In doing so, they influence practice beyond their immediate teaching domains. They attract others because of the profile characteristics listed above: they are focused on student learning, committed, responsible, aware, thoughtful, inquiring, and action-oriented.

Given prevailing school and societal norms that fly in the face of slowing down to think, question, and then demonstrate the courage and conviction to act, reflective practitioners represent a countercultural phenomenon. In effect, they can be considered "positive deviants" (Richardson, 2004). The concept of positive deviance grew from the work of Jerry Sternin when working with Save the Children. Sternin (as cited by Richardson, 2004, p. 17) explains,

Positive deviants are people whose behavior and practices lead to solutions to problems that others in the group who have access to exactly the same resources have not been able to solve. We want to identify these people because they provide demonstrable evidence that a solution for the problem exists within the community.

One example involved examination of children's nutrition in Vietnam in the 1990s (Dorsey, 2000). In many villages, children were starving. In one village, however, children were thriving, despite similar environments and resources across villages. Differences were noted across villages in terms of practices for feeding the children. Parents of the healthy children fed them four times a day, instead of just two, which helped digestion because the children's stomachs were small. They also fed the children small crabs and shrimps which were on the end of rice stalks, whereas parents in the other villages did not. The observers, Jerry and Monique Sternin, did not write a paper on raising healthy kids, duplicate it, and hand it out to villagers. They did not hold seminars on raising healthy children or make a 10-point action plan and tack it to huts and field posts. They *did* hold small gatherings that included parents of the healthy children and parents of the unhealthy children. In these gatherings, the parents shared their experiences and practiced the new feeding strategies. Over time, conversations and ongoing support led to changes in behavior and more healthy children. This approach contrasts significantly with typical development approaches in which "solutions" from an outside world are presumptively imported and forced into practice, regardless of how feasible or how likely such foreign ways are to be maintained in the substantially different local contexts.

Think of the implications for passing along wisdom in our own organizations. There are positive deviants in every school and system in which we have worked. Recently, the concept of positive deviance has begun to take hold in some schools (Richardson, 2004). Positive deviants can be thought of as schools or individuals that thrive in situations in which others do not. In the context of reflective practice, positive deviants, be they schools or individuals, "Just do it!," to borrow the slogan from Nike. People who are positive deviants seem to be innate reflective practitioners. They just continue to think, learn, and grow, despite what seem to be constraining forces and conditions around them. Perhaps it is the positive and productive nature of these deviants that serves as the powerful attractor, and that makes them effective agents of change beyond their immediate sphere of practice. Reflective educators, as positive deviants, have great potential to influence and to lead others.

Our list of reflective-educator qualities also includes a valuing of different forms of knowledge. Distinctions have been made between reflective educators (or reflective practitioners) and experts, in terms of how knowledge is viewed, generated, and valued (Schon, 1987; Webb, 1995). In addition to the historical, political, and sociocultural knowledge bases that surround us and that influence how we think and live (Kinchloe, 2004), generally speaking, there are two sources of knowledge educators bring to bear on practice: externally generated knowledge and internally created knowledge. Externally generated knowledge comes by way of the research community and usually offers generalized findings, directions, and strategies to be considered by practice communities. This is sometimes referred to as technical-rational, empirical, declarative, or content knowledge. Internally created knowledge comes by way of educators learning through reflecting on their practice and by customizing application of externally generated knowledge to unique contexts of practice, that is, specific schools, classes, and students. This is sometimes referred to as tacit, procedural, experiential, or contextual knowledge.

Reflective practitioners draw largely from an experiential or contextual knowledge base in which "it is impossible to disentangle knowing from doing" (Webb, 1995, p. 71). Content experts draw largely from a technical-rational knowledge base (Schon, 1983). They are masters of content but may not have the practice background that generates tacit knowledge about how to apply, use, or teach content in the classroom. They can share research findings but cannot necessarily model or demonstrate application in authentic settings. Webb (1995) explains that from the technical-rational knowledge perspective of content experts, "Professional practice rests upon an underlying discipline or basic science producing general theory and knowledge which the professional practitioner then applies to individual daily problems . . . [in] professional practice . . . knowing directs doing, and those who know are the experts (p. 71)."

This perspective explains some of the disconnect that educators may sense when learning from experts of content who cannot make the application to the classroom context. It also speaks to the frustration or cynicism that can arise among practicing educators when content experts assume an easy transfer of technical-rational knowledge to contexts of practice.

For some aspects of practice, educators draw on a technical-rational knowledge base, such as disciplinary expertise. Math teachers, for example, draw on the technical knowledge base of the discipline of mathematics. For many other aspects of daily practice, though, educators draw on their experientially and contextually derived knowledge from practice. Schon (1983) explains that when, as reflective practitioners,

> We go about the spontaneous, intuitive performance of the actions of every day life, we show ourselves to be knowledgeable in a special way. Often we cannot say what it is we know. When we try to describe it, we find ourselves at a loss, or we produce descriptions that are obviously inappropriate. Our knowledge is ordinarily tacit, implicit in our patterns of action and in our feel for the

stuff with which we are dealing. It seems right to say that our knowing is in our action. (p. 9)

Enriching this discussion of knowledge types is the thinking of Kinchloe (2004). He describes six types of knowledge that inform educational practice: empirical knowledge based on research; normative knowledge of what should be in terms of moral and ethical behavior; critical knowledge, which reflects sociopolitical and power dynamics; ontological knowledge that places oneself in historical and cultural context; experiential knowledge about practice; and finally, *reflective-synthetic knowledge,* which is the knowledge that emerges from individuals who reflect on and synthesize multiple types of knowledge to make appropriate decisions about educating and education. Kinchloe explains,

> Since our purpose is not to indoctrinate practitioners to operate in a particular manner but to think about practice in more sophisticated ways, a central dimension of teacher education involves reflecting on and examining all of these knowledges in relation to one another. A reflective-synthetic knowledge of education involves developing a way of thinking about the professional role in light of a body of knowledges, principles, purposes, and experiences. In this process educators work to devise ways of using these various knowledges to perform our jobs in more informed, practical, ethical, democratic, politically just, self-aware, and purposeful ways. At the same time they work to expose the assumptions about knowledge embedded in various conceptions or practices and in the officially approved educational information they encounter. (Kinchloe, 2004, p. 62)

Clearly, there are many types of knowledge influencing and informing educational decisions and practice. It is unnecessary and perhaps even counterproductive to differentially or exclusively value one type of knowledge over others. It is the job of educators to adopt a reflective stance, to continually learn and expand their understanding and repertoire of practice. In doing so they realize a paradox—both humility and joy—vested in lifelong learning: "Significant learning generally involves fluctuating episodes of anxiety-producing self-scrutiny and energy-inducing leaps forward in ability and understanding" (Brookfield, 1992, p. 12). Such is the journey of a reflective educator.

THE REFLECTIVE PRACTICE SPIRAL: LEARNING FROM THE INSIDE OUT

The Reflective Practice Spiral (Figure 1.2) presents one way to think about initiating and expanding efforts to embed reflective practices as a cultural norm in schools. It reflects an assumption that the place to begin is with oneself and that learning occurs from the inside out. As shown, the spiral

Figure 1.2   The Reflective Practice Spiral, Connecting the Individual, Partner, Small-Group or Team, and Schoolwide Levels of Reflective Practice

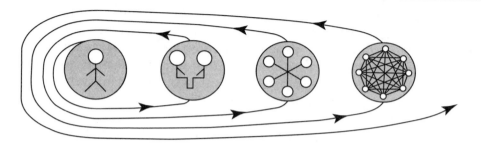

has four levels, beginning with the innermost level of individual reflective practice and extending outward to the partner level, then the small group or team level, and finally to the outermost circle, the schoolwide level of reflective practice. The spiral that moves through the levels represents the interconnectedness among the levels, resulting in a cumulative effect on schoolwide practices and learning. (A copy of the Reflective Practice Spiral is available as Resource 1.B.)

As mentioned earlier in this chapter, lived experience is perhaps the most powerful influence on the formation of beliefs, which are the driving forces behind actions. The learning and positive growth that individuals experience from engaging in reflective practices provides an informed, experiential foundation on which to advocate and commit to expanding the practice of reflection beyond themselves. As we develop our individual reflection capacities, we can better influence the reflection that occurs with partners and in small groups or teams of which we are members. As more such groups become reflective in their work, the influence and potential of reflective practice spreads throughout the school. A critical mass of individuals who have experienced positive outcomes from their own reflective practice and from reflection within groups and teams can better support widespread adoption. Each level in the Reflective Practice Spiral is described below, along with the respective potential benefits. Specific considerations and examples for teacher and administrator reflective practices at each level are addressed in Chapters 3 through 6.

Individual Reflective Practice

This is the level at which each of us, as an educator, has full responsibility and control. We can choose to be reflective in our work and our personal lives. Reflection with ourselves provides each of us with the opportunity to realize the following benefits:

- Improvements in our professional practices, given greater awareness of personal performance, practice dilemmas, possibilities that emerge from divergent and creative thought, and effects of our practices
- Enhanced student learning and learning capacities, given improvements in practice
- Increased personal capacities for learning and improvement, as the knowledge, skills, and dispositions for reflective practice become embedded in our way of thinking and doing
- Restored balance and perspective, given the time out created for reflection and learning
- Renewed clarity of personal and professional purpose and competence, given a sense of empowerment to align our practices with desired intents

Some ways to reflect alone include journaling, reviewing a case, reading literature, developing a teaching portfolio, exercising our bodies to free our minds, taking a personal retreat, and observing or listening to one's own practice through use of videotapes or audiotapes. Chapter 3 contains additional considerations and specific examples of reflective practice with oneself. When we begin to learn through personal experience about reflective practice and its potential, we are also beginning to increase our capacity to effectively support others in developing their reflective capacities.

Reflective Practice With Partners

Joining with another person in the process of reflection can result in greater insight about one's practice, especially when trust is high and the right combination of support and challenge is present. When reflecting with others, we realize the truth in the adage "What goes around comes around." Partner reflection can also introduce an element of fun. Humor, when appropriately interjected, reminds us not to take ourselves too seriously and that mistakes are an inevitable dimension of the learning process. In addition to the gains realized at the individual level of reflection, adding one or two partners to the reflection process can result in

- Expanded learning about our own practice, given the different perspectives of another person and when coached through the process of reflective inquiry
- Increased professional and social support and decreased feelings of isolation at work, given the presence of a strengthened collegial relationship

- An increased sense of who we are and how things work in our school, given the connection and exchange with another person who practices in our place of work
- Greater commitment to our work and our work environment, given an increased sense of competence, confidence, and connection to another person in our place of work

Some ways that two or three people can reflect together include interactive journaling, cognitive coaching, conversing about instructional design possibilities, talking through steps of an inquiry cycle related to specific events or dilemmas, reading and talking about articles or case studies, examining student work, and online dialogue. Chapter 4 contains additional considerations and specific examples of reflective practice with partners. The increased sense of competence, support, and connection that can emerge from reflection with a partner positions us on more solid ground to extend the practice of reflection to small groups and teams.

Reflective Practice in Small Groups and Teams

There is a big shift from reflecting alone or with partners to reflecting in a small group. Although the potential impact of reflection increases, so, too, does personal risk. Because more people are in a group, the sense of safety and connection between individuals is different than with partner reflection, often more variable and diffuse. Groups and teams also are frequently appointed or mandated, whereas partner reflection is often voluntary and self-organized. In appointed or mandated groups, there is frequently less control over who joins the group and their desire to participate. Composition and commitment affect interactions and outcomes.

Despite the risks involved in expanding reflective practice to such groups, good reasons exist to venture forth into this domain. When reflection becomes part of educational practice within small groups or teams, its members can realize the following gains:

- Enhanced learning and resources for learning about practice, given more people, each of whom brings varied experiences and expertise in life, learning, and education
- Increased professional and social support (including fun), given the expanded and more varied network of collegial relationships
- More effective interventions for individual students or groups of identified students, given shared purpose, responsibility, and expertise among members of a group
- An emerging sense of hope and encouragement that meaningful and sustained improvements in practice can occur, given group members committed to working and learning together

- Improved climate and collegiality, given greater understanding of our own and others' experiences and perspectives about our shared place of work

Some ways to reflect in small groups include action research, study groups, regular grade-level or content-area meetings to review and design instruction and assessment procedures, examining student data and work, and case-study reviews. Reflective practices can also enhance committee work by intentionally examining about past practices and future possibilities and by soliciting the perspectives of people representing broad interests in the work. Arguably, committees that form to address schoolwide concerns such as space, scheduling, extracurricular activities, and remedial supports for learning would be more effective if reflection and learning were an embedded part of the committee process. Refer to Chapter 5 for more considerations and specific examples of reflective practice in groups or teams.

At the small-group level of reflective practice, the potential to influence educational practices throughout the school gains momentum. Small ripples of change frequently become the impetus for much broader changes, even when that was not an original intent (Garmston & Wellman, 1995; Wheatley, 1992). The potential to improve educational practices significantly increases when increasing numbers of groups and teams embed reflective practices in their work. A culture of inquiry and learning begins to take hold on a grander, schoolwide basis.

Schoolwide Reflective Practice

The greatest potential for reflective practice to improve schools lies within the collective inquiry, thinking, learning, understanding, and acting that result from schoolwide engagement. Over the past decade, emphasis on schoolwide, as opposed to isolated, improvement efforts has increased (e.g., Calhoun, 1994). Isolated efforts (e.g., initiatives taken on by individual teachers, or applying to specific grade levels or content areas) typically result in only isolated improvements, with few cumulative gains realized once students or teachers move on from those experiences. Furthermore, effects do not spread to other groups of students without intentional efforts to design and implement new practices with those students. These are some of the reasons for the emergence of practices intended to promote professional community focused on increasing student learning (DuFour & Eaker, 1998; Fullan, 2000a; Hargreaves, 2001; Hord, 1997; King & Newmann, 2000; Louis & Kruse, 1995; Newmann & Wehlage, 1995). When reflection becomes part of educational practice on a schoolwide basis, the following gains are possible:

- Significantly expanded learning opportunities and resources for achieving schoolwide advances in practice aimed at student achievement

- Enhanced sense of common purpose and shared responsibility for all students
- Greater shared knowledge, planning, and communication about students among teachers throughout the school, resulting in greater instructional coherence
- Increased professional support realized from the expanded network of relationships and the extensive expertise revealed within the network
- Enhanced understanding of school culture, specifically what influences policy and practice and how schoolwide improvement efforts can be successful
- Increased hope and possibility for meaningful and sustained improvements in practice, given an expanded awareness of the commitments and talents of staff throughout the school and given the strengthened network among staff members
- Lessened sense of vulnerability to external pressures and, paradoxically, more reasoned consideration of opportunities that might result from external partnerships

Reflective practices at the schoolwide level can take many forms. An entire school staff may be involved in study groups on a common topic, such as reading in the content areas, instructional strategies, or performance assessment. There might also be groups or teams across the school with varied purposes. For example, interdisciplinary groups could form to share disciplinary expertise and to create a set of integrated student outcomes that would be addressed within each of the content areas. Cross-grade-level teams might explore the best practices for effective student transitions between grades or schools. Some issues require schoolwide attention and participation, so group composition should be intentionally designed to connect people across grade levels or curricular areas to bring forth different perspectives and relationships between individuals who may not typically cross paths during a school day. It is neither possible nor essential to include every staff member in every learning or shared-work initiative. What matters is that staff members are involved in some type of collaborative learning that coheres and contributes to overall educational goals and experiences for students. Chapter 6 describes additional considerations and specific examples of schoolwide reflective practices.

Moving Outward in the Spiral

There is greater potential to achieve schoolwide improvements in practice as reflective practices grow from the individual level of the spiral toward the school level. The potential at the outer levels is based on the premise that individuals continue to enhance their individual reflection and learning. Resources, information, perspectives, ownership, commitment, relationships, and shared responsibility and leadership increase substantially given greater numbers of staff members learning together.

As reflective practice spirals out from the center, challenges to effective implementation are greater. Complexity is dramatically increased as a result of the greater numbers of people involved. Interpersonal dynamics become a greater force. Logistics, such as scheduling time for reflection, become more difficult. Individual risk is greater because an individual's perspectives are exposed to a greater number of people with whom there may be varying degrees of trust, respect, and commitment. The surrounding context and climate of a school also have a greater effect as practices expand to include more people. There are long-standing structures that reinforce isolation. The history and established cultures within and across groups create invisible barriers to interaction. Multiple and often competing priorities for time and professional development can fragment focus, effort, and people. In short, as the individual moves out in the spiral, there is more potential but also more complexity and less control.

Recognizing the presence of significant, complicating variables at the school level can raise serious doubts about the feasibility of reflective practice. The inherently complex nature of schoolwide change can easily feel overwhelming. This is one of the reasons for proposing the Reflective Practice Spiral as a guiding framework. Each of us can choose to remain committed to our own professional learning and improvement by embedding reflective practices in our own lives. We can at least engage in reflective practices at the individual level. Choosing to assume a responsible, proactive stance toward our own development adds positive energy to our lives and to the environments in which we work. As individuals, we reap the benefits of continuous learning and we increase our professional competence. Learning also renews our spirit. Our human needs to learn and grow can be met, in part, through reflective thinking. A commitment to individual reflective practices benefits us as individuals and also has an indirect effect on others.

Beyond the individual, the potential for improvement in schools increases with each additional person who chooses to make a commitment to professional learning and improvement. Understandings about how organizations or systems evolve suggest that significant changes arise through the relationships and interactions among people (Garmston & Wellman, 1995; Wheatley, 1992). Also suggested is that change happens in ways we cannot predict or control. As each of us continues to learn, and as we reach out to connect and learn with others, relationships form and strengthen, thereby increasing the potential large-scale improvement. Gradually, we sense being part of a much larger whole that has the power and momentum to positively affect the lives of students. Schoolwide engagement helps keep energy high and hope alive.

Combinations of different groups of staff members learning together throughout the school result in expanded and strengthened relationships among all staff members. In effect, a web of relationships forms to facilitate communication and connection throughout the school community (see Figure 1.3). This web of relationships serves several very important functions:

- *A safety net is created for students,* who are less likely to feel anonymous and fragmented because staff members are in better communication about students, especially those who are struggling in school
- *A rich network of resources*—people and information—is formed and any member of the school community can tap it; if someone in our immediate network does not know something, we are likely to be connected to someone in another network who may know
- When we are more tightly coupled with others in our work, there is a greater likelihood of more *comprehensive, effective, and rapid response* to schoolwide issues, ranging from safety concerns to adoption of new curricula

To enhance the web metaphor for school improvement, consider that the threads of weaver spiders are one of the strongest organic materials that nature produces. In laboratories, scientists harvest the threads and weave them into bulletproof vests. Thus the web is an apt metaphor for the durable and protective community that emerges and spreads from the spinning of many individuals.

To envision how the web of relationships can accomplish these important functions, look at Figure 1.3 and think of it as representing a well-connected and effective community of educators in a school. Now picture

Figure 1.3   Visual Representation of Relationship Web Among Staff Members, Strengthened by Reflective Practices

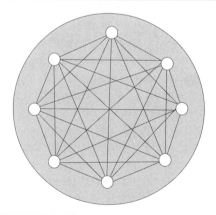

something falling onto the web. The specific something could be a student with unique challenges, a new program or curriculum, or new teachers. Because of all the interconnections, whatever falls onto the strands of the web is caught. The web flexes to accommodate its presence, so it does not fall to the ground underneath. Every connection (relationship) in the web knows that something new has arrived and can offer resources and support. Without these connections, whatever lands in the school (web) falls to the ground and is on its own to stand upright and establish the connections needed to survive. A web of relationships can embrace a new presence, connect it to the broader community, and bring forth resources needed to effectively interact with or respond to the new presence in the web. Reflective practice is one significant means of forming and strengthening the relationships, which are the verbal, social, behavioral, and emotional connections that constitute the web. (A copy of the Web of Relationships is available as Resources item 1.C.)

CLOSING

Education is about learning—not only student learning but also staff learning. Learning is a function of reflection, as depicted in Figure 1.4. "Adults do not learn from experience, they learn from processing experience" (Arin-Krupp, as cited in Garmston & Wellman, 1997, p. 1). Dewey asserted years ago that experience itself is not enough. Ten years of teaching can be 10 years of learning from experience with continuous improvement, or it can be 1 year with no learning repeated 10 times. Learning and improvement can no longer be optional. Reflection, therefore, must be at the center of individual and organizational renewal initiatives.

Reflective practice offers one powerful way for educators—individually and collectively—to stay challenged, effective, and alive in their work. The greater the number of people involved, the greater the potential to significantly improve educational practice and, therefore, the greater the potential to enhance student learning. When educators in a school join together to reflect and learn, they make a difference by harnessing the potential of their collective resources: diverse experience and expertise, shared purpose and responsibility for students, expanded understanding of students throughout the school, professional and social support, and hopefulness about meaningful and sustained improvement. Despite the hectic pace and the steady demands, increasing numbers of educators are making it a priority to create space in their professional lives for reflection and learning. In doing so, they are being nurtured to grow and are expanding their repertoire of effective instructional practices. They are moving from a culture of doing to a culture of learning with doing.

You are invited to use the Chapter Reflection Page (Figure 1.5) to make note of significant learning or insights sparked from reading Chapter 1. (A copy of the Chapter Reflection Page is available as Resource 1.D.) In the

Figure 1.4   Learning Occurs by Reflection on Experience. (Inspired by Judi Arin-Krupp)

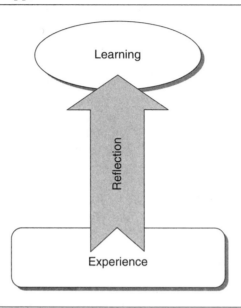

following chapter, Chapter 2, the focus shifts away from providing a background and framework for reflective practice to focus on fundamentals for generating capacity and for designing reflective practices. Chapters 3 through 6 will then focus more sharply on specific considerations and strategies for advancing reflective practices at each level of the Reflective Practice Spiral. According to Peter Block (2002), "the value of another's experience is to give us hope, not to tell us how or whether to proceed" (p. 24). We intend that the value in offering examples will inspire ideas, energy, and action, realizing that our examples cannot tell you how or whether to proceed. That decision must come from within.

Figure 1.5 Chapter Reflection Page

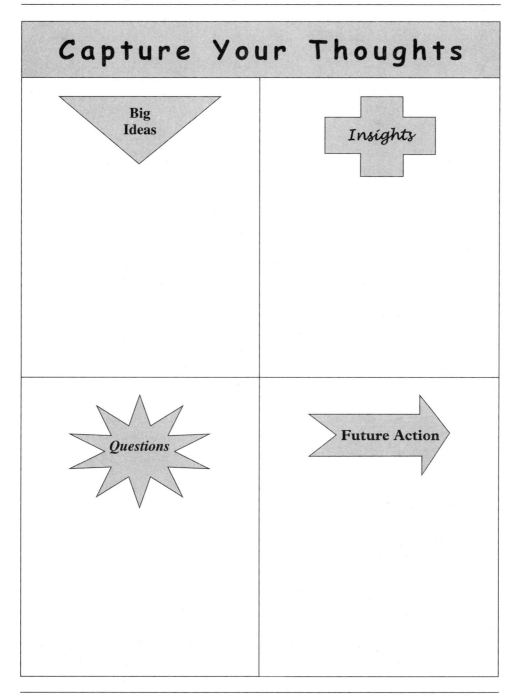

2

Fundamentals for Reflective Practice

We learn by conversing with ourselves, with others, and with the world around us.

—Sheila Harri-Augstein and Laurie
Thomas (1991, p. 3), *Learning Conversations*

The purpose of reflective practice is to increase learning at the individual and organizational levels (Kim, 1993) so that educational practice continuously improves and student learning is enhanced. According to Butler (1996), specific goals of reflective practice are

- To review a process to see if it achieved the desired goals or outcomes
- To make learning visible, to complete the learning cycle for each incident in our lives
- To give a more considered response to an event
- To achieve meaning and understanding inside actions
- To add value to self and to performance
- To move us from novice to expert (pp. 271–272)

To these goals we add explicit consideration of the impact of our actions on the people around us, not just impact of an instructional nature but impact of a human nature. Have we modeled and advanced equitable practices? Have we made earnest attempts to listen to and understand others and to question and challenge our own thinking? Have we been inclusive and fostered inclusive dispositions among students? Have we shown respect for different points of view and demonstrated civil discourse even in the face of disagreement? Have we acted in ways that align with our espoused values and beliefs?

Harri-Augstein and Thomas (1991) propose that educators accomplish such goals by engaging in learning conversations, which they describe as a means by which we increase awareness about our own learning processes and challenge our conditioned ways of thinking, being, and doing. Often such reflective processes are presented as cycles—learning cycles. For example, Rodgers (2002) describes a reflection process influenced by John Dewey's perspectives on reflective thinking. This cyclical process presumes rigor and adherence to scientific method: presence to experience, description of experience, analysis of experience, and intelligent action or experimentation. Osterman and Kottkamp (2004) also describe a similar reflective process, referred to as an experimental learning cycle. Jay and Johnson (2002) offer a comprehensive definition of reflective practice that serves as the foundation for their teacher education program. It, too, implies a cyclical process:

> Reflection is a process, both individual and collaborative, involving experience and uncertainty. It is comprised of identifying questions and key elements of a matter that has emerged as significant, then taking one's thoughts into dialogue with oneself and with others. One evaluates insights gained from that process with reference to: (1) additional perspectives, (2) one's own values, experiences, and beliefs, and (3) the larger context within which the questions are raised. Through reflection, one reaches newfound clarity, on which one bases changes in action or disposition. New questions naturally arise, and the process spirals onward. (p. 76)

As in the previous chapter, each of these conceptions underscores the centrality of action in reflective practice, action that is informed by deliberative thinking. Thinking is a precursor to learning. But without commitments to subsequent changes in how we engage with ourselves, others, and the world around us, no improvement will be realized.

With general goals and cycles of reflective practice in mind, more focused questions arise. How do we have reflective conversations in which learning happens? What are the various elements or dimensions of reflective practice? The purpose of this chapter is to introduce fundamentals for reflective practice that pertain to all levels of the Reflective Practice

Spiral—individual, partner, small group or team, and schoolwide. To do this, we address four questions:

- What adult learning principles support reflective practices?
- What personal capacities foster reflective practices?
- What makes reflective practice meaningful?
- What learning designs promote reflective practices?

Following this chapter, in Chapters 3 through 6, we offer specific examples of how these fundamentals of reflective practice are incorporated by teachers and administrators in a variety of educational practice contexts to address specific goals.

WHAT ADULT LEARNING PRINCIPLES SUPPORT REFLECTIVE PRACTICES?

> Adult learning is voluntary in all its dimensions—participation, acquisition, and outcome.
>
> —Mary Jane Even (1987, p. 22),
> *Why Adults Learn in Different Ways*

There is an extensive research base about conditions that foster learning in adults. When considering how to implement reflective practices in schools, what is known about adult learners and learning should guide the design process. When adults enter any learning situation, they immediately begin to filter information based on the depth of their knowledge about such situations, as well as on their relevant repertoire of life experiences. They identify commonalities and discrepancies and employ cognitive processes to make sense of the situation. This involves structuring the new information to understand it, integrating the new information with previous knowledge, and then working with this newly integrated knowledge to foster concept formation, generalizations, and application. The learning process is not linear. Adult learners continually cycle back and forth between current knowledge and new information, employing problem-solving and inquiry processes (Even, 1987).

Merriam (1993), an adult learning scholar, articulates core values about adult learning from which principles for facilitating reflective practices can be derived:

- The individual is at the center of education
- There is goodness in each individual, and there is a need to release and trust that goodness

Table 2.1   Conditions for Powerful Learning (Brandt, 1998)

In general, we can say that people learn well under the following conditions:

What they learn

1. What they learn is personally meaningful.
2. What they learn is challenging, and they accept the challenge.
3. What they learn is appropriate for their developmental level.

How they learn

4. They can learn in their own way, have choices, and feel in control.
5. They use what they already know as they construct new knowledge.
6. They have opportunities for social interaction.
7. They get helpful feedback.
8. They acquire and use strategies.

Where they learn

9. They experience a positive emotional climate.
10. The environment supports the intended learning.

SOURCE: Reprinted by permission from R. Brandt (1998). *Powerful Learning*. Alexandria, VA: Association for Supervision and Curriculum Development. May not be reproduced without permission. The Association for Supervision and Curriculum Development is a worldwide community of educators advocating sound policies and sharing of best practices to achieve the success of each learner. To learn more, visit ASCD at www.ascd.org.

- Learning should result in growth toward one's potential
- Autonomy and self-direction are signposts of adulthood
- There is potency in the individual to achieve self-direction and fulfillment in the face of social, political, cultural, and historical forces (p. 133)

Brandt (1998) draws from several sources (e.g., American Psychological Association, 1997; Caine & Caine, 1997) to summarize conditions that promote "powerful learning" (see Table 2.1). He emphasizes that the content of learning must be meaningful and relevant to learners. The process should include opportunities to reflect on past experiences and is also enhanced by social interaction. The context must be supportive emotionally and structurally.

Taken together, the works of Even (1987), Merriam (1993), and Brandt (1998) point to several implications for the design of reflective practices for educators. First, educators must be respected as self-directed learners and recognized as in charge of their own learning. Second, reflective practices must be grounded in the educator's context of practice. The context of practice provides meaning that both motivates the adult to learn and influences the shaping of knowledge and skill acquisition. Third, opportunities should be provided to examine underlying beliefs, values, and assumptions in order to achieve deeper understanding of teaching and learning processes. Fourth, when introducing new information or perspectives, the reflective learning process must allow opportunities to compare and contrast, link, and integrate old and new perspectives. In sum, significant learning for educators involves an active process of knowledge construction drawing from experience and other knowledge sources, making sense of new ways of thinking, and moving toward application in the context of practice.

In the rest of this chapter, we describe personal capacities that promote trust, which is core to creating contexts in which individuals feel safe inquiring about their professional practice. We introduce strategies for expansion of thought, which lies at the center of new knowledge construction. We present considerations about motivation and relevance in the reflective process. Finally, we overview numerous learning designs in which reflection is embedded.

WHAT PERSONAL CAPACITIES FOSTER REFLECTIVE PRACTICE?

Personal capacities for reflection refers to the skills and dispositions that enhance one's ability to reflect and learn from practice, as well as to support others in their ability to do so. Individual educators can choose to develop these capacities on their own, regardless of whether or not colleagues also choose to. It is a great support, however, to have others coengaged in such development. In this section, we identify personal capacities focused on two fundamental conditions for reflective practice: trust, and inquiry and thinking. We invite you to refer to our Theory of Action for Reflective Practice (introduced in Chapter 1) as you consider the new ideas in this chapter. Ideas about trust relate to the elements of *pause* and *openness* (see Figure 2.1); ideas about thought and inquiry link with the *inquiry* and *thinking* elements of our theory.

Fostering Trusting Relationships

The quality of relationships is a key determinant of the quality of reflection and the potential for learning (Ellinor & Gerard, 1998; Wheatley, 1992), whether done alone or with others. Relationships influence the emotion with which one approaches reflection, and emotion controls the gateway to learning (Wolfe, 1997). Trust, in particular, must be present for individuals to share their thoughts and be open to expanding their ways of thinking and doing.

Figure 2.1   Theory of Action for Reflective Practice

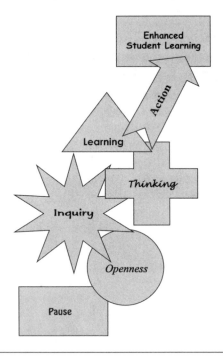

> Trust is perhaps the essential condition needed to foster reflective practice in any environment. If the reflective process is going to flourish in an organizational setting, the participants must be confident that the information they disclose will not be used against them—in subtle or not so subtle ways (Osterman & Kottkamp, 1993, p. 45).

Without trust, there is no foundation for a relationship focused on learning. Learning requires change. Change involves risk. "No one will talk about problems—personal or organizational—unless they feel safe, secure, and able to take risks" (Osterman & Kottkamp, 1993, p. 45).

Recent research offers convincing evidence that trust is an important requisite for learning and improvement in schools. A study of professional community in 248 elementary schools in Chicago found that "by far, the strongest facilitator of professional community is social trust among faculty members. When teachers trust and respect each other, a powerful social resource is available for supporting the collaboration, reflective

Table 2.2   Personal Capacities for Reflective Practice

Fostering Trust
What can I do to foster trust?

- Be present

- Be open

- Listen: with empathy, without judgment

- Seek understanding

- View learning as mutual

- Honor the person

- Honor the process

Expanding Thought and Inquiry
What can I do to expand thought and inquiry?

- Ask open questions
  Pay attention to intonation, syntax, presuppositions

- Respond with SPACE:
  Use silence, paraphrasing, accepting without judgment, clarifying, and elaborating

- Reframe
  Apply new frames to widen viewpoints

- Dialogue
  Engage in conversations that deepen understanding

dialogue, and deprivatization characteristics of professional community" (Bryk, Camburn, & Louis, 1999, p. 767). Bryk and Schneider (2002) explain that *relational trust* develops through interactions with people who share some common experience. In schools, relational trust evolves from social exchanges between and among members of a school community (e.g., teachers, students, parents, principals). Further, they explain, it is through daily interactions that individuals discern whether relational trust exists. Criteria for discerning such trust are identified as respect, competence, personal regard for others, and integrity.

What can you do to foster trust? To be in trusting relationships requires acting in trustworthy ways. One set of interrelated skills and dispositions that promote trustworthiness is described in the following paragraphs and outlined in Table 2.2. The choice to behave in these ways is difficult, given the pervasive norms of fast-paced doing in schools today. Developing and embedding these skills and dispositions as norms in our daily lives requires explicit, ongoing attention.

Be Present

Being present with oneself and others is an acknowledgment of value. Being present is to be aware of oneself, of others, and the surrounding circumstances. "To be aware is to allow our attention to broaden and expand to include more and more of our immediate experience. The central idea here is that we are capable of coming to understand what is happening as it is happening" (Isaacs, 1999, p. 144). Kahn (1992) describes how individuals who are psychologically present can bring themselves more fully to their work and to interactions with others at work, resulting in higher levels of productivity. He explains that

> The long term implication of such presence is that people who are present and authentic in their roles help to create shared understandings of their systems that are equally authentic and responsive to change and growth. This process is what allows social systems . . . to become unstuck and move toward new and productive ways of working. When individuals are open to change and connecting to work with others and are focused and attentive and complete rather than fragmented, their systems adopt the same characteristics, collectively. Individual and systemic wholeness, in these respects, are intertwined and complementary. (p. 331)

Raelin (2002) describes five skills of reflective practice: being, speaking, disclosing, testing, and probing. Similar to presence, he describes *being* as "the most unusual yet potentially powerful of the skills. . . . The object is . . . opening up to experience and to our interpersonal environment. We engage in such practices as suspending certainty, externalizing our thoughts, and exploring the tensions of opposites" (p. 70). Presence is a precursor to openness.

Be Open

Being open is a state of mind that allows consideration of multiple perspectives. It requires hearing different views as valid ways of thinking, not as threats. "Openmindedness is an active desire to listen to more sides than one, to give full attention to alternative possibilities, and to recognize the possibility of error even in beliefs that are dearest to us" (Zeichner & Liston, 1996, p. 10). Exposure to different views fosters inquiry by providing additional information, which may contrast with one's own views (Diss, Buckley, & Pfau, 1992; Hatton & Smith, 1995; Levin, 1995). In the absence of openness, reflection merely validates and perpetuates one's current views. At the core of being open is a belief that there are multiple ways of experiencing, making sense of, and acting in the world. Also recognized, if not anticipated, is the complexity that often results from remaining open and seeking a richer understanding of phenomena. In our fast-paced daily lives, we often make hasty decisions or accept superficial (sometimes incorrect) explanations or understandings. Being open guards against such tendencies.

Listen With Empathy and Without Judgment

Related to openness is the ability to listen well, without judgment and with empathy. Listening builds trust. Trust fosters relationships. Relationships provide the context for shared reflection, learning, development, and leadership, all of which are closely linked. If we do not listen well, we do not learn well and we do not connect well with others. If, as leaders, we do not learn and we do not connect, we also do not influence (lead) others. We can assert positional authority, but without engaging the hearts and minds of others, professional and organizational practices will not be advanced.

Our tendency is to listen from memory, screening and interpreting what is being said through our own filter of experiences, values, and beliefs (Carlson & Bailey, 1997; Isaacs, 1999). When we listen this way, a speaker's intended meaning may be lost or misinterpreted. Listening well requires an awareness and suspension of our own thoughts so the focus is on the speaker's experience and intended meaning (Garmston & Wellman, 1999; Lee, 1995). "To suspend is to change direction, to stop, step back, and see things with new eyes. This is perhaps one of the deepest challenges humans face—especially once they have staked out a position" (Isaacs, 1999, p. 135). This explains, in part, why it is so difficult to listen well. The listeners' own ways of thinking or acting are at risk of being changed or influenced (Rogers, 1986).

Empathetic listening involves an even deeper sense of genuine connection with another person, a feeling of strong connection not only to the words but also to the emotion felt and expressed by that person. "Empathic relationships generally confer the greatest opportunity for personal, and thus professional, growth in educational settings" (Rogers as described by Butler, 1996, p. 265). Listening is perhaps the greatest gift we can offer one another, and in the process, we foster the growth of a reflective community of educators.

Seek Understanding

Understanding is an outgrowth of listening well. Understanding does not require agreement, although full understanding often lays the groundwork for identifying points of agreement. Seeking to understand other people's thoughts and actions leads to a better appreciation of who they are, how they view their circumstances, and the ways in which they contribute or hope to contribute. And when engaged in authentic inquiry, both the speaker and listener experience increased depth of understanding. Understanding is one of the most respectful and powerful ways of

connecting with another person (Covey, 1989). When educators feel understood by their peers, they can more easily let go of needing to be right.
They can release their tight hold on their views, on their realities. They can
also more easily let go of judgments and negative assumptions. Mutual
understanding promotes trust, which, as emphasized previously, is a
requisite condition for inquiry and reflection.

View Learning as Mutual

To view learning as mutual means that partners in a reflective
process are learners and derive benefit. Schools are hierarchically structured organizations with unequal value implicitly assigned to individuals
depending on age, years of experience, degrees held, and even grade level
or content area taught. Too often, younger and less experienced teachers
who do not hold graduate degrees are socialized into thinking they are of
less value in their school community. Of course, the reverse can also be
true when more experienced teachers are stereotyped as lacking an interest in continued growth and change A mutual-learning stance sidesteps
the hierarchy and assumes value in the varied perspectives and experiences of each individual. Research in the area of mentoring has shown
this to be the case. Often, the experienced teachers who serve as mentors
gain as much or more than their less experienced mentees. Educators
committed to reflective practice can "approach all situations [and people]
with the attitude that they can learn something new" (Zeichner & Liston,
1996, p. 11).

Honor the Person

Perhaps the greatest threat to reflection and learning is to in some
way dishonor a person. Reflective educators interested in building up
their organizations must choose to honor people by offering the same
degree of respect that they wish to be shown, even when different views
are held. Talking behind someone's back, sharing information that was
offered in confidence, or building coalitions that exclude are acts of dis-
honoring people and breaking commitments to work and learn together.
In our efforts to be inclusive and to widen the circle, we must not assume
that *my* way of learning or expressing meaning is *the* way for others, also.
Here is a recent example from practice. A colleague shared that a teacher
kept showing up at meetings to learn more about embedding literacy practices into content area instruction in a high school. This teacher never
missed the meetings. While others verbally participated, he sat quietly and
listened. Privately, the facilitator inquired of the man how he felt the meetings were going. He indicated that his presence, albeit in silence, was his
means of demonstrating support. Respecting his presence and his silence
was honoring who he was and was one way to continue extending him a
culturally sensitive invitation to continue participating in the group.

Honor the Process

Process has developed a bad reputation among many educators. Granted, engaging in too much process without attaining meaningful outcomes is not time well spent. Developing capacities for reflective practice, however, takes time, explicit attention, practice, and feedback. There is no fast lane to creating a reflective learning community. Momentum and efficiency are slow to develop. Trusting relationships develop over time as individuals demonstrate trustworthy behaviors toward one another. Collective thinking capacities also develop over time as individuals learn how to reflect and think together.

How do we learn to think together to solve problems, create options for learning, and reflect on results? Recall the learning curve presented in introductory psychology courses. At first, engaging in new ways of thinking and doing feels awkward, inefficient, and even ineffective. There is a propensity to disengage early in the learning process because it doesn't feel right and because better results are not readily apparent. Over time, however, new ways of thinking and doing become more fluid, automatic, and embedded into practice. The learning curve holds true for adults just as it does for young people. Remind others so they also do not become discouraged or impatient. Stay the course. Remember the Chinese proverb "Sometimes you must go slow to go fast." The benefits of reflective practice come slowly to fruition.

Expanding Thought and Inquiry

Within the context of trusting relationships, expanded ways of thinking and genuine inquiry can emerge. "It is only through the process of inquiry that awareness, understanding, and competence are developed and realized" (Bright, 1996, p. 177). Thoughts, however, are stubborn or, stated more graciously, they are self-protective and self-validating (Carlson, 1997).

> Our thought system is like a filter that information passes through before it gets to our awareness. It is a complex, perfectly woven pattern of thought, linked together into concepts, beliefs, expectations, and opinions. It is our thought system that enables us to compare new facts or situations with what we already know from past experience. . . . Thought systems contain our view of "the way life is." They are the psychological mechanisms that convince us when we are right, accurate, or justified. (pp. 19–20)

Grounded in and reinforced by experience, our thoughts are not readily disposed to questioning.

When conflicts arise between new information and prior knowledge, prior experience can serve as either a hindrance or a facilitator to inquiry and thinking. In the case of conflicting information, Hashweh (2003) explains there are three possible outcomes: a conservative outcome in which there may be some change in thinking but, for the most part, existing views are preserved; a transitional outcome in which the individual remains in a state of conflict; or an accommodative outcome in which cognitive structures are reorganized and new learning occurs.

As educators experience new circumstances or roles, they are likely to experience conflict. In response to such conflict, reliance on previous ways of thinking and acting may be counterproductive. A bigger toolbox is needed. As one of this book's authors describes metaphorically, early in his career as an administrator he had one main tool, a hammer. He explains, if you are really good with a hammer, you tend to see every problem as a nail—and he did. The result was not always as successful as he would have liked. The more tools one has available, the greater the likelihood that appropriate tools can be effectively matched with particular presenting situations.

Underscoring the difficulties encountered in changing thoughts, some question whether it is reasonable to assume that thinking can be taught or changed. In response to such queries, we adhere to the least dangerous assumption: all educators can become more effective in their practice. This means we believe that educators can learn to think in ways that result in new understandings and practices *and* that, given supportive conditions, most will. We now describe four complementary strategies that increase the likelihood of inquiry being fostered and thinking being influenced: ask open questions, respond with SPACE, reframe circumstances and perspectives, and engage in dialogue. (These strategies also are listed in Table 2.2.)

Ask Open Questions

At the heart of reflective practice is inquiry. Inquiry is an active search for understanding, which is facilitated by carefully constructed questions. Perkins (1992), in his book *Smart Schools*, wrote, "Learning is a consequence of thinking" (p. 8). Our corollary is: thinking is a consequence of questions. A powerful question can alter all thinking and behaving that occurs afterward (Goldberg, 1998). Statements tend to spark analytic thinking and judgment. Questions, on the other hand, tend to spark creative thinking and generate a search for answers, a negotiation of meaning, or a continuation of dialogue. Inquiry helps people to construct their own meanings and become partners in helping others to construct the same.

Because language constructs everyone's reality, the language chosen when asking questions has a major impact on emotion, the learning environment, and ultimately personal identity as a learner. Intonation, syntax, and presuppositions are key linguistic elements in posing effective questions (Costa & Garmston, 2002). Each is described briefly here.

The nonverbal quality of *intonation* sends a message of intent. Intonation refers to how the message sounds. Intonation tends to be a more accurate discriminating variable than the content of a question. When asking questions, speakers need to align intonation with inquiry. Grinder (1993) identifies two kinds of voice intonation. One is referred to as *credible voice,* the other as *approachable voice.* Credible voice is used when giving directions or making statements that need to be viewed as credible or directive: "Get off the desk, now." This voice has a flat intonation pattern and drops at the end. The tone communicates no openness to being questioned. Approachable voice is used when asking questions or wanting input. "How might we design an experiment to test that hypothesis?" This voice has an intonation pattern that fluctuates up and down, and it ends with a rising tone. An approachable voice invites genuine inquiry and should be used when posing questions intended to prompt reflection.

A second element of asking questions is *syntax,* or how the question is structured. The nature of responses provided depends on the nature of the questions asked. If questions ask for recall, answers tend to be short and to the point: "What is the life cycle of a mosquito?" There is no elaboration. If the syntax of questions suggests making comparisons, contrasting different events, analyzing, or some other means of active processing of thoughts, answers are longer, with greater breadth and depth. If the syntax is structured to engage consideration of positive potential (such as, "What might be the best possible results when doing this presentation?" or "If you taught the perfect lesson, how would it look?"), people start to construct a positive future. When the mind is actively involved in constructing responses, the likelihood of behaving in congruent ways is increased. If people cannot internally or verbally construct positive outcomes, they encounter difficulty in moving forward to accomplish their desired goals.

A third element of asking questions to promote reflection and metacognition is *presupposition.* Presuppositions are very powerful. They work whether they are negative or positive. They are powerful because individuals and groups act as if presuppositions are true. For instance, a newly hired high school principal was informed by a staff member, "It's too bad that 250 of these students won't be here in the spring." The principal was shocked by this statement (a presupposition), but, sure enough, in the spring, 250 students had dropped out. If people believe that some kids cannot learn and that departure is inevitable, they will be correct. Many of the kids about whom this presupposition is held will choose to disengage and, ultimately, leave. Henry Ford is reported to have said, "Whether you think you can or think you can't, you are right." Presuppositions that are stated positively can foster more positive results.

Most of the time, educators are either planning for a future event or reflecting back on something that has already occurred. Following are examples of questions that may be helpful in promoting reflective thinking in these circumstances. As you read the questions, consider how intonation, syntax, and positive presuppositions might affect responses.

- How do you think the lesson went? What happened that caused it to go that way?
- When you think about what you had planned and what actually happened, what were the similarities and what were the differences?
- As you think about the results you got, what were some of the ways you designed the lesson to cause them to happen?
- When you reflect back on the lesson, what might you do differently next time?
- As you think about the last time you taught this lesson, what are some of the outcomes you want to have happen again?
- What are some of the professional goals that you are working on for yourself?
- Who or what are the resources for you as you work toward your professional goals?

Respond With SPACE

The way in which a person responds to another person influences thinking and inquiry just as much as questioning does. Costa and Kallick (2000a) use SPACE as an acronym for the response strategies described here.

If the intent of responding is to promote reflective thinking, time must be provided to think. Sometimes, this requires *silence*—the first element of the SPACE acronym—on the part of the listener. A fitting Estonian proverb says, "Silence is sometimes the answer." We tend to want answers quickly. But for reflection to occur, less is frequently more. Clues for determining whether partners are processing come from watching the eyes. When someone is thinking, the eyes are usually up or moving. When done thinking, the eyes come back to center and refocus on others. If people are interrupted with more questions or information while in the midst of thinking, they never have a chance to complete their thoughts. Silence allows people to think. Watch the eyes. You will know it is okay to respond when the speaker pauses and her attention and eyes have turned back toward you. Silent counting is another strategy that can help take longer pauses, although it is hard to listen when counting. One teacher hangs up reminder notes in her classroom that say, "Less talk, more visuals." We can each find ways to remind us that silence is sometimes the respond called for.

Paraphrasing, the next element of the SPACE acronym, requires listening. When listeners paraphrase, the speakers know that they have been heard. Paraphrasing is *not* parrot-phrasing. In other words, listeners should not say exactly the same thing the speakers just said. Such responses can be interpreted as mocking restatements or as lacking sincere interest, which damages rapport. Paraphrasing is taking the main concepts or ideas and saying them back to check out whether or not you have correctly interpreted the meaning and intent of the speaker. Some sentence stems to use are

- Let me see if I understand; you said . . .
- I want to make sure I got all the points; you said . . .
- You said [this], and then you said [this], and then . . . Is that right?

Paraphrasing communicates a genuine attempt to try to understand. If listeners have the wrong meaning, the speaker can correct through restatement.

Accepting nonjudgmentally is the third response strategy described by the SPACE acronym. If listeners want a stream of meaningful thoughts from speakers, they must accept what is being said. Interrupting with one's own viewpoints or responding with apparent disagreement will inhibit thinking and sharing. Judgment, whether it is praise or rejection, shuts down thinking (Deci, 1995; Kohn, 1993). Listeners can accept nonjudgmentally without adhering to the same views. Acceptance and disagreement are communicated not only through words but through body language and facial expression. Nonverbal communication accounts for the majority of communicative intent. Relaxed body posture, relaxed facial expression, and head and eye orientation toward the speaker provide nonverbal cues that what is being said is being heard and accepted without judgment.

Clarifying is the next SPACE response behavior that can increase reflection and metacognition. If a teacher says, "I want students to know the times table," a principal might respond, "How will I know when a student knows the times table?" By asking clarifying questions, teachers can distill in their own minds the desired student responses and indicators of learning. This kind of reflection happens only when people take the time to ask naive questions that internally illuminate the meaning. When asking clarifying questions, be sure to use proper intonation, such as approachable voice, so clarifying does not sound like interrogating or accusing.

Extending is the last response strategy of the SPACE acronym and one that is easily and frequently used. The following sentence stems, for example, call for an extension of thinking:

- Say more about . . .
- Tell me more about . . .
- Some other possible connections are . . .

Using these stems gives people a chance to extend their thinking beyond what they have already considered and discussed. Another strategy for extending thinking is to ask take-away questions. For instance, "As we end our conversation, what are the possible connections to the team goals?" Or "I wonder if we were to ask the students what they thought, how they might respond?" Take-away questions frequently cause continued thought and reflection. It is not unusual for people to show up the next day and say, "I have been thinking about our conversation and . . ." This is a sign that people are actively participating in a reflective process.

Reframe Circumstances

Consistently referred to in the literature on reflective practice is the need for reframing or frame-breaking. This is a process of coming to see things from a different point of view or from within a new framework. Often we are cued to reframe a situation—or, more accurately, to reframe our perceptions of a situation—when we feel stuck, perplexed, or upset. For example, an interaction with a colleague or student may not have gone well, or a new approach for absenteeism does not seem to be working, or questions linger about the outcomes of a recently taught course. Choosing to reframe presumes the possibility that current views may be incomplete and inaccurate. Butler (1996) explains, "To dislodge personal theories, to break the framework for understandings that govern personal and professional performance and to create newer versions involves, necessarily, a period of discomfort" (p. 276).

In Raelin's (2002) model of reflective practice (introduced earlier in this chapter), he identifies *being* as the skill that allows one to be in a framing mode. He describes framing as "how we think about a situation, more specifically, how we select, name, and organize facts to tell a story to ourselves about what is going on and what to do in a particular situation" (p. 72). Stories are typically recounted in one mode or frame. Coming to understand the stories more fully or in alternative ways often requires reframing. Following are some sample questions to prompt reframing. These and more reframing questions are available as Resource 2.A.

- How might I think about this situation differently?
- What am I not considering?
- What judgments and assumptions are blocking alternative ways of seeing this situation?
- What learning principles have I disregarded in my lesson design?
- Why am I holding on to this view—what function does it serve, and what might I be defending?

Tightly held views block us from considering different explanations and from learning new ways of thinking and practice. For learning to occur, firmly entrenched views must be let go. "Learning is and should be, on some occasions, a disturbing and unsettling process . . . deep learning involves frame breaking and discomfort" (Butler, 1996, pp. 275–276). It is not unusual, therefore, to enlist another person to coach different ways of thinking about specific situations.

Jay and Johnson (2002) introduce comparative reflection as a way to "reframe the matter for reflection in light of alternative views, others' perspectives, research, etc." (p. 77). They pose specific questions intended to support the reframing process:

- What are alternative views of what is happening?
- How do other people who are directly or indirectly involved describe and explain what's happening?

- What does the research contribute to an understanding of this matter?
- How can I improve what's not working?
- If there is a goal, what are some other ways of accomplishing it?
- How do other people accomplish this goal?
- For each perspective and alternative, who is served and who is not? (p. 77)

When reframing, then, we can only begin where our thinking tendencies bring us. In other words, we start with where we are. We may even stubbornly hold on to these views for a while, convinced that the problem or issues are "out there." We blame what is external to us, defending what we know or believe that we know. From this place of comfort we must intentionally and courageously move ourselves to uncover and question our assumptions, to consider alternative explanations, and to act based on new and previously unconsidered findings. Discovery of such findings is both humbling (we didn't know it from the start) and exhilarating (we now have more options for advancing our practice). By way of example, we offer below just three of the many types of reframing that educators could invoke in their practice: reframing with a lens on relational and human dimensions; reframing that widens the cultural proficiency lens; and reframing that shifts from *how* questions to *what* and *why* questions.

One type of reframing, that we refer to as *relational reframing*, involves shifting from a dominant academic or cognitive focus when working with students to being more inclusive of relational and human dimensions. Max van Manen, widely acclaimed for his technical, practical, and critical reflection typology (see Chapter 1), also writes about the pathic dimension of teaching. He explains:

> pedagogical competence . . . is largely tied into pathic knowledge. Teacher knowledge is pathic to the extent that the act of teaching depends on the teacher's personal presence, relationship perceptiveness, tact for knowing what to say and do in contingent situations, thoughtful routines and practices." (van Manen, 2002, pp. 216–217)

Van Manen (2002) reminds us about the significance of pathic knowledge in pedagogical effectiveness, which underscores what most educators already know and what accounts for many of their decisions to teach. Relationships and connection are precursors to teaching and learning. Instruction is mediated by personal and relational factors.

Here we share examples to illustrate the significance of reframing meaning and purpose within teacher-student relationships. The first involves a junior high special education teacher whose focus with students with disabilities was almost exclusively teaching academic skills. Every period of the school day, a new group of students showed up in her separate classroom to receive academic instruction in a small group setting. She was urged to consider a wider array of services and supports for her students because they were having a range of difficulties in their general education classes. Her priorities remained academics in the pull-out setting until, with encouragement, she observed some of her students in general education settings. She returned from the observations in tears. She had no idea how difficult it was for her students and how significant was the discrepancy between what she had chosen as priorities and what was required in the regular classes in terms of organization, management, study skills, social interactions, and academics. This experience gave rise to a different way of framing her role in the lives of these students. Her focus shifted to consider the question "What can I do to increase the possibility that my students will be more successful in the general education classes?" In this case, observation had a powerful effect because the teacher had a connection with the students being observed. She could feel their discomfort and frustration, which gave rise to a pathic response.

Another even more poignant example involved a team of general and special educators and related service providers. They were debating whether a student with significant physical, medical, and cognitive disabilities should continue attending their school, his neighborhood school. Even though the student had attended that school for several years, they questioned whether the placement was still appropriate, given uncertainty about what he was learning and a gradual decline in his functioning. They could not measure, or in other ways discern, growth. The debate came to an abrupt halt when they were reminded of the student's degenerative disease and that recent declines indicated he did not have long to live. Instantly, a shift occurred from focusing on whether the student was learning to asking, "How do we support this student and his family in our school community for as long as he will be here with us?"

A second application of reframing as a tool for reflective practice involves consideration of educational matters through a *cultural proficiency* lens. This reframing addresses a critical dimension of teaching practice, shifting from judgment to understanding in our interactions with students and colleagues whose backgrounds and cultures differ from our own. Attwood and Seale-Collazo (2002) identify the difficulty of "understanding student resistance beyond the temptations of blaming the student or yourself." In conflicts with students, particularly students whose cultures, experiences, and interests differ from one's own, educators can easily (and sometimes unconsciously) assume a position of blame, blaming students and themselves. Perspectives must shift from viewing students as problems to understanding what knowledge and experiences students bring to school and, as important, to understanding our own assumptions about learning and about students. Milner (2003) explains, introspective behavior could lead teachers to better understand and relate to their students of color because they better understand themselves as racial beings. . . . Many White teachers do not see themselves as racial beings and often (idealistically) dismiss notions of race. Reflection in cultural contexts could prove effective as they grapple with ways to better meet the needs of diverse learners. . . . Indeed, students of color often operate in classrooms . . . that do not meet their affective, social, and intellectual needs. . . . Much of this ineffectuality is a consequence of racial mismatches in cultural contexts: Teachers do not understand the experiences and life worlds of their students. (p. 180)

Milner (2003) recommends journaling as a relatively safe means by which teachers can "think through often uncomfortable, complex, and challenging issues they may not be ready to discuss or expose to a group" (p. 178) to increase awareness of themselves as racial beings. Further, he advocates that specific questions be offered to guide reflection about race in cultural contexts, at least initially, when teachers just begin engaging in reflection about race and culture. Milner poses the following questions to support reframing of culturally grounded conflicts:

- How will my race influence my work as a teacher with students of color?
- How might my students' racial experiences influence their work with me as the teacher?
- What is the impact of race on my beliefs?
- How do I, as a teacher, situate myself in the education of others, and how do I negotiate the power structures around race in my class to allow students to feel a sense of worth?
- How might racial influences impact my and my students' interests in the classroom? How might I connect lessons to those interests?
- To what degree are my role as teacher and my experiences superior to the experiences and expertise of my students, and is there knowledge to be learned from my constituents?
- How do I situate and negotiate the students' knowledge, experiences, expertise, and race in relation to my own?
- Am I willing to speak about race on behalf of those who might not be present in the conversation, both inside and outside of school, and am I willing to express the injustices of racism in conservative spaces? (Milner, 2003, p. 178)

A third example of reframing involves a shift in the type of questions that are asked. Peter Block (2002), in his book *The Answer to How Is Yes: Acting on What Matters,* suggests a paradigmatic way of reframing questions: moving away from *how* questions and toward *what* and *why* questions (or at least achieving a better balance between these types of questions). *How* questions, he explains, carry the risk of passing quickly over *what* and *why* questions, which are questions that give our lives and our work purpose. *How* questions often presume the answers are "out there," vested in the external world around us, not inside us. *How* questions reinforce our cultural propensity for doing more and more and more! Block explains,

> We live in a culture that lavishes all of its rewards on what works, a culture that seems to value what works more than it values what matters. I am using the phrase "what works" to capture our love of practicality and our attraction to what is concrete and measurable. The phrase "what matters" is short hand for our capacity to dream, to reclaim our freedom, to be idealistic, and to give our lives to those things which are vague, hard to measure, and invisible. (p. 4)

It is true that *how* questions can grow from a genuine desire to understand and support something new. Yet, *how* questions can also deflect individual responsibility and ownership of presenting situations. As every initiator of a new idea or practice knows, asking *how* questions is a strong defense against taking action.

The following example illustrates how the *how* question failed to change practice for a group of paraprofessionals. Through modeling and demonstration, they were taught how to teach students with disabilities to do more for themselves in daily classroom activities. For example, instead of the paraprofessionals gathering all the materials for an instructional activity, they were instructed how to prompt students to prepare for the activities themselves, without adult assistance. After being so instructed, one paraprofessional responded, "We don't have to learn how to do this because we already do these things for the students." In this situation, their role frame of "doing for" and "taking care of" the students (instead of teaching them) was firmly grounded in past experience and expectations. They did not view the students as capable of independence and so felt no need to teach the students to participate, even partially, in classroom activities. Such frames are not easily broken. Again we wonder what new insights and actions might have emerged if the paraprofessionals had opportunities to reflect around more positive and participatory possibilities for students. What might be valuable in terms of their participation in family and community activities? What kinds of interactions might be valued by their peers?

In some situations, reflecting on our own learning experiences provides a springboard for reframing how we might support student learning. Consider the scenario that was just shared about paraprofessionals supporting students with special needs. What if the paraprofessionals had been asked to reflect on how they learned to drive a car? What did it feel like? How much practice and what kind of assistance were needed early in their learning versus later in their learning? How long did it take to learn? At what point did they feel the thrill of competence? Their experiences would likely mirror stages that most everyone goes through when learning new skills. First we acquire new skills, then we gain fluency, and then we generalize them to other settings. Finally, we "own" those skills. We can use them at different times and places. We are independent and feel competent and efficacious performing them. We reached this point because someone believed that we would be independent and gave us the right amount of assistance at the right time and then faded their support over time. Considering *what* and *why* questions prior to *how* questions can open the door for deeper understanding and commitment to effectively supporting student learning.

Block (2002) does acknowledge that *how* questions, in the right context, are valid and useful. But too often "they become the primary questions, the controlling questions, or the defining questions" (p. 24). Instead he urges questions that are more inviting of our own human deliberations and more empowering of our own free will. He provides examples of reframing *how* questions to *what* questions such that reflections about personal meaning, purpose, and responsibility are elicited. When someone asks, "*How* do I get others to change?" the intent is external. How do I get someone else to do something different? Because we do not have control over the behavior of other people, we must shift or reframe our focus on what we can do. The focus shifts from external to internal. Here are his examples:

• From . . . *How do you do it?*	To . . . *Is it worth doing?*
• From . . . *How long will it take?*	To . . . *What commitment am I willing to make?*
• From . . . *How much does it cost?*	To . . . *What is the price I am willing to pay?*
• From . . . *How do you get those people to change?*	To . . . *What is the transformation in me that is required?* and *What is my contribution to the problem I am concerned with?*
• From . . . *How do we measure it?*	To . . . *What measurement would have meaning to me?*
• From . . . *Where else has this worked?*	To . . . *What do we want to create together?*

SOURCE: Block, 2002 (pp. 15–32).

Readers are strongly encouraged to read Peter Block's book *The Answer to How Is Yes: Acting on What Matters*, for in-depth consideration of both the original and the reframed questions.

In a recent interview (Sparks, 2003), Block captures the essence of his reframing as "trying to shift the focus from skills and methodology to issues of spirit, of will, of courage" (p. 52). Applied to our present focus on reflective practices in schools, before rushing to a series of *how* questions (such as, How do I engage in reflective thinking? How can we find time to meet? and How long would it take to go schoolwide?), readers might consider engaging around the following *what* and *why* questions:

- What do I value about being reflective and thinking about my practice?
- What kinds of questions do I have about my practice?
- What contributions might reflective practice make to our school community?
- Am I willing to be open to examination of my practice, my thinking about practice, and the effects of my practice on others?

Reframing is one of the most powerful tools in a reflective educator's toolbox. It offers one strategy for challenging our values, beliefs, and assumptions and paving the way for considering alternative explanations and achieving more accurate, thorough understandings. The previous examples illustrate the power of reframing in the lives of educators and the students and communities they serve. More examples are offered in Chapters 3 through 6. (A list of questions to support reframing is provided as Resource 2.A.)

Engage in Dialogue

The power of dialogue to promote reflection and learning has been widely claimed (Bohm, 1989; Ellinor & Gerard, 1998; Garmston & Wellman, 1997, 1999; Isaacs, 1999). Dialogue has been described as a "conversation with a center, not sides" (Isaacs, 1999, p. 19) and as a "living experience of inquiry within and between people" (p. 9). It is a process of sharing and thinking together for the purposes of expanding thinking, promoting understanding, making connections, and generating possibilities. "Thinking together implies that you no longer take your own position as final. You relax your grip on certainty and listen to the possibilities that simply result from being in relationship with others—possibilities that might not otherwise have occurred" (Isaacs, 1999, p. 19). Dialogue is also a way to get unstuck by uncovering assumptions and beliefs that block effective thinking and action (Ellinor & Gerard, 1998).

Dialogue is frequently contrasted with discussion (Ellinor & Gerard, 1998; Garmston & Wellman, 1997, 1999; Isaacs, 1999). As depicted in Figure 2.2, dialogue can be thought of as an inclusive and opening-up process in which participants discover new perspectives and connections and arrive at fresh understandings, insights, and connections. There is no pressure to come up with one answer or one point of view. Dialogue holds and reveals many possibilities without constraint. Discussion can be thought of as a narrowing and eliminating process. The purpose of dialogue is to increase understanding and possibility; the purpose of discussion is to narrow options and make decisions. Both processes are necessary ways of conversing, but the distinction needs to be made about when each is most

Figure 2.2   Illustrated Comparison Between the Processes of Dialogue and Discussion

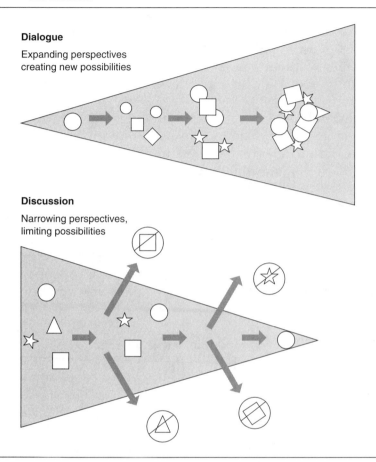

appropriate. Moving to discussion and decision making before adequate dialogue often leads to decisions that lack sufficient information and to decisions that do not stay made. Underlying the thinking about dialogue is a theory that shared meaning leads to shared thinking, which leads to aligned action.

Some decisions are not important enough to warrant a group going through an extensive, participatory process of dialogue before decision making. For example, the color of copy paper or the contents of the vending machine would not be worthy of extended periods of conversation. But important and complex decisions that affect students and staff call for consideration of many diverse perspectives. For example, how should new students and families be welcomed to school? How might our schedule be revised to allow more time for team learning? What do we need to consider when forming flexible instructional groups? In what ways might we rethink counseling and course options and sequences to ensure equitable access by all our students? What principles should ground decision making about dealing with financial cutbacks in our district? For these types of substantial decisions, all the resources in a group should be tapped for at least two reasons. First, decisions should be made on the richest set of information. Second, people can usually live with decisions when they feel their viewpoint has been respected and understood and when the reasons for an ultimate decision are communicated and understood.

For an illustration of the difference in outcomes that can be realized when using an inclusive dialogue (instead of a focused discussion) prior to making a decision, refer to the diagram of two groups in Figure 2.3a and Figure 2.3b. Each diagram shows a group of 12 people, each of whom is indicated by the circled letters, seated in a circle. In the top circle, only person A and person H share their respective perspectives with the rest of the group (represented by the letters A and H in the center of the circle). In the bottom circle, all of the 12 individuals share their respective perspectives with the group (represented by all the letters in the center of the circle). Now consider that each group makes a decision about how to proceed based on the perspectives shared (i.e., the perspectives in the center of each circle).

- Which group had more people actively participating?
- Which group probably learned the most during its conversation?
- Which group had a richer set of perspectives on which to base a decision?
- Which group might have discovered several new possibilities for moving forward?
- Which group's members are more likely to honor and abide by the decisions made?

This exercise visually illustrates two different ways that groups can converse and the likely consequences of each type of conversation. The group in the bottom circle could be thought of as having engaged in a dialogue. The group in the top circle is more likely to have moved quickly to discussion and thereby limited the number of perspectives shared.

Unfortunately, in schools, many conversations about important topics look like that of the group in Figure 2.3a. Only a few perspectives are shared, resulting in poorer-quality decisions and in decisions that are not honored by all group members. Not surprisingly, therefore, some topics appear repeatedly on group agendas. Often groups will argue there is not enough time to dialogue before making decisions. These same groups, however, out of necessity allocate time to revisit "decisions" that have not been honored. Often, we end up spending time addressing the same issues over and over and over again. A proactive stance that allows time for dialogue about important issues on the front end may ultimately be more efficient and effective.

Figure 2.3a   Group Considering the Perspectives of Just Two Members

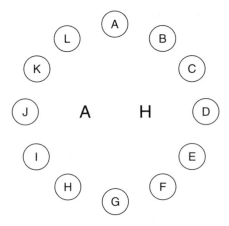

Figure 2.3b   Group Considering the Perspectives of All Members

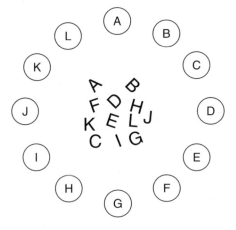

WHAT MAKES REFLECTIVE PRACTICE MEANINGFUL?

> Adults learn, retain, and use what they perceive is relevant to their professional needs.
>
> —From McGregor et al.(1998, p. 4), *Professional Development for All Personnel in Inclusive Schools*

That the focus of reflection must be relevant to practice cannot be overstated. Knowledge, processes, and skills that improve educators' effectiveness with students are powerful motivators for learning. The primary rewards of teachers are known to lie in the accomplishments of students

(Lieberman & Miller, 1999; Rosenholtz, 1989). Without a meaningful focus, efforts to establish reflective practices in school will not be successful. What constitutes meaningful? Here we describe four influences on meaning: topic (content), type of reflection, opportunities to strengthen relationships, and opportunities to learn.

Topic refers to the content focus of reflection. To improve student outcomes, the focus of reflective practices must in some way be related to student learning (Bryk et al., 1999; Newmann & Wehlage, 1995). Within this broad domain, more specific emphases are targeted depending on specific context and student needs. A specific topic or focus may be precipitated by feelings such as dissonance, dismay, frustration, surprise, curiosity, and conflict (Clarke, 1995). Scribner (1999) identified internal factors that motivate teachers to learn, all of which predominantly focused on core instructional elements, including content knowledge (especially among secondary teachers), pedagogical skill deficits, challenges to classroom management, and gaps in student-centered knowledge. In their work with principals, Barnett and O'Mahoney (2002) identified three areas of high interest for reflective practice: identifying student learning outcomes and monitoring progress; developing strategic leadership capacities; and improving the performance of school-based teams. Some authors assert that learning for professionals should be largely self-directed (Bailey, Curtis, & Nunan, 1998; Butler, 1996) so that topics are valid and of interest to participants. All of this supports the assertion that improving personal practice serves as a motivation for professional learning. Table 2.3 presents an illustrative sampling of topics that might be meaningful emphases for reflection.

Type of reflection refers to the specific aim of reflection within a given topical focus. As mentioned in Chapter 1 and throughout the literature on reflective practice, three types of reflection have been identified: technical, practical, and critical (Grimmet, MacKinnon, Erickson, & Riecken, 1990; Hatton & Smith, 1995; Taggart & Wilson, 1998; van Manen, 1977). A technical focus of reflection examines methods or technique; a practical focus examines both goals and methods of practice; and a critical focus examines not only goals and methods but also outcomes from a moral, ethical, and social perspective. With this latter focus, "reflection is an intellectually active, critical, and extending process by which teachers appreciate the implications of their classroom decisions in terms of the immediate needs of students and the broader goals of society" (Lasley, 1992, p. 26). Table 2.4 offers examples of questions to guide these types of reflection.

As discussed in Chapter 1, we caution against presuming a hierarchy of reflection. For example, technical reflection is sometimes considered the lowest level and critical reflection the highest level. We would argue all types are needed and beneficial, each serving a different purpose and all serving the purpose of equitable opportunities and furthering social justice. It is not just critical reflection that serves this end. According to Fendler (2003),

Table 2.3   Sampling of Topics to Promote Meaningful Reflection

Focus on students

- Understanding individual student strengths, challenges, learning styles, and interests
- Observing or listening to students to determine problem-solving, organizational, and learning strategies
- Reviewing student work to determine overall levels of performance and specific interventions
- Analyzing patterns of social interaction among students
- Determining effective student groupings to support learning, participation, access, and equity
- Reviewing curricular materials to determine appropriateness, given student abilities, interests, and background, as well as broader community values

Focus on self

- Understanding of conceptual underpinnings of curricular emphases and how all the parts fit together to create a meaningful whole
- Determining the effectiveness of various instructional strategies within specific content areas and given unique contextual factors
- Paying attention to individual as well as group learning needs and strengths
- Examining personal assumptions, biases, or conflicts with students, peers, or parents
- Revisiting personal purpose, values, and beliefs and their alignment with personal educational practices
- Determining defining elements of my own culture and how that may be influencing my interactions with students and colleagues of color
- Assessing my cultural proficiency and identifying areas and strategies for growth
- Being inclusive and supportive of parents, community members, and colleagues
- Assuming responsibility for team and schoolwide initiatives

Focus on staff

- Determining assignments for instructional teams focused on specific groups of students
- Developing supportive mentoring and induction experiences for staff members who are new to the school
- Intentionally including colleagues in reflection and learning efforts

Focus on school

- Assessing cultural competence, including organizational policies and practices and their impact on equity across all student groups
- Engaging conversations about race and other types of cultural difference and the impact on student, collegial, and community relations

(Continued)

Table 2.3 (Continued)

- Creating the schoolwide schedule to embed collaborative learning opportunities for teams of teachers
- Examining space to determine appropriate use, given instructional needs of students
- Designing effective communication systems to connect and keep informed all members of the school community
- Examining student data and setting priorities for educational improvement initiatives
- Focusing site-based governance practices on issues of increased student learning

Focus on community

- Extending meaningful opportunities for parent and community involvement
- Seeking ways to foster understanding and competence of different cultures represented in the school community
- Inviting community involvement in determining district and school goals and in actions to achieve the goals
- Encouraging participation by community resource personnel
- Sharing information and improvements with the surrounding community

The alleged opposition between technical reflection and social reconstructionist [critical] reflection is a false dichotomy . . . both traditions of reflective practice may constitute political activism. . . . Teachers . . . who engage in reflective traditions that appear to be instrument or technocratic may do so precisely because of a heartfelt commitment to social reconstruction. . . . Because they believe that the efficient mastery of subject matter by their students is the most effective means of redressing social inequities. Educators from all political persuasions engage in a wide variety of reflective practices. (p. 21)

Also consider that the career stage of a teacher can play into the type of reflection engaged as well. Novice teachers (early-career teachers) and expert teachers are known to differentially reflect. When practice-related questions or new circumstances arise, expert teachers have a much richer experiential base of knowledge (tacit knowledge) on which to draw than do novice teachers. Reporting on his classic teacher expertise studies, Berliner (1986) explains that

Experts possess a special kind of knowledge about learners that is different from that of novices . . . and of a very different order than is subject matter knowledge . . . it is knowledge that influences classroom management and is the basis for transferring subject matter. (p. 10)

This excerpt points to a more sophisticated tacit knowledge on the part of expert teachers that enhances their ability to support *transfer* of subject

Table 2.4   Sample Questions to Prompt Different Types of Reflection
(Lasley, 1992)

Reflection Questions: A Technical Focus

- What practices are and are not effective in the classroom?
- What problems require attention?
- What approaches can be used by the teacher to correct problem situations?
- Is the class organized and well managed?

Reflection Questions: A Conceptual Focus

- What is the espoused philosophical or theoretical basis for current practice?
- Are the teacher's classroom practices consistent with the teacher's espoused philosophy?
- Does current practice appear to foster or diminish student attentiveness to assigned tasks and learning?

Reflection Questions: A Dialectical Focus

- Is the philosophy of the teacher consistent with the needs of the students?
- What teacher practices enhance or diminish student growth?
- What student needs are not addressed by current teacher and school practices?
- How should schools be reordered and restructured?
- And what must teachers do to facilitate such restructuring?

SOURCE: Adapted with permission from T. J. Lasley (1992). Promoting teacher reflection. *Journal of Staff Development*, 13(1): 24–29. May not be reproduced without permission.

area knowledge to students. They are not just teaching content, they are expertly crafting the means by which content is made accessible to students. Expert teachers' richly developed schemata of student differences and context variations result in designing more effective learning environments and strategies than do novice educators (Sparks-Langer & Colton, 1991). Experts also see a broader context for problems that emerge and can draw on their tacit knowledge to determine effective interventions and supports. Berliner (1986) adds that expert teachers, when presented with novel situations about which they must determine a course of action, take a bit longer to respond than do novice teachers, presumably because of the wider, deeper, and more connected knowledge bases from which they draw.

Early-career teachers tend to focus their attention at the more technical level of reflection (Ross, 1990; Sparks-Langer, Simmons, Pasch, Colton, & Starko, 1990). Leat (1995) explains that early-career teachers need to focus primarily on the immediate classroom context, including classroom management and relationships with students. He found that too much emphasis on reflection at other levels (e.g., theoretical or critical) could be the source of considerable stress. Reflection at higher and deeper levels tends to occur more frequently in experienced teachers, although Pultorak (1996) did find that when novice teachers engaged in a structured interview that posed questions aimed at eliciting critical reflection, these teachers developed in their ability to critically reflect over time. Regardless of the level of reflection or the career stage of an individual teacher, reflection is viewed as the process by which teachers continue to improve their practice and move from novice to expert (Butler, 1996; Steffy, Wolfe, Pasch, & Enz, 2000).

The final two influences on making reflective practices meaningful are closely related: *opportunities to strengthen relationships* and *opportunities to learn.* The opportunity to learn with colleagues is of high interest to many educators. Such collaboration can satisfy associational needs. For example, members in study groups focused on the topic of literacy reported that their primary interest in participating was the opportunity to learn with and get to know other educators (Henry et al., 1999). Chapters 4, 5, and 6 offer numerous examples of ways that educators have constructed meaningful learning experiences together.

Ultimately, the determination of meaningfulness is individually constructed. For some educators, topical focus will be the largest determining factor. For others, the opportunity to learn with colleagues may prove more influential. For many, a combination is important. Regardless of initial motivating factor, most important is to begin.

WHAT LEARNING DESIGNS PROMOTE REFLECTIVE PRACTICE?

There are many ways to design and structure professional learning to foster reflective practices. Teachers seem to engage in different learning designs or structures depending on the focus of the learning objective. In a study by Scribner (1999), teachers viewed collaborating with peers as the most beneficial way to learn about instructional strategies and classroom management. To learn about a subject area, individual inquiry and access to outside expertise (e.g., information delivered in workshops) was viewed as most helpful. To learn more about social factors influencing students and the school, teachers relied most on their own experience.

By structures we mean how the reflective learning process is organized. Think of structures for learning in both big or strategic and small or tactical ways. Big structures are designed based on responses to questions such as these: What is the overall learning goal? Who and how many people are involved? What kinds of activities are involved in the learning process (e.g., writing, watching videotapes, observing in classrooms, shadowing or interviewing students, examining student work products)? What is the schedule for learning over time? How will outcomes of the reflective learning process be incorporated into practice? Focused or small structures refer to the specific ways in which reflective thought is prompted or guided. Small structures are designed in response to questions such as the following: What are the specific desired outcomes of the reflective process (e.g., lesson plans, revisions of student assignments, designs to promote classroom community, understanding student experiences and perspectives)? Have the participating educators been involved in reflective learning cycles previously? Is the topic or content focus of reflection new to the participants?

In terms of possibilities for big structures, we refer you to the National Staff Development Council (NSDC; see www.nsdc.org), which offers many resources on designs to foster excellence in professional learning in which reflective practices are embedded. We draw your attention to two resources. First, the Summer 1999 issue of the *Journal of Staff Development*, titled "Powerful Designs of Learning," offers a menu of designs for professional learning. Each learning design is described, examples are provided, and additional resources are identified. A sampling of the learning designs featured in this issue is briefly summarized in Table 2.5. Second, NSDC recently published an extensive monograph and accompanying CD-ROM, titled *Powerful Design for Professional Learning* (Easton, 2004), that includes 21 learning designs, descriptions, tools, and examples in use. It is a remarkably useful resource.

In terms of smaller structures, reflection can occur alone or with others and can be structured or guided to varying degrees, depending on the purpose, the context, and the individuals involved. Employing more than one form of reflection can also be beneficial (e.g., Haefner, 2004; Perry & Power, 2004; Pultorak, 1996). Reflecting alone and with others each has its advantages, although the potential of collaborative reflective practice is particularly great (e.g., Risko, Vukelich, & Roskos, 2002). Recall that one of John Dewey's distinct criteria for reflective thinking was that it should occur in community, with others (Rodgers, 2002). There is also emerging consensus that guided or structured reflection, sometimes including specific instruction about types of reflection and reflection strategies, yields more satisfactory results, especially when individuals are new to engaging in reflective practices and when critical reflection is a desired intent (Dinkelman, 2000; Pultorak, 1996; Risko et al, 2002; Spalding & Wilson, 2002; Yost, Sentner, & Forlenza-Bailey, 2000). It is not safe to assume that educators know how to or will be inclined to reflect on their practice with others even when they are teamed to do so (Supovitz, 2002). Stated more positively, when provided with structures and guidelines, more substantial thinking and outcomes are likely. This is one reason we have included sample reflection protocols and tools in the Resources for your use.

CLOSING

Opportunities for educators to reflect on and learn from practice are limitless. Every experience presents an opportunity for growth, and even the most accomplished educators can improve their practice. In this chapter we identified what we view as fundamental considerations for educators

Table 2.5   Sampling of Designs to Promote Staff Reflection and Learning
(NSDC, 1999)

Action Research	"Action research is a form of disciplined inquiry that . . . can be as simple as raising a question about some educational practice and collecting information to answer the question, or can be as complicated as applying a *t*-Test to determine whether or not post-test results from an experimental group are statistically significant" (Glanz, 1999, p. 22).
Cadres	"Cadres are small groups that coalesce around specific issues, research options, and recommended course of action" (Rapaport, 1999, p. 24).
Cases	"Case-based professional development involves using carefully chosen, real-world examples of teaching to serve as springboards for discussion among small groups of teachers" (Barnett, 1999, p. 26).
Coaching	"Coaching provides a model of respectful collegial reflection about instructional decisions" (Harwell-McKee, 1999, p. 28).
Examining Student Work	Examining student work involves "structured conversations about the assignments teachers give to students, the standards students must achieve, and student work" (Mitchell, 1999, p. 32).
Journaling	"Journal writing . . . [is] a place for learners to record observations, toy with various perspectives, analyze their own practice, interpret their understanding of topics, keep records, make comments, or reconstruct experiences" (Killion, 1999, p. 36).
Mentoring	Mentoring "provides the newcomer with support, guidance, feedback, problem-solving guidance, and a network of colleagues who share resources, insights, practices, and materials" (Robbins, 1999, p. 40).
Portfolios	A portfolio is "a collection of items . . . gathered over time which forms the basis for discussion by colleagues or members of a group" (Dietz, 1999, p. 45).
Shadowing Students	"Shadowing is the process of following a student and systematically recording that student's instructional experiences. The technique . . . provides a rich display of what happens in the classroom and provides a deeper understanding of the connection between pedagogy and student performance" (Wilson & Corbett, 1999, p. 47).
Study Groups	Study groups involve "a small number of individuals joining together to increase their capacities through new learning for the benefit of students" (Murphy & Lick, 1998, p. 4).
Tuning Protocols	Tuning protocols involve "a group of colleagues coming together to examine each other's work, honor the good things found in that work, and fine tune it through a formal process of presentation and reflection" (Easton, 1999, p. 54).

SOURCE: All the excerpted definitions cited in Table 2.5 are from articles in the Summer 1999 *Journal of Staff Development* feature issue titled "Powerful Designs for Learning." Contact the National Staff Development Council for additional information (www.nsdc.org).

in pursuit of enhancing their reflective practices. To support integration and application of these building blocks for reflective practice, we offer these questions:

- What is *your* vision as a reflective educator? Why does becoming more reflective matter to you right now? What ideas about adult learning principles and meaningful learning seem most useful in applying to your reflective practice journey, and why?
- Are there certain experiences or views of yourself, your school, your students, or your colleagues in which it might be helpful to apply a reframing lens? How might you view a situation in a different way that brings in some new or changed perspectives that allow for more opening up of teaching and learning opportunities?
- What do you do right now to foster trust, empathy, and openness with colleagues? What might you develop further in yourself, and why? (You may want refer back to Table 2.2.)
- What can you do to expand your inquiry capacity? Recall the strategies such as open questions, SPACE, reframing, and dialogue. What is already in your toolbox, and what else might help you to further grow in thinking deliberatively?

With ongoing development of our personal capacities to create trusting relationships and to expand our thinking and inquiry, we can achieve higher levels of competence and effectiveness as reflective educators. Ultimately, reflective practice becomes part of our core values and beliefs, which are central to any sustained development by individuals or organizations (Butler, 1996). We come to view ourselves as reflective educators. Being reflective becomes part of our identity. As long as we are reflecting, we are learning. As long as we are learning, we are growing. As long as we are growing, we are moving closer to our human potential for contributing to this world in our chosen role as educators. Despite the prevailing norms of isolation and the hectic pace of life in schools, we can feel optimistic about the potential of reflective practice to transform schools into communities in which educators and students embrace continuous learning and improvement.

You are invited to use the Chapter Reflection Page (Figure 2.4) to make note of significant learning or insights sparked from reading Chapter 2. The next four chapters provide considerations for and specific examples of how reflective practices can be initiated at the individual (Chapter 3), partner (Chapter 4), small-group (Chapter 5), and schoolwide (Chapter 6) levels of the Reflective Practice Spiral.

Figure 2.4 Chapter Reflection Page

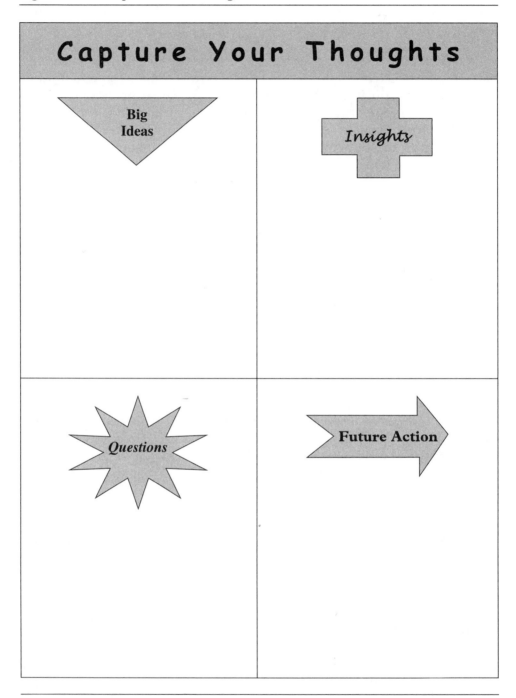

3

Individual Reflective Practice

From the perspective of the individual teacher, it means that the process of understanding and improving one's own teaching must start from reflection on one's own experience.

—Kenneth M. Zeichner (1993, p. 8),
*Connecting Genuine Teacher Development
to the Struggle for Social Justice*

You may be asking yourself, How does reflective practice specifically relate to me in my life as an educator? Reflection is a highly personal practice that offers great potential for illuminating meaning, purpose, and learning in your professional life. To be reflective means choosing with intention ways of thinking, being, and doing. To be reflective means choosing enrichment around our day's activities. It means committing oneself to continuous growth as a person and as a professional. In our work lives, each of us encounters circumstances, both planned and unplanned, that can be better understood and learned from when our commitments to personal reflection are honored. Each of us interacts with people with whom we can connect and together create new and improved realities for the children in our charge as educators.

The place to begin with reflective practice is with ourselves, the only part of the Reflective Practice Spiral over which we each have control and total responsibility. Think about the life-saving advice offered to passengers before each flight on a commercial airline. You are instructed to put on your own oxygen mask first so that you may better assist others. The greater your personal reflective capacities and practices, the greater your potential to influence colleagues in your school to become more reflective—to help them "put on their oxygen masks." Others respect and are drawn to individuals who are thoughtful, who strive to continuously learn and improve, who are flexible in their approaches to teaching and leading, and who stay clearly focused on what matters most: students being included and learning well. Self-development is the core of professional development or, "more profoundly, [it is the process of] personal being and becoming" (Butler, 1996, p. 265).

"Much of what happens in teaching is unknown to the teacher . . . and experience is insufficient as a basis for development" (Richards & Lockhart, 1994, pp. 3–4). To make the subtleties of our teaching and leadership practices known and to develop new insights and understandings, we must choose a reflective stance. In Chapter 1 the individual level in the Reflective Practice Spiral was introduced. The purpose of this chapter is to delve more deeply into the potential, meaning, and practice of reflection as individuals.

This chapter and the following three chapters (Chapters 4, 5, and 6) focus on the *how* of reflective practice and are organized in a parallel way. First, there is a brief review of the respective levels of reflective practice (i.e., individual, partner, small groups, schoolwide). Next, we add to the fundamentals of reflective practice presented in Chapter 2 by describing considerations pertaining to the respective level of reflective practice. These considerations are followed by a presentation of examples from the world of practice and then a menu of additional ideas to consider for use. In reviewing the examples and ideas, you are likely to see potential for application at other levels in the Reflective Practice Spiral. Each chapter closes with questions to assist you in getting started with reflective practice at that particular level.

One note of caution: Many of the examples and ideas in Chapters 3 through 6 offer structures or protocols intended to foster reflection. The structures, however, will not result in reflection, learning, or improvement unless inquiry, deliberative thinking, and action are engaged. Changes in structure—big (organizing) and small (protocols)—provide only the *opportunity* for learning and changes in practice. Positive, discernable results depend on what happens within the structures. As you consider applications, consider reviewing Chapter 2 for more specific ideas about meaningful topics, adult learning principles, and individual capacities and strategies for reflection. This information provides the foundation for successful application of the examples and ideas presented here and throughout the rest of the book. Also intended to support your growth are reflection protocols derived from many of the examples in this chapter. These protocols are located in the Resources section at the end of the book and may be enlarged and copied for professional-development purposes.

SPECIAL CONSIDERATIONS FOR INDIVIDUAL REFLECTIVE PRACTICE

One of the first considerations for reflecting with ourselves is finding and *guarding* time and space in our lives for significant pauses. Our surrounding culture does little to support time out for thinking and learning, particularly time alone. Creating space in which to think conflicts with the norms of doing and the value placed on decisiveness in our organizations. Raelin (2002) poses unsettling questions in this regard: "Is it possible that the frenetic activity of the executive is a drug for the emptiness of our organizational souls? [T]hat constant action may merely serve as a substitute for thought?" (p. 66). Personal uncertainty about whether the benefits of reflective practice will outweigh the costs also makes it difficult to give ourselves permission to claim time to reflect. When you find yourself wavering, consider the following reassurance: "It is in the quiet and solitary times of reading and writing that the insights from life take on a more systematic form" (Webb, 1995, p. 76). How powerful it would be if more of us—teachers and administrators—adopted and modeled reflective ways of practice, thereby lending value and credibility to this pursuit. A first step in claiming time for reflection involves truly believing that personal time for reflection is critical for your spirit and practice as an educator.

Assuming that a commitment to yourself—your all-alone self—is important to you, the task becomes one of finding your own way to claim space for reflection. Some people mark time on their weekly calendars. Others build thinking space into daily routines—going for an early-morning run, listening to their thoughts along the daily commute, closing the door and turning off the lights during a prep period, hanging out a bit longer in the shower (or laundry room), walking right after work, or journaling, accompanied by a cup of tea, after their children are in bed.

A discussion of honoring the need for time for oneself is not complete without also stating the importance of living a balanced life, which includes attending to basic needs like good sleep, good nutrition, and the importance of family, friends, relaxation, and play. (Time out, just so you know, is the theory and vision—the authors are certainly not claiming consistent application! The vision does, however, inspire us to continue efforts to bridge this theory-to-practice gap.) We know that, like exercise, rest, nutritious food, and fun, reflective practice is good for us, but commitments to healthy personal practices are not easily sustained. This is one reason that it can be easier to maintain a regular schedule of reflection

Figure 3.1   Theory of Action for Reflective Practice

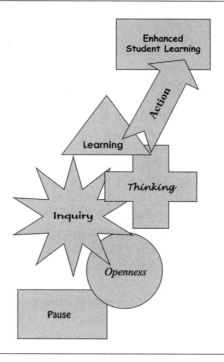

when we partner with another person (see Chapter 4). Often it is easier to honor a commitment to other people than to ourselves.

We now share several additional considerations that influence our individual journeys as reflective educators and, specifically, the ways in which we engage in the Theory of Action for Reflective Practice (see Figure 3.1). We view these considerations as serving to deepen personal inquiry and thought that leads to greater learning about ourselves and to grounded actions as a professional educator. We begin with a substantial examination of *identity*, the ways in which who we are in our work, consciously and subconsciously, drives both our thoughts and actions. A framework for considering issues of identity is offered as a reflection tool and may offer support in considering other ideas within the chapter. Next we raise consideration of *ethics* embedded in our daily work. The essential place of *courage* is then considered. To engage seriously in examining our thoughts and practices, big and small, is not an endeavor for the faint of heart. The importance of *care* is addressed next, followed by a discussion of *voice*. Care and voice are examined from a both/and perspective. Finally, we emphasize again the place of continuous practice in improving and embedding our reflection capacities in daily life. These considerations for individual reflection, summarized in Table 3.1, will be now be explored.

Table 3.1   Considerations for Individual Reflective Practice

Fostering Trust (review from Chapter 2)
. . . openness, listening and understanding, mutuality, honoring

Expanding inquiry (review from Chapter 2)
. . . asking open questions, responding with SPACE

Reframe
. . . taking a different point of view

Dialogue
. . . thinking together

Time
. . . finding and honoring time for oneself

The Basics
. . . remembering our basic needs

Identity
. . . clarifying our identity

Ethics
. . . asking ethical questions and considering moral dilemmas

Courage
. . . examining what it means to be courageous

Caring for Others and for Self
. . . seeking balance to keep us centered

Voice
. . . strengthening our own voice and being open to others'

Practice, practice, and more practices

Identity

> Identity encompasses how a person understands his or her rela-
> tionship to the world, how that relationship is constructed across
> time and space, and how the person understands possibilities
> for the future.
>
> —B. Norton (2000, p. 5), *Identity and Language*
> *Learning: Gender, Ethnicity, and Educational Change*

Who am I in this work as an educator? How do I hope to contribute in
my school community and in other parts of my life? How are the school
and other learning environments shaping our children's identities? In our
daily lives, each of us assumes multiple roles—teacher, parent, son, principal, granddaughter, friend, sibling, and colleague are a few examples. Roles
are the labels used to define certain functions, relationships, or classes of
responsibility. Identity and role are not the same thing. Identity and culture

are not the same thing, even though identity is shaped by the various cultures, such as race, gender, class, and work cultures, of which we are a part. Identity is more personal and individual than either role or culture. Our identity is who we are and how we see ourselves as a person in particular contexts. "For an individual, identity is a framework for understanding oneself" (Garmston & Wellman, 1999, p. 162). Why is this important to our discussion of reflective practice? There are at least two reasons to consider identity. First, our individual identities are operative influences on what we believe, how we think, and how we behave in the context of our practice. Second, because identities are shaped by social interactions and forces around us, we are compelled to consider the effects of our school and classroom environments on both children and adults in schools. We begin by sharing a model that offers a way of reflecting on how our identities influence our beliefs, thinking, and behaviors.

Identity Intertwined With Development and Action

A model which underscores the centrality of identity on thinking and doing was originally conceived by Gregory Bateson (1972) and has since been adapted by Robert Dilts (1996) and Bob Garmston and Bruce Wellman (1999). Dilts refers to the model as *Levels of Change and Leadership;* Garmston and Wellman refer to it as *Nested Levels of Learning.* Drawing from both of these models, we offer the following levels and descriptions. *Mission* is the vision or purpose of an organization; it is the big goal of our work. *Identity* refers to a person's sense of self; it is the *who* of our work. *Values and beliefs* encompass what we view as highly important. They provide the rationale underlying our capabilities; they are the *why* of our work. *Capabilities* are considered the strategies and mental maps that give direction to our behavior; they are the *how* of our work. *Behaviors and skills* are specific actions or reactions that we exhibit in accomplishing our work—the *doing* of our work. *Environment and structure* define the physical surroundings and the external constraints and opportunities; they comprise the *where* and *when* of our work. Questions that can be used to elicit thinking about each of these levels and their interconnectedness are shown in Table 3.2 along with sample responses. (A copy of this framework, with the third column left blank to allow for writing your own responses, is available as Resource 3.A.)

Here is the operative thesis of the model: "Each level [when moving up the table] is more abstract than the level below it, but each has a greater degree of impact on the individual or system" (Dilts, 1996, p. 4). This means identity and beliefs, for example, are more likely to influence strategies and skills than vice versa. To build generative capacity within people and within systems, we view it as important to focus on both the upper and lower levels in the model. Too often we focus only on the lower levels. Some examples help illustrate application of this reflective framework. If

Table 3.2   Personal Development Model for Professional Purpose and Practice, With Sample Responses

Level	Reflective Question	Sample Response
Mission or Overarching Purpose	What am I working toward? What are we creating or aiming to achieve?	Equity in schooling; ensure opportunities, access, and support so that all children have a sense of belonging in their schools and are successful in their learning; foster academic, social, and emotional growth.
Identity	Who am I in this work? How do I hope to contribute?	Facilitator of teacher and student learning; connector of people and resources; lifelong inquirer and learner.
Values and Beliefs	What do I believe about or value in this work? Why should we proceed in this way?	Inclusivity is the foundation for constructive growth; learning alone and together foster positive interdependence; humans want to learn, grow, and contribute; competence builds confidence.
Capabilities, Strategies, Mental Maps	How do I or will I accomplish this work? What strategies will guide my actions?	Relationships must be established as the pathways for learning; students must be understood as individuals and viewed in life context; opportunities, expectations, and instruction all must be intentionally provided.
Behaviors and Skills	What do I do to advance this work?	Observe, listen, inquire; identify individually relevant zones of proximal development; adapt expectations and strategies to create and build on success. Plan–design–implement–reflect cycle.
Environment and Structure	What structures and surroundings support this work?	Proximity; intentional mix of whole-group, small-group, and individual work; flexible time structures; time to confer with instructional colleagues.

SOURCE: The levels (column 1) and questions (column 2) in Table 3.2 are adapted with permission from R. Dilts (1996). *The new leadership paradigm*. Santa Cruz, CA.; and from R. Garmston & B. Wellman (1999). *The adaptive school: A sourcebook for developing collaborative groups*. Norwood, MA: Christopher-Gordon.

we want to teach children to read, we should focus not only on the strategies and skills of reading but also on the child's identity as a reader. A child who claims, "I am a reader!" is more likely to continue engaging in efforts to expand and refine the enabling strategies and skills of reading. A child who views herself as not able to read ("I am not a reader") is much less likely to be drawn to reading. If we want to teach children how to learn cooperatively, we must do more than just put four desks together; we must teach the strategies and skills of cooperative work and must reinforce values around cooperative work. If we want teachers to become more facilitative and less directive, we must not only teach them the kinds of questions that engage more thinking and engagement by students, but must also support their learning about why such engagement enhances their effectiveness as teachers. (Application of this framework interfaces with another framework described in Chapter 2, Peter Block's "Shift from *how* to *what* and *why* questions.")

We are not suggesting that identity is the exclusive focus in learning work but that it be addressed along with matters of why, what, and how. Typically emphasized in learning work are the lower levels, the "doings." We have found this model to be instructive and compelling for many educators seeking to understand who they are in their work and how they can contribute to growth in others. The model offers insight about the interconnectedness of identity, beliefs, strategies, and skills. It helps to explain why low-level instruction or development activities sometimes fail to produce generative gains. It provides a structure for understanding our thoughts and actions and gives permission and encouragement for engaging in questions of meaning and purpose in our work and our lives. Provided in the Resources is a protocol (similar to Table 3.2) to guide individual thinking about each level. Our daily thoughts, interactions, and work are deeply rooted in our personal identities, our sense of who we are.

Social Influences on Identity Construction

A second reason to examine identity in our work as educators involves the social influence on identity construction. Because identity is shaped by social forces around us, it is critical to consider the types of learning environments in which children and adults live, work, and play. For children, place in the classroom's social order affects both their identity and their access to learning opportunities, especially social learning opportunities with other children. This social dynamic creates a formidable challenge for children who are not native English speakers as they attempt to negotiate participation and position in classroom communities (Hawkins, 2004). Lacking subtle language finesse, the children are at risk for being marginalized from or by their English-speaking peers. Hawkins explains, "Identities are, thus, deeply linked to the positioning work that is always operant throughout social encounters and interactions, and possibilities and constraints are determined, in large part, through the power and status relations of the participants in the interaction" (p. 19). One does not freely choose an identity. Social exchanges and discourse have a strong influence on the identity shaped in particular contexts.

According to Hawkins, implications for educators include reframing the essence of their work from "teaching English to offer[ing] students access to the range of knowledge, abilities, and forms of languages (discourses) that will enable them to lay claim to the social identities that afford them a participant status in the social communities of their choice, and to provide scaffolding (and a truly supportive environment) for the attainment of these" (p. 23). Such reframing work (e.g., a shift from "teaching English" to empowering life outcomes may be prompted by looking at children's learning environments through the Personal Development for Professional Practice Model lens (Table 3.2) or using other reframing tools.

The extension of social influence on identity formation applies equally well to grown-ups in schools. Each new teacher, just like each new student, walks through the door with an indeterminable amount of potential to both learn and contribute in valuable ways in the school community. The ways in which newcomers are socially acculturated significantly influences their identity formation within the community and, therefore, their learning and contribution. In Etienne Wenger's (1998) social learning theory, referred to as Communities of Practice, identity is inseparable from practice, community, and meaning. In the particular case of newcomers, they must find their identities. Wenger explains that

> theories of identity are concerned with social formation of the person, creation and use of markers of membership (e.g., ritual, rites of passage, social categories); [and] address gender, age, class, ethnicity; learning is caught in the middle. It is the vehicle for the evolution of practices and the inclusion of newcomers and the vehicle for the development and transformation of identities. (p. 13)

According to Wenger, both participation and nonparticipation in a community shape our identities, which in turn influences how we locate ourselves in a social landscape: what we care about and what we neglect, what we attempt to know and understand and what we choose to ignore, with whom we seek connections and whom we avoid, how we engage and direct our energies, and how we attempt to steer our trajectories. Reflective questions arise, then, about how we intentionally welcome, socially support, and professionally acculturate newcomers to our practice communities in ways that are likely to maximize participation and contribution.

Wenger, like Hawkins, urges a broader and deeper view of education and our relationship to it—a view that is not limited to considerations of instruction, assessment, students, or even schools. He conceptualizes education in its broadest and deepest sense with its most encompassing purpose:

> Education concerns the opening of identities, exploring new ways of being that lie beyond our current state. Whereas training aims to create an inbound trajectory targeted at competence in a specific practice, education must strive to open new dimensions for the negotiation of the self. It places students on an outbound trajectory toward a broad field of possible identities. Education is not merely formative, it is transformative. (Wenger, 1998, p. 263)

Wenger emphasizes that students need places in which to engage, experiences through which to create an image of themselves in the world, and means by which they affect the world around them such that their actions matter. Wenger's views serve as powerful considerations in reframing education, our chosen profession, and reframing—by means of enlargement—our chosen roles as educators.

There are a number of excellent structures and strategies described later in this chapter that could support reflection on one's identity—for example, journaling about the questions in the Personal Development for Professional Practice Model, or experimenting with images and personal metaphors. But first we continue our examination of considerations for individual reflection by looking at the issue of ethics. This discussion may especially resonate with the upper three levels of the Personal Development Model: values/beliefs, identity, and mission.

Ethics

> Teaching at its core is a moral profession. Scratch a good teacher and you will find a moral purpose.
>
> —Michael Fullan (1993, p. 12)
> "Why Teachers Must Become Change Agents"

What does it mean to be a moral profession? How do issues of right and wrong come into play in the lives of educators? What do we do when conflicts arise between our own ethics and the ethics of others around us? Are there universal ethical standards, or are all ethics relative? There are no singular, agreed-upon answers to these questions. Indeed, philosophers and ethicists have engaged around these types of questions since the beginning of human history. Despite the continuing ambiguity, Rockler (2004) reminds us that "On any school day, professional educators face a myriad of problems that contain moral dilemmas. For [educators] to act responsibly, they constantly must examine ethical questions" (p. 15). Further, he asserts,

The study of ethics has become more urgent as people seek to determine ways to live ethically meaningful lives in the most complex times in human history. Persons now face the most destructive forces to ever confront humankind. Professional educators need to engage in the process of moral reflection more than ever before. (p. 46)

We bring up ethics in the context of reflective practice not to offer any absolute resolutions, but to affirm the presence of moral dilemmas in everyday educational practice and to affirm the struggle in which one engages in reflecting on best courses of action when faced with such dilemmas. We will draw from Michael Rockler's *Ethics and Professional Practice in Education*, presenting just a few of the ethical issues that he raises, along with some related questions. (As a point of clarification, Rockler uses the terms *moral* and *ethical* interchangeably.)

- *Ethics and political decisions.* Do vouchers diminish a sense of connection among people that is necessary for a democracy? On the other hand, what about individual rights to choose? What are the effects of educational outcomes being determined primarily by single-measure performance on standardized tests? What should be the priorities for allocating public resources? Under what conditions is it appropriate to increase individual taxation to achieve a greater societal good?
- *Ethics and diversity.* What ethical conflicts might exist between commitments to cultural diversity and adoption of standardized curricula? How are tensions between cultural assimilation and cultural difference resolved so that identity is not threatened and so that underclass status is not reinforced? What are the effects of teaching only English to children whose first language is not English? Should all students learn the same things? If not, how do we decide, and who decides?
- *Ethics and relations with students.* What discussions between educators and students are kept in confidence? What circumstances warrant conversation among educators, or between educators and parents, regarding individual students? What are appropriate boundaries in relationships between educators, students, and their families?

These are just a few of the domains in which educators can find themselves faced with ethical dilemmas. Best responses are often determined locally when educators, along with others in schools and communities, choose to engage in reflective thinking around the presenting issues. Personal or individual values cannot be the sole means of decisions about ethical practices in schools, because they are not uniform among people.

"Part of the reason for ethical standards comes from the need to create a social arrangement by which people can live together in relative harmony" (Rockler, 2004, p. 28). To pause, to be open, to inquire, to deliberate, and to act with an aim toward relative harmony is complex, courageous, and critically important work.

Courage

Angeles Arrien (1993) writes about courage in her book *The Four-Fold Way*. She says that one part of leadership is being a warrior. As leaders for education, we have to fight for what is most important in schools. We must stand up for what matters most regarding the health, well-being, and well-learning of the children we serve. How do we show up and be fully present in our daily pursuit of meaningful and substantial learning? How do we summon the courage to do what we know is right? A principal colleague once explained that in his culture, Native American, members have a spear to put in the ground when deciding on an issue of major importance. The spear symbolizes the final stand on what one views as important, the point at which one is not willing to concede without engaging in conflict and standing up for one's values and beliefs. Educators are called on to advocate for learning as the central focus in schools.

Ira Chaleff (1995), in *The Courageous Follower,* describes the interdependence of formal leaders and their organizational colleagues, whom he refers to as followers. He explains that leaders and followers orbit together around the purpose of the organization, clarifying that followers do *not* orbit around the formal leader. One of the essential roles for all members of an organization is to keep practices aligned with purpose and to keep formal leaders grounded in purpose. To serve effectively in this role, members must be courageous. Chaleff explains, "Courage is the great balancer of power in relationships. An individual who is not afraid to speak and act on the truth as she perceives it, despite external inequities in a relationship, is a force to be reckoned with" (p. 18). Also consider what effective leaders know: that to be good leaders, they must be willing to follow.

Parker Palmer (1998) has written extensively about courage in his book *The Courage to Teach*. He affirms the very human side of teaching. He describes seasons embedded within the careers of teachers, with fall symbolizing the throwing of seeds, winter as a place of darkness and shadow, spring as the bringing forth of new life, and summer as standing grounded and firm. Each of us, teachers and administrators alike, can relate to the ebb and flow of this seasonal metaphor. It takes courage to stand in front of or sit alongside students or adults to teach, lead, present, facilitate, consult, and coach. Sometimes we do so standing grounded and firm. Other times we are less graceful and confident. In any season, going forth in our chosen work requires courage, which comes in part from clarity about who we are. The cover of Palmer's book states a simple premise:

"Good teaching cannot be reduced to technique[;] good teaching comes from the identity and integrity of the teacher. . . . The connections made by good teachers are held not in their methods but in their hearts—the place where intellect and emotion and spirit and will converge in the human self." We extend this premise to administrators, as well.

For educators, authentic pursuit of a conscious and reflective life requires strong hearts and minds. As with the lion in *The Wizard of Oz*, the capacity to be courageous is within each of us but is not always summoned. Chaleff (1995) contends that "Our 'courage muscle' will develop to the degree we exercise it" (p. 20). The will to continue strengthening our courage muscle comes from an inner knowing that good teaching and good leading come from within. As we continue through the seasons of our work and continue our commitments to learn and improve, we can take heart in Palmer's reassuring message that we teach and we lead grounded on who we are.

Caring for Others and for Self

> Caring is the greatest thing. Caring matters most.
>
> —Baron von Hugel

Many would agree with Baron von Hugel's words: when looking back at our lifetime and considering what matters in our time on earth, caring may be what matters most. The importance of caring and compassionate responses to others is a theme shared by people, cultures, and religions around the world. And, when considering our work in schools, it is clear that a teacher's caring and pathic responses are critical aspects of a student's experience in school.

Recall from Chapter 2 van Manen's (2002) description of teachers' pathic knowledge that includes their "personal presence, relational perceptiveness, tact for knowing what to say and do in contingent situations, thoughtful routines and practices" (p. 217), and other ways of knowing that are relational and emotional, in contrast to cognitive and quantifiable forms of knowing. Being physically and emotionally present with students, listening with one's ears and heart, applying patience, "stepping into their shoes," and establishing genuine relationships are all examples of a teacher bringing the pathic dimension into teaching. Caring and connecting matter. As teachers and administrators, it is so important that we show students that we see them and we care for them. And, as most educators know, there is never an end to the ways in which we could show caring or further individualize support for students. There is no end. There are no boundaries, except those we define, necessarily so, for ourselves.

Like nurses and other direct-care professionals, as educators we are considered part of the caring professions, professions in which much energy is spent in care and support of other human beings. This carries with it the inherent reward of building connections and promoting growth. It also carries the inherent challenge of feeling overwhelmed by the many human needs faced on a daily basis. On some days as we drive away from work, our thoughts turn to the children or grown-ups for whom we wish we could have done more. Especially today, during times of increased demands, increased diversity of student needs, and an overall press to do more with less, educators can easily move into feeling overly responsible and overwhelmed. Left unchecked, these thoughts can easily turn into feelings of guilt and inadequacy.

In some respects it seems odd that people who care so much may also be the ones who feel guilt so much. Only partially in jest, Andy Hargreaves (1994) suggests that the degree of burden educators feel is proportional to the size of their tote bag carried to and from work each day. He explains that educators are particularly susceptible to feelings of guilt as a result of a combination of factors, including a commitment to care and nurture, the open-ended nature of teaching, pressures of accountability, and a persona of perfectionism. The ever-present cycle between expectations and constraints further exacerbates the feelings of not doing enough for those about whom we care. Perhaps twinges of occasional guilt or feelings of discomfort are not harmful, as they engender responsible, compassionate, and caring responses. Moments of guilt or disequilibrium may be a catalyst for further reflection and learning. But ongoing (excessive) guilt is an emotional trap, unhealthy, and a direct path to burnout. In many cases, excessive guilt is a sign that a teacher has lost balance in caring for his or her own needs in some way. Guilt can be a cue to step back and redefine one's responses. We're not saying don't care; rather, we're suggesting that as you care deeply about your students, your colleagues, and your work, don't forget to care for yourself.

Ways to attend to this balance of care of others and care for self varies from person to person. Here is how Carl, a second-grade teacher in an urban school, helps thoughtful colleagues keep feelings of guilt in check. When he hears extremely hard-working colleagues begin to spiral downward with feelings of being ineffective in this way or that, when he feels that a colleague is being too hard on him- or herself, he has a ready mantra: "You are a good enough teacher. You are good enough." Core to this mantra is the idea of letting go of perfectionism. Often, guilt and feelings of inadequacy come from expecting everything from oneself, expecting to be perfect. So Carl has found this a useful construct to apply when competent teachers are beating themselves up. He also has a strong personal orientation toward the "here and now" in his teaching and in his personal life. He seeks to be fully present with his students when he is with them, and to be focused on his students when he is planning for them. Likewise, he seeks to be fully present with his family when he is not at work. He attempts to be mindful and present in all of his relationships.

Relevant to our purposes here is the realization that work in a caring profession provides us with both human rewards and struggles. Such work can be a source of great joy and also great angst. We intend that by putting issues of care, guilt, and balance on the table, educators will not feel alone in this struggle and may, over time, come to better understand these dilemmas and potentially choose constructive responses. Such responses include enlisting the support of trusted colleagues to reflect on what is reasonable, possible, and most productive so that we sustain the energy and health required to engage in this caring profession. In moving more into reflection and examination of one's teaching and teaching practice, we suggest that teachers strive for a healthy tension around care for students and care for oneself. It doesn't need to be a win/lose or either/or dichotomy, in which either we care for our students or we care for ourselves. We believe that a both/and paradigm can be useful here: both care for students and care for oneself.

Voice

Another example of both/and thinking involves keeping tension around both clarifying one's own voice and opinions on educational issues, and continuing to stay open to other people's perspectives. Both are important. Some educators have difficulty finding their own voice as they engage in reflective practices (Canning, 1991; Costa & Kallick, 2000b). It is easy to fall into routine ways of doing things without much consideration of how we really think or feel. We can also become accustomed to others telling us directly or implying indirectly what is expected and what we should do. The busier and less present we are, the more likely these things are to happen. Our hierarchical orientation in education supports expertness and can diminish recognition and value of our own wisdom. "Self-knowledge involves what and how you are thinking, even unconsciously. Many people are not used to engaging in the 'self-talk' that is necessary for hearing their inner voice" (Costa & Kallick, 2000b, p. 60). Consider, for example, the following questions:

- What do I think about this?
- If I were to make the decision, what would I identify as important, and why?
- What would be the most productive way for my colleagues and me to move this issue forward?

Finding our own voices is an asset in that we come to know our innermost thoughts, questions, and desires regarding our work. We can also tap and share our knowledge of practice. By sharing these discoveries with others, we enrich our conversations, deliberations, and collective action with our colleagues. To keep our own voices in check, we must also be intentional in our efforts to remain open and consider other perspectives.

Our past experiences inform our present thoughts and can therefore limit, as much as inform, our perceptions of present realities. Our own view of the world is so much a part of who we are that it serves as a filter for our thinking. As a Zen proverb states, "We see the world as we are, not as it is." We must become aware of our biases and make a conscious effort to attempt seeing things from another perspective. In an effort to remain open, we can ask ourselves,

- What are some other ways of thinking about this?
- Has this always been the case, or have there been times when something different has happened? Why?
- What influences on thinking and behaving have I not considered?
- How do my beliefs guide me to think this way, and how might other beliefs alter my thinking?
- If I trusted people's intentions, would I interpret their responses differently?
- Are there other people who could help me see this differently?
- Why do I hold on so strongly to this one view?

Practice, Practice, and More Practice

Finally, like every other set of skills and dispositions, reflection capacities develop, strengthen, and become more integrated into how we think and behave with practice. Lots of practice. Lots of consciousness. Lots of intention. And lots more practice and reflection on practice. Reflecting on our own is a good place to begin being mindful of individual capacities described in Chapter 2: be present, be open, listen without judgment and with empathy, seek understanding, assume mutuality in learning, honor the person, question, respond, reframe, and create dialogue. We can practice all of these capacities on our own, then carry them with us into learning conversations with others.

INDIVIDUAL REFLECTIVE PRACTICE: EXAMPLES FROM PRACTICE

In this section, we offer several frameworks (i.e., mental models) for use in fostering reflection with ourselves. Such frameworks may be especially helpful to reflective practice newcomers in guiding intentional reflection experiences. Eventually, all of us develop our own ways of prompting inquiry and reflection about our practice. The first example offers a big-picture organizer for thinking about how reflective practices might be more embedded throughout your day. The remaining examples offer a variety of reflection processes and sample protocols which we encourage you to adapt to your needs.

Insert Reflective Practices Everywhere!

One evening while listening to our colleague RoAnne Elliott encourage a new generation of staff developers, we heard her advise, "Insert learning processes everywhere!" This idea is both simple and profound. By closely examining our daily routines and activities, we can undoubtedly identify opportunities to insert reflective practices. As we prepare for the day, we can insert reflection prompts, such as, What dispositions do I want to model today for my students? How can I keep my mind open to different viewpoints? What do I hope to have accomplished by the end of the day? At the start of committee meetings, participants could be asked to think about the dispositions or behaviors that will foster productive use of the meeting time. Faculty meetings could begin with partner sharing about an unexpected instructional success or challenge and the thinking it prompted. They could end with a take-away question likely to prompt continued thinking after the meeting ends. Walks to the faculty lounge or around the school during lunch could be filled with free-flowing observations about how teachers are enriching their curriculum to foster equitable practices.

When does reflection happen, or, more to the point, when could it happen throughout an already full and often hectic day? How can we reframe our hectic days as opportunities to learn and, just as important, how to reprioritize our time to make good on these opportunities so that our own reflection, learning, and development serve as the cornerstone of our practice? Andrea Forcier, a sixth-grade teacher in Minnesota, shares a variety of ways she embeds reflective practice into her daily routines in ways that are not burdensome but that prompt deliberative thought and foster improvements in her practice. Like many educators, she finds herself reflecting in the car, at night in bed, and even in the shower. One unique aspect of her reflection, however, is the intentional involvement of her students as partners in reflection. After teaching a lesson, she invites her students to share not only what they learned but to also offer feedback about what helped their learning and how the lesson could be improved. Jumping off from her students' reflections she asks herself, Did the kids engage and enjoy it? Was it at an appropriate level? Should I just ditch this and find or create something else? Is there another teacher who teaches this material that has a great way of doing it? In preparation for future use, she makes changes in lessons immediately, not only to capture specific ideas that emerge but to document the reasons and thinking underlying the changes as well. Andrea has also taken the initiative to engage her peers in reflective practices. Although there are on regularly scheduled opportunities for Andrea and her colleagues to meet and reflect together, she seeks out their ideas and gathers them to examine student work. By including teachers with varied backgrounds (e.g., science, English, art, special education), the critique and learning is greatly enriched. Driven to continuously reflect, learn, and improve, Andrea has embedded opportunities to reflect on her practice and to engage others—children and peers—in doing so throughout her week.

In Figure 3.2 we offer a framework for taking inventory of your current state of reflective practice and for considering possibilities for embedding more reflection and learning opportunities. (Refer to Resource 3.B for a copy of this framework.) Our point is not to elicit reflection fatigue, a state of mind brought on by obsessive questioning and thought. Rather, it is to recognize the many opportunities for reflection and learning that already exist in our daily practice. By reframing some daily experiences as opportunities to reflect and learn, we exercise the potential to increase both the meaning and effectiveness of our practice, without necessarily allocating a lot more time. There are daily opportunities to reflect by ourselves and with others. In the column farthest to the left, you may wish to replace the Reflective Practice Spiral levels with a chronological, period-by-period framework. At its core, the work of educators is learning work. This learning work involves intentionally prompting reflection among colleagues, as well as in ourselves.

A 4-Step Reflection Process

The 4-Step Reflection Process, outlined in Table 3.3, guides reflection-on-action and reflection-for-action, both focused around a specific event or circumstance. (Refer to Resource 3.C for a copy of the 4-Step Reflection Process that can be used for professional-development purposes.) It is similar to a reflective process introduced by Smyth (1989). It brings the reflector through a sequenced process of thinking: description (what?), analysis and interpretation (why?), overall determination of meaning (so what?), and projections about future actions (now what?). This sequence of thinking is easily embedded into a personal reflection repertoire. This 4-Step Reflection Process and the example that follows, "Letting Your Reflections Flow," were used in a reflective practice initiative in a high school. They were formatted on single pages and placed in faculty mailboxes. These mailbox prompts, as they were called, served as gentle reminders to take a time-out for reflection and offered a structure for engaging in reflection.

Letting Your Reflections Flow

David Bohm (1989) refers to dialogue as "a stream of meaning flowing among us and through us and between us" (p. 1). Although *dialogue* is often used to refer to interactions between people, it can also refer to a person's internal exploration of various viewpoints and assumptions—an inner dialogue. Most of us must learn how to dialogue with ourselves. It is not an intrinsic skill to any of us, although we each have the potential to do it. Following are several different prompts for engaging in dialogue with yourself. Before you begin, you may wish to review the introductory

Figure 3.2   Personal Inventory for Reflective Practice

	CURRENT REALITIES In what specific situations do you find yourself...	REFLECTION PROMPT How much reflection and learning is going on?	POSSIBILITIES How might reflection and learning be advanced?
	Reflective Educator ... Take Inventory		
	...on your own?		
	...in dyads or triads?		
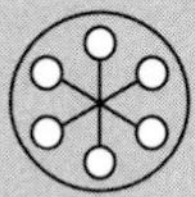	...in small groups or teams?		
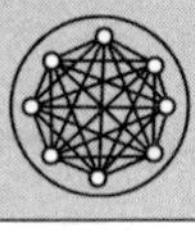	...in large groups (e.g., school or organizational level)?		

description on dialogue located in Chapter 2 (pp. 52–55). A recommended mode for dialogue with yourself is writing. However, be careful not to pressure yourself to write in technically correct ways. The purpose is expression of thought, not coherent and carefully sequenced articulation. Select a prompt, and let the dialogue begin.

Have a Written Dialogue With Yourself
About What It Means to Be a Teacher

When did you first think about being a teacher? What influenced your thinking in this way? Did particular teachers or other people influence your thoughts about becoming a teacher? How do you want to contribute to the lives of children? What are your hopes and visions? What do you want students to learn from you and with you? What do you need to continue learning from them? What are the underlying beliefs and values that guide your teaching? Where do you struggle with alignment between beliefs and values and actual behavior? Why? Explore potential reasons for this. How do you want to be as a teacher? What do you want to learn more about that will enhance your teaching? How can you remain true to these desires?

Table 3.3   A 4-Step Process for Guiding Reflection

Think about a significant event, interaction, lesson that occurred in your classroom or school, with students or adults, that you feel is worth further reflection. You might choose a positive and encouraging experience, or you might choose a more unsettling and challenging experience.

Now consider the following series of questions to prompt your thinking about the experience. You may wish to write down your thoughts. You may even want to share your thoughts aloud with another person.

1. *What happened? (Description)*

   - What did I do? What did others (e.g., students, adults) do?
   - What was my affect at the time? What was their affect?
   - What was going on around us? Where were we? When during the day did it occur? Was there anything unusual happening?

2. *Why? (Analysis, interpretation)*

   - Why do I think things happened in this way?
   - How come I chose to act the way I did? What can I surmise about why the other person acted as she or he did? What was going on for each of us?
   - What was I thinking and feeling? Or was I thinking at the time? How might this have affected my choice of behavior?
   - How might the context have influenced the experience? Was there something significant about the activities? Something about the timing or location of events?
   - Are there other potential contributing factors? Something about what was said or done by others that triggered my response? Are there past experiences—mine or the school's—that may have contributed to the response?
   - What are my hunches about why things happened in the way they did?

3. *So what? (Overall meaning and application)*

   - Why did this seem like a significant event to reflect on?
   - What have I learned from this? How could I improve?
   - How might this change my future thinking, behaving, interactions?
   - What questions remain?

4. *Now what? (Implications for action)*

   - Are there other people I should actively include in reflecting on this event? If so, who, and what would we interact about?
   - Next time a situation like this presents itself, what do I want to remember to think about? How do I want to behave?
   - How could I set up conditions to increase the likelihood of productive interactions and learning?

Identify a Specific Event or Experience and
Write About It From as Many Perspectives as Possible

What happened from my viewpoint? What happened from the viewpoint of others? How might someone in the balcony look down on and interpret the event. How can I view this as understandable difference instead of trying to identify winners and losers? Does there have to be a right way and wrong way?

Select Any Topic and Do Some Freewriting

You may want to think metaphorically. Learning to reflect is like planting a seed, patiently watching it, and hoeing away the competing and unwanted weeds. For example, Bohm's depiction of dialogue as a stream of meaning could be envisioned as a river. Dialogue is like a river. Or teaching is like planting and tending a garden. Write down your thoughts, feelings, beliefs, and observations about the selected topic. Write about connections between your topic and other things. Don't evaluate or judge thoughts as they pour out. Just let them flow! Later, look back at all your thoughts. Ask yourself, "I wonder what this means? What are the connections between this and that? Are there new insights or perspectives I hadn't really thought about before? How did this experience of freeing up my mind expand my thinking? What additional questions are raised?"

Reflection Directions

Reflection has direction. Figure 3.3 depicts four different directions that guide reflection. As you begin or extend your process of individual reflection, practice these different ways of reflecting. You can reflect within to inquire about personal purpose and why you are the way you are. Why are you a teacher? How did you come to be here? What are your intentions? How do you stay centered? What nurtures your creativity and zest for teaching? How do you want to be with your students and colleagues?

You can reflect back on circumstances or events that have already occurred, a process referred to as *reflection-on-action* (Schon, 1983; Webb, 1995). This is one of the most frequently employed forms of reflection. It occurs after an event, when you are removed from it and the doing is done (temporarily). The mind is then freed up to reflect on the doing:

> During [reflection-on-action], personal experiences are reflected on, a reevaluation occurs. . . . During this activity, new data are linked to what is already known, relationships within the data are established, ideas and feelings are tested for their authenticity, and thus new personal practical knowledge and understanding are established. The outcome of this is the state for the design of future action; in other words, it is the input for reflection to action. (Butler, 1996, p. 274)

Figure 3.3   Reflection Directions

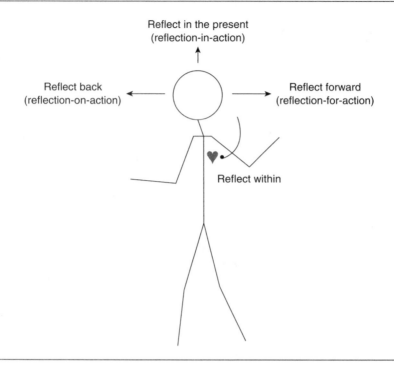

You can reflect in the present as events are occurring, an activity referred to as *reflection-in-action* (Butler, 1996; Schon, 1983). This is one of the most difficult but potentially powerful forms of reflection. It is difficult because of the hot-action nature of teaching (see Eraut, 1985, quotation in Chapter 1). It is powerful because it is the means for making adjustments in the process of teaching, based on a keen awareness of what is going on in the present:

> Reflection-in-action . . . is possible if and only if there is mental processing capacity available to get outside the act of generation of the performance and to watch its effects and evaluate them. This means being able to accumulate and evaluate immediate feedback within the performance context . . . it allows modification of the performance plan to make it more efficacious. (Butler, 1996, p. 273)

The abilities to reflect in action and to make adjustments accordingly are readily apparent in master educators, both teachers and administrators. The minds of master teachers, for example, are not totally consumed with delivering instruction and keeping students engaged. Their minds are freed up to observe student responses, to notice subtle indicators of confusion, to identify unusual responses. Reflection-in-action requires a high level of consciousness. High-performing athletes also offer salient examples of reflection-in-action, making minor adjustments as they perform. Teachers ask themselves, How are students responding? Who is not responding? When did student engagement trail off? Why?

You can reflect forward, a process referred to as *reflection-for-action* or *reflection-to-action* (Butler, 1996). In this type of reflection, you envision the effect of specific interventions or actions on a group of students, the classroom as a whole, a group of colleagues, the learning environment, and the school as a community. Reflection-for-action has the potential to identify future ways of thinking or behaving that are likely to produce desirable results. As mentioned above, reflection-on-action is the major input source for considering reflection-for-action.

Journaling

Journaling makes invisible thoughts visible. It provides a means of describing practice and of identifying and clarifying beliefs, perspectives, challenges, and hopes for practice. It is a way to put your thoughts on paper. It offers a private place for honest accounting and review. You can go back and read entries many times. It sometimes helps to recall previous thoughts and different times in your life. If you have journaled about past problems, when you face another, you may be able to find references, analogies, and solving strategies that have worked previously. Journaling can be a quiet or energizing time of reflection. A middle school principal once explained that journaling was a way to dump thoughts and feelings, which helped him get rid of old problems. He was able to write about an issue, think about it, and then let it go. He also used his journal as a way to document events.

Some people use a carefully chosen, beautiful journal. Some use sticky notes. Others use whatever loose sheets of paper might be available, then deposit these papers in a place of easy retrieval for review at a later time. "[M]aking entries in confidential journals can help us as teachers see where we divert from our lesson plans, what procedures seem to work well for students, which activities are less successful, and so on" (Bailey, Curtis, & Nunan, 1998, p. 549). Entries in journals can include various items, such as date and time, a short description of what happened (with greater detail given about important aspects of an event), and an analysis (Posner, 1996). The significance and implications may be included, as well. Benefits of journaling have been identified as expanding awareness, understanding, and insights about teaching practice; making connections between theory and practice; and generating new hypotheses for action (Taggart & Wilson, 1998). Journaling helps to clarify your thinking. It can also be done using an interactive format with partners (see Chapter 4).

Here we share three varied examples of how high school teachers, each journaling in her own way, engaged in a schoolwide small-learning-communities literacy project. Later in the chapter we share specific ways that journaling has been used with student teachers at the preservice level of teacher development.

Visual Diary

Monica, a high school art teacher, shared her way of journaling—a visual diary. She uses the visual diary to record her daily reflections on teaching. But instead of sticking with words, she depicts meaning with a variety of visual representations that capture the events of her day. She drafts sketches, diagrams, and mind maps. She uses pictures from magazines or that students have drawn that have particular meaning. She finds sayings in articles or magazines, or she creates words and phrases from letters cut out of the newspaper. She includes poetry that students write or poems she finds meaningful. She sometimes also includes topics she wants to share with her colleagues. Monica shares her visual diary with her students as a model for reflection and as a model for the kind of journaling she expects in her classes from her students.

Monica shared this method of reflective journaling with other teachers, and the idea has spread. Some use this technique of reflective journaling to record their thoughts for the monthly faculty table talk, a time for faculty to sit with peers from other departments and share what they are learning and working on. Other teachers have taken the visual diary idea as a technique to use with their students to encourage student reflection.

Calendar Prompts

Another journaling technique was created by Susan, a science teacher, and is incorporated into her planning book. At the beginning of each month she creates a monthly calendar with question prompts to which she wants her students to respond. Susan then uses these same prompts to reflect on ideas she wants to share with her students, as well as to help clarify her own thinking on topics prior to responding to her students' reflections.

Lesson Plan Sticky Notes

A math teacher, Leslie, developed yet another way to prompt reflection through journaling. Keeping a notebook or journal did not fit her style of learning, but she did want to record the ideas, successes, challenges, and questions that surfaced as she implemented new literacy strategies into her classes. Her way was to keep sticky notes on her lesson plan book. As she practiced new teaching strategies or noticed changes in the behavior or learning patterns of students, she would jot it down on the sticky notes. To track her thinking and observations, she then used her collection of sticky notes to support her evaluation of the success and failures of the week and to ground her plans for implementation the next week. Leslie also used her lesson plan book sticky notes when reflecting with another math teacher. Because this was the first time both math teachers had taught the new curriculum, they met weekly to plan together, discuss student behaviors and concerns, evaluate student work, troubleshoot potential challenges, and create their embedded weekly literacy lessons. The sticky notes assured that Leslie's insights were not forgotten, but used for reflection-on-action and reflection-for-action.

Five States of Mind

The five states of mind described by Costa and Garmston (2002) offer another framework or mental model for guiding reflection on your own. Briefly described here are the five states of mind, with related questions that prompt reflection.

Efficacy involves having an internal locus of control and knowing that you can make a difference.

- Am I thinking efficaciously in this situation?
- How am I assuming responsibility for my role in this situation?
- As I think about what happened, what are things I did that I want to make sure you do in the future?
- How did I decide to make that change in plans?
- What might I tell a colleague about my learning?

Flexibility involves thinking outside the box, choosing to look at things from a different perspective.

- Am I thinking flexibly? Or am I limited to only one way of thinking?
- How might I do that differently the next time?
- What are some different outcomes I might want to incorporate into my aims of practice?
- What new ideas am I learning about that can increase my impact?

Craftsmanship is a focus on continuous improvement, a desire to always get better at what you do.

- Is this better than what we or I used to do?
- How can it be improved?
- What did I see or hear that tells me the goals were reached?
- What are some of the elements that I would plan more specifically next time?
- How will I assess the students'/colleagues'/parents' performance?

Consciousness is being aware of your own process of thinking; the contexts or environments around you; and the relationships among various thoughts, actions, and circumstances.

- What am I aware of?
- What is not here that needs to be?
- What don't I know? As I planned this activity and now, as I think about what happened, what were the most important lessons I learned?
- What do I want to pay more attention to and learn more about?
- How do I know when and how to make midcourse corrections in the moment?

Interdependence recognizes that you are never working alone, because you are always involved in an interdependent relationship whether you want to be or not.

- Who else might help? Who else is or might be involved?
- What would my friend Diane do?
- Who else could I talk with about this activity?
- How do I plan together with colleagues for future applications?
- What are some of the lessons I have learned from my mentors?

Thinking through this framework prompts internal reflection that can assist getting unstuck when what we are doing isn't working. One of the authors of this book has the five states of mind posted on the wall in his office. When stuck, he looks at the posted states of mind and goes down the list, one by one, thinking about the problem, his actions so far, and what he may have forgotten to try. Sometimes it is important to look for what is not there as much as what is there. Thinking about the questions posed above prompts reflection-on-action and reflection-for-action.

Internal Reflections for Principals

To say that the daily life of a principal is continuous in-action work is perhaps an understatement. From the moment you arrive at school until you hit the pillow at night, you can never be too sure what will come your way. Over the years I (Bill) have accumulated strategies and mental maps to guide my thinking and action. Here are some examples.

What Are Your Nonnegotiables?

A personal reflection question for principals is "What are your nonnegotiables?" What is it that you will not negotiate away for yourself, your staff, your students, your parents, and so forth? These are things you feel so strongly about that you would be willing to go to the wall for them. What would you be willing to be fired for? With more and more demands and fewer and fewer resources, priorities get very clear because you cannot do everything for everybody. So, before you are tested—and you will be tested if you have not been already—what are your nonnegotiables?

It May Not Be Easy, but Is It Right?

The life of a principal will regularly place you in conflict situations. We create some of these situations ourselves, but most are created by others. As a decision maker, many times you will have someone unhappy with your decisions, and thus you will incur criticism. In the final analysis you must do what you think is right. It may not be easy, but is it right?

JIT Worrying

I have developed a process of JIT worrying. In the business world the acronym JIT stands for "Just in Time." I have found that if I worry too soon, I must worry twice—once about what might happen (reflecting forward) and then again when the issue actually does happen (reflection-in-action). I do, however, create scenarios ahead of time. Envisioning actions to take if the results are good or bad provides more options for me to consider. In the end there is probably no benefit in worrying twice, if at all.

Can You Live With the Critics?

Angeles Arrien (1993) provided this question to ask yourself: Is your self-worth as strong as your self-critic? We can terrorize ourselves by what we think about. Stop the inner terror. Self-reflection can create possibilities or, conversely, put you into a downward spiral. Spend time answering the question and thinking of the possibilities before assuming the worst-case scenario.

What Is Your BATNA?

Fisher and Ury, in their (1981) book *Getting to Yes*, provide five steps for processing issues. The first step is determining your BATNA: Best Alternative to a Negotiated Agreement. If there is no decision or no compromise for an issue, what is your alternative? Your BATNA is not something that is made public unless you want it to be. A private BATNA offers you an opportunity to think, playing scenarios out in your mind based on what might happen, and anticipating the consequences of your actions. This is not easy work, and it is very important.

No Deal Is an Option

Peter Block (1987) said there are five possible outcomes in any negotiation: win-lose, lose-win, lose-lose, win-win, or no deal. In the first three scenarios there is a loser, and normally that means an emotional and substantive loss. The result can damage relationships for a long time. Of course, we all want the fourth option, win-win. But Block introduces a fifth option: no deal. Sometimes it is better to walk away rather than agree to something that you will be unhappy with later.

How Do You Manage Up?

Dee Hock (1996) said you should spend 40 percent of your time managing yourself, 30 percent of your time managing up, 15 percent managing your peers, and 15 percent managing your direct reports. It is doubtful that these percentages hold in education as they do in business. Nevertheless, the concept of managing up is a good one to consider. If there is a mismatch of supervisory styles, how do you react? Let's say you are very concrete and your boss is a free thinker; you probably just want the boss to tell you what to do. Another possibility is that you are a creative person and your boss is a concrete sequential wanting to know every move you make. To manage up, you must decide if you need to direct your boss in order to get your work done. For examples about how to manage up, visit www.fastcompany.com, and search for Boss Management.

INDIVIDUAL REFLECTIVE PRACTICE: MORE IDEAS TO CONSIDER

There are many creative ways to reflect that we sometimes discover for ourselves. Not everyone benefits from prompts or prescribed processes, such as those described above. Some find that meditation and prayer open their minds and hearts to different ways of thinking. For others, exercise or music has the effect of creating space for new thoughts and insights to emerge. Still others listen to audiotaped books as a way to both ground and expand thinking about practice. We even know of individuals who simply go to sleep and let their unconscious minds take over the processing of problems or complexities of practice, later resulting in more conscious insights or understandings. Oftentimes, they wake up in the middle of the night with clear minds and new ideas. Undoubtedly, we are on the front end of discovering myriad ways to enrich and expand our thinking capacities, which will unleash exponentially our ways of doing. Below is a menu of ideas for reflecting on your own that may spark an interest for you.

Self-Observing

Bergsgaard and Ellis (2002) introduce the practice of *self-observing* as a means by which educators become more conscious observers of their thoughts, feelings, and behaviors to gain insight into their teaching practices. They propose that mental activity in human beings takes three forms, which sometimes work independently of one another and other times work interactively. One form, *organic impulse,* they describe as an immediate response, such as emotion, to a presenting stimulus. Another form, *idea generation,* refers to the thoughts which emerge consciously or unconsciously that result in meaning or interpretation. Often, emotional responses and emergent ideas reinforce a thought–emotion cycle that can spiral and be difficult to control. The third form of mental activity is *self-observing,* is described as "the condition of consciousness characterized by awareness, objectivity, clarity, acceptance, and being in the present as well as by the absence of opinion, preference, prejudice, and attachment" (p. 56).

To illustrate self-observing, Bergsgaard and Ellis offer an example. A student gets up and leaves class. The teacher demands he stop and return to his seat. The student leaves despite the command. She follows him down the hall, at which point he informs her he is feeling sick. Her thinking and behavior shifts instantly. The teacher acted on fear (an impulse) that was exacerbated by concerns (idea generation) of losing control. The authors offer commentary on this scenario:

> What is most remarkable . . . is that the strongest, most stressful feelings for the teacher were not based on the simple reality of one human being leaving a room, but issued out of ideas based upon assumptions and illusions that provoked emotion which provided a further acceleration of the idea development process. (p. 59)

The authors suggest that practice at self-observing could have resulted in the teacher recognizing she was feeling threatened and rather than acting on emotions might have demonstrated more informed and sensible actions.

Bergsgaard and Ellis suggest five strategies for developing the practice of self-observation. *Contemplative observation,* they explain, is derived from Buddhist meditations and has been described by Richard Brown (1998) as a method that

> synchronizes the observer with the learning environment; awakens and clarifies perceptions, thoughts, and emotions; and develops knowledge and compassion. In contemplative observation, we observe not only what is happening in the environment, but also what is simultaneously occurring within ourselves. (p. 70, as quoted by Bergsgaard & Ellis, 2002, p. 61)

The authors suggest that a second strategy, *journaling* (introduced earlier in this chapter), can be used to gain insight about how organic impulse and idea generation are evoked within ourselves. The other three strategies are interrelated. *Breathing techniques* assist in quieting the mind and slowing down the pace of thought and action, thereby allowing reconnection with authentic instead of perceived realities. *Relaxation responses* support the state of nonattachment, the ability to let thoughts pass through one's mind without attaching emotion. They explain that

> . . . when this practice awareness of breathing and the Self is brought forward into the classroom, what appeared to be a charged, frantic and chaotic environment can be viewed by the objective but compassionate observer as individual human beings all interacting out of their own needs in ways that make sense to each. (p. 64)

Finally, *meditation* is proposed as a way to "tap into the mindfulness and awareness that leads to the Self-Observing" (p. 64). The process of self-observing, in particular, reinforces the early steps of reflective practice cycles (e.g., pausing and openness) and lays the groundwork for later steps of gaining new insights which lead to improved teaching and learning practices.

Reflection in the Design of Web-Enhanced Lessons

Koszalka, Grabowski, and McCarthy (2003) developed the ID-PRISM protocol for assisting educators in the process of creating web-enhanced learning environments that integrate learning objectives and technology resources. Refer to their protocol, shown in Table 3.4. The acronym stands for *instructional design: possibilities, realities, issues, standards, and multidimensional views.* Underlying the design of the protocol are five research-based characteristics of effective reflective practices:

- Inquiry, shown as the big-picture framing questions
- Recipes or tools that offer structured guidance for reflection
- Strategic sequencing of the protocol's elements from unconstrained thinking to more focused planning
- Contextualizing that engages teachers in consideration of web-enhanced instructional possibilities related to the specific learning constraints and opportunities in their classrooms
- Action planning that creates a bridge to implementation by specifying actions or steps

Essentially, the ID-PRISM protocol serves as a scaffolding tool for teacher learning on embedding effective use of technology to enhance student learning. Readers are encouraged to consult this resource for an in-depth description and a rich set of examples.

Table 3.4   The ID-PRISM Reflection Tool for Web-Enhanced Learning
(Koszalka et al., 2003)

Possibilities

What are the possibilities for your ideal teaching and learning environment?
- The best strategies and resources I currently use in my classroom . . .
- Using real-world experiences during learning . . .
- Student activity during ideal learning events . . .
- Ideal informational and people resources available for learning . . .
- Based on my beliefs about teaching and learning, my ideal classroom . . .

Realities

What are the school-infrastructure realities that impact the creation of your ideal
Web-enhanced learning environment?
- As I think about my current classroom . . .
- To move toward my ideal classroom . . .

Issues

How do teaching and learning issues impact the creation of your ideal Web-enhanced
learning environment?
- Internet access can support my teaching . . .
- Internet access can support student learning . . .
- Internet access would affect social interaction in my ideal classroom . . .
- An acceptable use policy (e.g., censorship, copyright, etc.) in my ideal
  classroom . . .
- Assessment and evaluation of my students in my ideal classroom . . .

Standards

How do educational standards and curriculum requirements impact the design of
your ideal Web-enhanced learning environment?
- My goals and expectations for learning in my ideal electronic learning
  environment . . .
- Resources that will support my goals include . . .
- Educational standards and curriculum requirements influence my
  teaching . . .
- Teaching consistency across grade levels is . . .

Multidimensional Perspectives

How do learning, learners, and the environment impact the learning design of your
Web-enhanced learning environment?
- The relationship among learning, learner, and the environment in my ideal
  classroom . . .
- Based on my beliefs about teaching and learning, to create my ideal
  classroom . . .

Reprinted with permission from T. A. Koszalka, B. L. Grabowski, & M. McCarthy (2003). Reflection through the ID-PRISM: A teacher planning tool to transform classrooms into web-enhanced learning environments. *Journal of Technology and Teacher Education, 11*(3), 347–75. Norfolk, VA: Association for the Advancement of Computing in Education (AACE), www.aace.org.

What Question Did You Ask Today?

Questioning is a powerful reflection tool. It positions us as active learners and can open our minds to new possibilities and ways of thinking. When Isido Rabi, the winner of the 1994 Nobel Prize in physics, was young, each day after school his mother would ask him, "What did you ask today in class?" Her question stood apart from typical questions parents often ask their children, such as, "How was your day?" or "What did you learn today?" Later, when reflecting on his achievements, Rabi attributed his success to his mother's daily question and the stimulus it created for thinking creatively and moving beyond surface understandings (Bonder, 1999).

Questions emerge from our need for information, as well as from our curiosity to understand commonalities, discrepancies, surprises, and relationships among ideas and perspectives. Pausing to craft a question sharpens our thinking about what we already understand, do not understand, and want to understand. As we reflect on both the question and what is learned, new knowledge is created. What we learn helps us discover breaks in our logic or discrepancies in our associations. Some questions do not have answers but stretch our thinking as we consider the possibilities. Questions do not have to be asked of someone else. We may ask ourselves a question and then hold it in our thoughts to play with ideas. When we choose to ask questions of others, the potential exists not only to learn, but to create conditions that open up conversations for others to reflect and learn.

Race Reflection

Cultural diversity and equity are primary considerations in the process of continuous renewal and improvement in schools. A significant challenge in our profession arises from the limited experiences of our predominantly Caucasian teaching force with culturally diverse populations. This does not mean that White teachers cannot be effective with students of color, as explained by Gloria Ladson-Billings (2000) in her book *Dreamkeepers.* Each of us, however, brings our lived experience as our underlying theory of how the world works and our cultural norms and expectations. If we lack experience interacting in diverse cultural contexts, our underlying theories for understanding and acting in the world are devoid of those influences.

In Chapter 2, we shared some of Richard Milner's (2003) work regarding reflection around race and culture. He recommends journaling as one way that educators could safely begin exploring their thoughts and examining their actions and interactions with students around the construct of race. You are referred back to the reframing section (Chapter 2, pp. 46–52), which includes some of Milner's specific reflection questions on race and culture. Also recommended is direct interaction with Milner's full text (full

Figure 3.4   Sample Reflection Map on Classroom Management Lecture

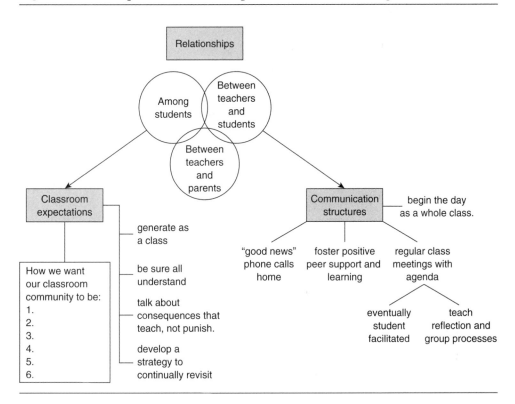

citation located in the reference list) to add depth of consideration to racial influences on education generally, and on teaching and learning specifically.

Mapping

Mapping could be considered a form of journaling. Journaling is a linear or sequential presentation of written information—one sentence or thought after another. Mapping is a more fluid presentation that shows connections and relationships between ideas and information. Similar to graphic organizing, mapping is a way to visually represent an event, meeting, lesson, curricular unit, reading, or presentation. A map can clearly communicate the big ideas at a glance. For example, a presenter may have shared and expanded on three main ideas about classroom management: relationships, classroom expectations, and communication structures. Figure 3.4 illustrates how a map of that presentation may have looked. Mapping allows different emphases on information by altering the size, boldness, and location of words and pictures. It also easily depicts relationships among the main ideas, as well as between each main idea and its respective subpoints. The process of constructing maps requires higher-order thinking about the content and creates a framework onto which future information can be added.

Teacher Narratives

Teacher narratives are "stories written by and about teachers that form the basis of narrative inquiry" (Sparks-Langer & Colton, 1991, p. 42). They are a somewhat more disciplined form of writing than journaling. Journaling is more free-flowing. Teacher narratives usually have more structure and focus, because they are intended to communicate a story. Either keen observers or teachers themselves write real stories about teaching. The stories illuminate the realities, dilemmas, joys, and rewards of teaching. Reflecting on teacher narratives yields several benefits: insights about motivations for teacher actions, about the details and complexities of teaching, and about teachers themselves (Sparks-Langer & Colton, 1991).

Teacher narratives can be specifically designed for use as case studies, in which specific problems of practice would be presented that require reflection for analysis and solution finding. Case studies have the advantage of portraying realities of practice without requiring in vivo observations, which are time-consuming (Taggart & Wilson, 1998). Autobiographical sketches, also called *personal histories* (Sparks-Langer & Colton, 1991), are a specialized form of teacher narratives. The stories are of a more personal and in-depth nature, offering insight "into the past to uncover preconceived theories about teaching and learning" (Taggart & Wilson, 1998, p. 164).

Weekly Journal Seeds for Student Teachers

As part of work with preservice teachers, a university instructor developed "Weekly Journal Seeds" as a structure to support student teachers in more meaningful examination of articulated teaching competencies (which appeared all too theoretical) and to prompt deeper examination of the teaching context, including consideration of some of the unique and at times ambiguous aspects of their teaching situation. The Weekly Journal Seeds were e-mailed to student teachers on Monday of each week. Most weeks there were at least three seed questions, with one question designed to prompt exploration of their teaching context, one question overtly linked to the teaching competencies identified for their licensure area, and one question framed around an inspirational quote from the supervisor's personal "quote collection."

To personalize the design of the Journal Seeds, the university supervisor considered the flow of the student teaching experience (including certain events that needed to occur, such as a midterm and final conference), the parameters of the student teaching (what was required and what was flexible), the wide range of student teacher backgrounds in the program (some already had licenses and years of teaching experience, whereas others were newcomers to teaching). The university supervisor brought her own experiences and creative intuition into the process, as well. Following is a sample of the journal seeds sent during the first week of the students' practica:

- What have been the highlights of your start-up week(s) so far? What success stories do you want to remember? What are some specific things you did as a teacher that you believe contributed to some successful student and class situations? What have been the surprises, challenges, and headaches?
- As you anticipate this school year, what are your biggest hopes and dreams for your students? For yourself? For you and the teaching team with whom you work?
- A lot of scheduling and adult communication go on in your position, especially at the start of a school year or new semester. Tons of effort, right? So far, how is it going with communication/consultation/collaboration (as described on the competency checklist)? What specific positive qualities and actions do you add to the collaboration in your classroom/school? Certain strategies or skills you'd like to learn more about? Other noteworthy joys or concerns in the area of collaboration right now?
- Quote to ponder: "The one who teaches is the giver of eyes" (Tamil proverb). What does this quote mean to you? Does this or another quote resonate with some of your core beliefs as a teacher?

To date, student feedback suggests that the journal seeds are supportive of focused examination of the teaching week for teachers who are regular users of e-mail.

Teaching Portfolios

Teaching portfolios have been described as "a purposeful collection of any aspect of a teacher's work that tells the story of a teacher's efforts, skills, abilities, achievements, contributions to students, colleagues, institution, academic discipline or community" (Brown & Wolfe-Quintero, 1997, p. 28). Items that might be included in a teaching portfolio (Bailey et al., 1998) are (a) a personal statement of teaching philosophy, strengths, interests, and challenges; (b) a description of teaching goals and responsibilities (e.g., courses, specific assignments); (c) any materials developed by the teacher (e.g., lesson plans, syllabi, assignments, audiovisuals, tests); and (d) evidence about teaching performance and effectiveness (e.g., student feedback, student-performance data, colleague and peer perspectives, supervisor feedback), and the teacher's interpretation or analysis of the evidence.

Teaching portfolios offer numerous assets in the process of reflection (Bailey et al., 1998; Brown & Wolfe-Quintero, 1997). First, the process of reviewing and selecting items for the portfolio is itself a reflective process. "The very process of developing a portfolio can help [teachers] gather together their thoughts about their professional strengths and synthesize them into a cogent collage" (Brown & Wolfe-Quintero, 1997, p. 29). Second, teaching portfolios contain multiple and varied data about teaching and its effects. Multiple perspectives add breadth and depth to the analysis process. Third, the time spent reflecting on the teaching portfolio as a whole "inevitably enlarges a teacher's view of what teaching is" (Brown & Wolfe-Quintero, 1997, p. 29). Finally, teaching portfolios provide one way of documenting the nature of one's teaching at one point in time. In reviewing portfolios over the years, one realizes one's growth. Use of teaching portfolios not only serves to document growth but also contributes to it.

Instead of creating a comprehensive portfolio that addresses an entire scope of teaching, smaller portfolios can be developed that focus on one specific area of teaching (e.g., one course or curricular area). This allows a focused review of specific areas and facilitates an easier revision process because the materials for each area are gathered together. Another idea is to include a partner in the portfolio's design and review process, the same way in which a teacher assists a student in portfolio design, selection, and review. Another person adds the invaluable dimension of an outside perspective and serves as coach to support reflection and inquiry.

Metaphors

Metaphorical thinking is a way to illuminate features through comparison. "A metaphor holds the most meaning in the smallest space" (quote attributed to Scott Card). It has been described as

> attending to likenesses, to relationships, and to structural features . . . identifying conceptual categories that may not be obvious or previously acknowledged . . . making knowledge in one domain a guide for comprehending knowledge in another, with some transfer or meaning taking place in both directions. . . . To be a metaphorical thinker is to be a constructive learner, one who actively builds bridges from the known to the new. (Pugh, Hicks, Davis, & Venstra, 1992, pp. 4–5)

Developing metaphors requires creative thinking and has the potential to shift thinking in ways that analytic thinking cannot. Metaphors can be used to simplify and clarify problems, summarize thoughts, develop alternative ways of thinking about a topic or event, and communicate abstract ideas (Taggart & Wilson, 1998). Cross-cultural metaphors can have a powerful effect. Here are some examples:

- Not learning is bad; not wanting to learn is worse (African proverb)
- Children need models more than critics (French proverb)
- A poor person shames us all (Gabra saying)
- No matter how far you are down the wrong road, turn back (Turkish proverb)

Johnston (1994) described one example of the use of metaphor to promote reflection. She requested that each of three students completing a master's program "write a metaphor that described her experience in the program, paying particular attention to capturing ways in which she had changed or not changed during the two years" (p. 15). One student wrote about being a "contractor," explaining that initially she followed pre-designed plans but that over time, she and the future homeowners worked together to create customized plans. Another student wrote about being a tree in a drought, whose roots system had to seek out new sources of nutrients. The third student captured her experience as an artichoke with each petal being an element of practice that can be understood only when peeled away and examined. (Use of metaphors to promote reflection in the context of groups is presented in Chapter 5.)

Reading With Reflection

Ideas for individual reflection would be incomplete without emphasizing the value of reading and reflecting on the information. Although one emphasis of reflective practice frequently is on generating internal knowledge and making sense of one's teaching practice, external sources of knowledge are also important, if not essential. Given the isolating tendencies in the teaching profession, such as teaching in the same school or district for one's entire career, educators particularly must make concerted efforts to stay informed about findings from research and about practices occurring elsewhere in education. There are many ways to teach and learn. The greater one's repertoire, the greater the likelihood for success with all students.

The amount of professional literature is overwhelming. Fortunately, much of it can now be readily accessed through electronic journals and libraries. Professional journal subscriptions provide current literature conveniently delivered to your doorstep. Although there may be little time to read volumes of information, scanning for particularly relevant articles and using a highlighter or making notes in the margins can accentuate significant learning. Keeping sticky notes close by facilitates jotting down key ideas and transferring them to a calendar or plan book for application or follow-up. Listening to professional publications and presentations on audiotape in the car is also convenient. Reading professional literature is one important source for new information, ideas, and renewal.

Personal Reflections on Meaning in Life

Amid the busy-ness of everyday life, there are times when we find ourselves deep in thought about who we are, how we contribute or would like to, what is important to us, and to whom we are especially grateful. There are also times when we are noticeably out of balance and must intentionally create the space to consider these life-meaning perspectives. Are we human doings, or human beings? In what ways are we both doings and beings? Envision yourself high up on a mountain slope, looking up, down, and all around into vast open space. Or maybe you are nestled in a windbreaker and sitting on a cool, sandy beach watching the waves rhythmically rise and fall then spread out across the sand. In both spaces you are removed from the typical daily hustle and bustle and you are keenly aware of the natural world around you, a world with its own rhythms and energies of which you seldom take notice. You are small in comparison. You can just *be* in this place. You are not called to *do.* Here is a list of questions, from which you might select a few to prompt reflection. And, of course, we encourage you to add to the list. (Refer to Resource 3.D for a copy of these questions.) We also invite you to consider with whom you might share some of your responses.

- What is it that I want to do with my most precious thing: my life?
- If 80 percent of what I do has little noticeable impact and 20 percent provides me with the best results, what things in the 80 percent am I going to stop doing?
- Is my self-worth stronger than my self-critic, and how do I know? Is my self-critic preventing me from moving toward my most valued life pursuits?
- How do I use my gifts and talents to foster caring, commitment, and interdependence in my work?
- What am I willing to get fired for?
- What words of wisdom would my parents or grandparents offer as I sort through what matters most and how I can contribute?
- How do my children think of me, not only as a parent, but as a person? A citizen? What lessons do I hope to have taught them through modeling?
- Who are the people that bring joy to my life? And to whose life do I bring joy?
- Who have been the most important mentors in my life? Have I thanked them lately? What is stopping me?
- If I had one week to live, what would I do?
- In one sentence, what would I want written in my obituary?

GETTING STARTED WITH INDIVIDUAL REFLECTIVE PRACTICE

The decision to be a reflective educator is a commitment to your own growth and demonstrates a high level of professional responsibility and personal leadership for continuous development of your practice. It is how you develop the expertise and insights that accumulate into wisdom. It is a commitment made in a life context that reluctantly yields space for thinking and creating. We are confident that it is a decision you will not regret. In fact, we believe that becoming more reflective is likely to heighten your awareness of the deep-seated yearning to make sense of your world and become the best you can be. Webb (1995) describes the paradox of subtle urgency for reflection in our life of practice:

> Reflection-on-action remains the endangered species of reflective practice. It is the most easily lost due to pressure of work and its loss has no immediate, transparent effect. My experience continues to tell me, however, that the quiet times of reflection-on-action are critical for the survival of my own reflective practice . . . this puts the onus on one's self to make the time and organize one's life in such a way that reflection-on-action can continue to have an impact on professional practice. (p. 77)

The longest relationship that you have is with yourself. Why not make the best of it! Becoming more reflective is a way to learn more about who you are, what is important to you, how you think, what you say and do, and who you are as an educator. Choosing reflection supports your desire for excellence and effectiveness in your work.

To further guide your thinking about developing your reflection capacities and your own preferred means of reflection, we invite you to contemplate the following questions. (Refer to Resource 3.E for a modified set of these questions.)

- Thinking about your own development as an educator, what are you most interested in learning more about? Why does this seem important to you?
- What about the considerations of identity, ethics, courage, care, and voice? Which of these issues seems most important to ponder further right now, and why? Do you have any thoughts on how you might step into examining such an area of your identity and/or beliefs and values?
- As you reflect on your practice, what are your big questions? What parts of the curriculum are students missing? How can you maximize the learning strengths of all your students?

- What would be the best way to go about addressing these interests and questions? What ways of reflection are best aligned with your learning styles (e.g., journaling, exercising, reading, mapping)?
- How might you create space in your life to reflect and learn on a regular basis?
- Are there additional people you want to include in your process of reflection?

The Chapter Reflection Page (Figure 3.5) can be used to jot down your thoughts in response to these questions.

CLOSING

You can teach and lead based only on who you genuinely are (Palmer, 1998). In these demanding times, it is easy to slide to a place of feeling as if you are never enough. But who you are every day, how you create meaningful learning experiences for students and colleagues, the positive energy you choose to bring to your work—these things are enough. They are more than enough: they are an enormous gift to the world around you. By maintaining a focus on reflective capacities that expand and improve your personal practices, your influence on others expands, as well. Just remember to have your own "oxygen mask" securely in place before assisting others.

Figure 3.5   Chapter Reflection Page

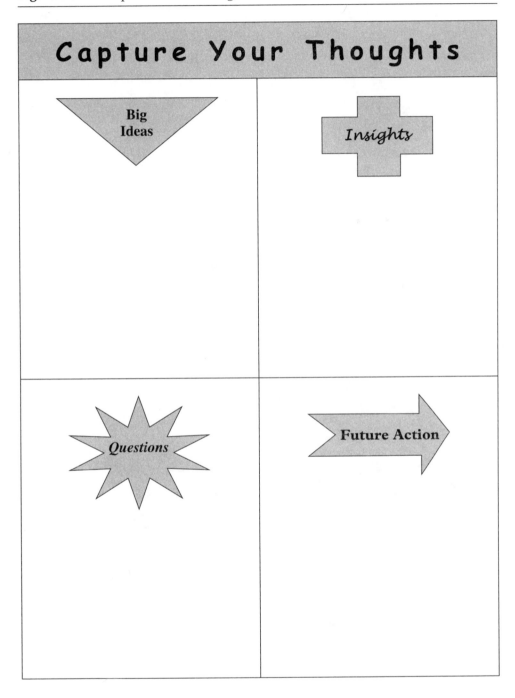

4

Reflective Practice With Partners

Awareness of one's own intuitive thinking usually grows out of practice in articulating it to others.

—Donald Schön (1983, p. 243),
The Reflective Practitioner: How Professionals Think in Action

As human beings, we are drawn to interactions with others. These interactions provide a means of understanding who we are in the world around us and in our professional and personal lives. Reflecting on educational practice with another person has the potential to greatly enrich our understanding and to support improvements in our practice. Because we filter our experiences through our own views of the world, however, reflecting alone can result in self-validation and justification (Bright, 1996; Butler, 1996; Levin, 1995; Zeichner, 1993). Reflection with another person offers a safeguard against perpetuating only our own thoughts. Bright (1996) explains,

> Because it is the practitioner's understanding which is the window through which a situation is understood and interpreted, an essential feature of "reflective practice" is the need for the practitioner to

be aware of her own processes in the development and construction of this interpretation . . . to understand how she understands a situation. . . . As intimated earlier, "reflective practice" is not easy, and the "self-reflexive" element of it makes it even more difficult. Paradoxically, this suggests the role of others in this self-reflective process because colleagues and clients may be very perceptive in detecting assumptions and bias present within a practitioner's practice. (pp. 177–178)

When reflecting, a partner can assist us in gaining awareness of fixed assumptions and viewing events from another perspective (Bright, 1996; Butler, 1996). Reflecting with a partner addresses the major concern about reflecting solely with ourselves, which is reinforcing only our own views and perceptions. Compared with reflection in groups, partner reflection offers the advantage of more privacy. Trust, therefore, is more readily fostered. Trust and safety are always issues when interacting with others, especially when revealing one's questions and thinking.

Recall from Chapter 1 (see p. 21–22) the potential gains that can be realized at the partner level in the Reflective Practice Spiral. In addition to offering new insights, reflecting with a partner has the potential to strengthen collegial relationships, decrease feelings of isolation, and increase a sense of connection in and to one's place of work. Reflection with partners can increase skills and confidence in the reflective practice process, thereby bolstering courage and commitment to expand reflection to the arena of small groups (Chapter 5) and even schoolwide (Chapter 6)— the outer levels of the Reflective Practice Spiral.

In this chapter, we focus on how to engage in reflective practices with partners. We use the term *reflective practice with partners* (or *reflection partners*) to refer to two or three people (dyads or triads) who collaboratively engage in a reflective learning process focused on improving educational practice, with the ultimate objective of enhanced student learning. We distinguish between reflection with partners and reflection in groups or teams (the next chapter) in the following ways. Reflective practice with partners (in contrast to groups/teams) is smaller and participation is usually voluntary, which means that the individuals involved usually are self-directed and motivated to reflect together. They often have connections through shared interests, areas of practice, or individual styles. In this chapter, we expand the how-to information shared in Chapter 3 (individual reflection) to include partners. Again, we offer considerations, examples, ideas, and suggestions for getting started with reflective practice with partners, and again, we refer you to the reflective practice Theory of Action (Figure 4.1) as a reminder of key elements of a reflective process intended to produce improved actions. Much of the substance of this chapter is intended to enlarge the openness, inquiry, and thinking dimensions of the theory.

Figure 4.1   Theory of Action for Reflective Practice

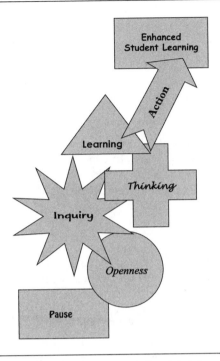

SPECIAL CONSIDERATIONS FOR REFLECTIVE PRACTICE WITH PARTNERS

It is not safe to assume that adults who learn well by themselves will learn well with others. Think about the kind of specific support teachers provide when students are expected to work together compared to when they work alone. Likewise, with adults, intentional consideration of learning design is helpful. We offer design considerations related to the purpose of partner reflection, with whom to reflect, and ways to reflect together. In particular we extend previous discussions about listening, thinking, and coaching. A summary of considerations for partner reflection is offered in Table 4.1 for your reference, including relevant topics described earlier in the book. All these considerations interact with one another. The desired focus of reflection, for example, may influence who is selected as a reflection partner. Conversely, the choice of a reflection partner may influence the choice of topic for reflection. Topical emphases for reflection are infinite; reflection partner options may be less plentiful.

Table 4.1   Considerations for Reflective Practice With Partners

Clarify Purpose and Process

- Something I would like to learn more about is . . . because . . .
- Things that help me to be reflective are . . .

Strengthen Listening

- Intentional pause: a requirement for both listening to oneself and listening to others
- Empathic listening: listening and understanding (from Chapter 2)
- Suspension: develop the ability to suspend beliefs in order to listen
- Increase awareness of listening blocks: comparing, mind reading, filtering, judging, dreaming, identifying, advising, sparring, being right, derailing, and placating

Expand Thinking and Inquiry

- Theory of Action for Reflective Practice (Figure 4.1)
- Open questions, SPACE, reframe, and dialogue (from Chapter 2)
- A shift from *how* to *what* and *why* questions (from Chapter 2)
- Reframing and reexamining experiences through a new lens (from Chapters 2 and 3)
- Reiman's Guided Reflection Framework: apply "matching responses" to affirm and encourage; apply "mismatching responses" to challenge

Coach

- Reflection and inquiry embedded in practice context
- Direct support for knowledge development and skill transfer to practice
- Nonevaluative; judgment-free data and inquiry (Sanford, 1995)

For some people, the choice of a partner precedes identification of a specific reflection focus.

What Is the Purpose of Your Partner Reflection? What Is the Focus?

As with any type of reflection, the overarching purpose of partner reflection is to expand thinking and understanding about practice in order to increase effectiveness as an educator. Partner reflection may focus on a specific area of teaching or leadership practice, a shared teaching or leading situation (e.g., coteaching or cofacilitating), or a specific aspect of your partner's practice. It may also focus on external sources of knowledge or circumstances. We refer you back to Table 2.3 (p. 57–58) for a sampling of topics. Numerous factors influence what you and your reflection partner identify as a focus, and some of those factors are described in this section.

To begin with, the amount of teaching experience, as briefly mentioned in Chapter 2, influences reflection emphases. Early in one's career, the learning and development process usually concentrates on creating a supportive learning environment, becoming familiar with the curriculum, and establishing instructional practices. Later on, learning and development expands to include more complex instructional issues (e.g., differentiating instruction to meet a wider range of abilities and interests), productive collaboration with colleagues, mentoring of new teachers, and contributing to school-level organizational and improvement work. As we enter middle and late adulthood, our interests typically shift to larger work and life issues, such as the effects of external state, national, and global events and trends on humankind, as well as issues and questions of our own contributions and legacies to our families, profession, and communities.

In addition, the specific focus of reflection, such as a particular initiative or teaching practice, is influenced by the "stage" of implementation for an individual educator. Is this an instructional practice that I just started last week? Or have I spent the past 6 months working with the practice and am now moving toward refining my understanding and use? Concerns and questions change over time based on the individual's level of experience with a given practice or initiative. We share the Concerns-Based Adoption Model (CBAM) (Hall & Hord, 2001) as a framework for considering one's changes throughout the learning process. The Stages of Concern component of CBAM (shown in Table 4.2) suggests that when teachers begin implementing a new instructional strategy, their initial concerns focus on expectations and then shift to management. At the management stage, teachers benefit from clear examples, strategies, and materials to be used in implementation. As implementation progresses, concerns and interests shift to the effects on students and then a desire to collaborate with others and refine practices. Implications for partner reflection are to anticipate an evolution of concerns and interests for reflection depending on how much use or practice educators have with a particular initiative.

Dyads and triads also offer an excellent opportunity to inquire about the process of learning through reflection. A focus of reflection may be shaped by questions partners have about their own reflective process (in a sense, metareflection). Partners may wonder,

- How does the reflection process influence my thinking?
- What conditions are conducive to my reflection? What conditions inhibit my reflection?
- Why am I drawn to reflect on certain aspects of my teaching practice and routinely ignore other aspects?
- How do I increase my reflection as I am teaching or leading (reflection-in-action), instead of primarily afterward (reflection-on-action)?
- Are my personal reflection capacities (being present, being open, listening) developing?

Table 4.2   Concerns-Based Adoption Model: Stages of Concern
(Hall & Hord, 2001)

Stages of Concern			Expressions of Concern
IMPACT	6	Refocusing	I have some ideas about something that would work even better.
	5	Collaboration	I am concerned about relating what I am doing with what my coworkers are doing.
	4	Consequence	How is my use affecting clients?
TASK	3	Management	I seem to be spending all of my time getting materials ready.
SELF	2	Personal	How will using it affect me?
	1	Informational	I would like to know more about it.
	0	Awareness	I am not concerned with it.

SOURCE: From Gene E. Hall & Shirley M. Hord (2001). *Implementing change: Patterns, principles, and potholes* (p. 61). Boston, MA: Allyn & Bacon. Copyright © by Pearson Education. Reprinted by permission of the publisher.

Such questions ground continuous improvement and are well suited for reflection with partners.

Without a compelling purpose, time for partner reflection is not likely to be honored. If you are not learning, or if you are not learning about something that interests you, the time allocated for reflection will soon become filled with other activities. Time spent learning together is too valuable to be spent on issues of lesser importance or, worse, issues that detract from your growth, such as gossip or an obsession on circumstances beyond your influence or control.

Early in the process of reflecting together, partners should articulate their learning desires and needs. Here are some specific ideas for deciding on topics and desired outcomes. One way to proceed is to take a few minutes individually and then share responses to the following prompts: (a) "Something I would like to learn more about is . . . because . . ."; (b) "Things that help me to be reflective are. . . ." The first prompt identifies potential content emphases for reflection. It may also target personal reflection capacities for improvement described in Chapter 2—for example, "I would like to get better at listening without feeling the need to respond." The second prompt gets at conditions that promote reflection, ranging from the surrounding environment (e.g., noise, light, temperature, seating) to ways of interacting (e.g., time available to process before responding).

At the beginning of each reflective interaction, it is useful for partners to clarify what they hope to gain from the specific interaction. Is the primary intent to obtain insight, to identify a range of options, to make a decision, or to just get thoughts out in the open to begin clarifying issues? At the end of each interaction, it is also helpful to recap the territory covered and to identify key ideas or outcomes that emerged. Sample formats and prompts for closing reflections are offered later in the book (Figure 5.6 on p. 169).

With Whom Might You Reflect?

Initial reflection partners often are self-selected because the motivation to reflect in dyads or triads is inside-out (self-initiated), although partners or partnership are sometimes mandated (as in mentoring). Initial partners typically share an interest in some aspect of practice and may have similar experiences and viewpoints. Over time, however, there may be a desire to learn with and from someone who has different experiences and views, recognizing that comparison and contrast serve as stimulants for thinking and for new understandings.

Access is an important consideration in partner selection. If you plan to meet face-to-face, how proximal is your potential partner? Long and stressful drives will inhibit access. Are there common times during the day or week that would work? How frequently do you and your partner want to meet? Some partners use a combination of face-to-face and electronic means of reflection. The Internet enables quick, easy access any time.

As already emphasized, trust is the foundation for collaborative reflection. Trust is difficult to build and easy to destroy. If we behave in trustworthy ways, we are more likely to attract partners who do as well. One indicator of trustworthiness is congruence between actions and words. Desirable reflection partners demonstrate such integrity. They also focus on students, learning, and their purpose as educators. Or, as a German proverb tells us, they know that "The main thing is keeping the main thing the main thing." In seeking partners, choose people who produce energy rather than drain it. Negativity and cynicism are unproductive and diminish your spirit. Seek people who are open to growth, yours and theirs. Be wary of people with expert tendencies. No one knows it all. Everyone can improve. Strong partnerships spark great growth potential. A checklist of considerations for partners is offered in Table 4.3. The list includes characteristics to continuously develop within yourself so that you, too, serve well as a reflection partner.

How Do You Reflect Together?

In Chapter 2 we introduced the importance of listening and how difficult it is to listen without our own thoughts filtering what we hear. We also introduced reframing as a way to think differently about events and circumstances. Finally we introduced the notion that changes in thought,

Table 4.3   Characteristics to Consider for Reflective Practice Partner

Essential characteristics: Characteristics that I would choose to be present in any reflective practice partner.

Someone who

—— stays focused on student learning

—— is committed to continuous improvement

—— is trustworthy

—— contributes positively to the overall climate

—— is a good listener

—— is curious

—— is open to examining practice—hers and mine

—— will inquire about and help expand my thinking

—— will encourage and support changes in practice

—— has integrity

—— aligns actions and words

—— is accessible enough to allow regular opportunities to reflect together

Variable characteristics: Characteristics that I may intentionally choose as similar to or different from me, depending on my learning needs and desires.

—— years of teaching experience

—— type of teaching experience (e.g., level, content area, school demographics)

—— teaching style and philosophy

—— life experience

—— age

—— gender

—— ethnicity, culture

—— personality

—— learning style

understanding, and knowledge involve cognitive restructuring, especially when we are confronted with situations that create dissonance. In this section, additional information is offered for developing listening and thinking capacities. Then, ideas about the practice of coaching are presented. Listening, thinking, and coaching are central to fostering reflective practice with partners.

Listening

Listening seems simple enough. Beyond putting down the newspaper and physically orienting toward the speaker, how hard can it be to just listen? Turns out it is a lot harder than we might anticipate. (An old adage suggests that this is why we have two ears and just one mouth.) Listening well is what enables us to hear and understand what someone says to us. Listening and being listened to create a sense of connection and trust between individuals. It is a powerful means of establishing rapport. When we truly listen, we listen with our ears, our eyes, our bodies, and our hearts. Deep listening is very honoring of a relationship. Stephen Glenn said, years ago, that people want three things: to be listened to, to be taken seriously, and to know that a person has a genuine interest in what you are saying.

Reflective practice with partners holds enormous potential for learning about ourselves, our thinking, and our practice. It also serves as a major source of encouragement and support for growth. If we cannot listen well, the potential for learning and support will not be realized for ourselves or others. Here we add to the listening section in Chapter 2 (pp. 39) by describing the skill of suspension and by identifying common blocks to listening.

Suspension is a thinking skill that fosters listening. We invite you to read the suspension excerpt in Table 4.4. As you read this excerpt, underline, highlight, or make notes in the margin about words, phrases, and ideas that resonate for you. Share with a partner what you identify as significant. Some of the words and ideas that stand out for us are *notice our own thinking . . . suspension is a way of emptying the cup . . . choosing to temporarily put aside your views . . . dialogue as a finite game . . . others have opinions that are true for them . . . as challenging as it is, it increases our learning.* When we are initially learning suspension, the idea that we can be more aware of our thoughts but choose *not* to engage around them is often an "aha" experience. That we can choose to let our feelings and thoughts pass is a freeing notion—hard to do, but worth attempting. Sometimes there is no particular need to engage passing thoughts or feelings and make them bigger than they are or allow them to take us off in tangential directions. They can be put aside, allowing space to attend more fully to others. As you engage in partner reflection, pay attention to your thinking and practice the skill of suspension.

Mastering suspension will also assist you in minimizing common blocks to listening. The Web site of the International Listening Leadership Institute (http://www.listeningleader.com/) used to name 12 blocks to listening: comparing, mind reading, rehearsing, filtering, judging, dreaming, identifying, advising, sparring, being right, derailing, and placating. As you read this list, which blocks could you relate to? There are some to which many of us seem prone, particularly as we gain experience in our professional roles. Being right, giving advice, and making comparisons are common culprits. Who among us doesn't like to be right or give advice? Who among us doesn't tend to compare and contrast our thoughts and experiences with those of our speaking partner? The problem is, these tendencies maintain a focus on ourselves and divert attention from our speaking partner. Later in this chapter we describe an activity that creates an opportunity for partners to practice the skill of listening and be mindful of the interference created by a failure to suspend blocks to listening.

Thinking

Thinking, of course, is integral to the process of learning. Theory and research abound on the topic of thinking. What is thinking? How does one think? What prompts thinking? What supports thinking at higher levels, resulting in concept formation? Alan Reiman (1999) proposes a reflection framework based on the work of Vygotsky and Piaget, two eminent cognitive psychologists, and then provides a synthesis of findings from studies in which the framework was used. Our intent in summarizing Reiman's work is to deepen understanding about the complex processes involved in thinking and in supporting others' thinking.

According to Reiman, Vygotsky viewed knowledge construction as co-created through interaction with other people. His work emphasized the significant role of a "capable other" in providing appropriate types and levels of support to foster growth in others. Capable others are viewed as individuals who have a more in-depth and complex understanding of the subject of interest. Vygotsky also created the term *zone of proximal development* (ZPD), to refer to the space in which learning is most likely to occur. In the ZPD, the task at hand is of interest to the learner (motivation); it is sufficiently complex to engage the learner (a challenge), but not so complex that the learner cannot engage with it.

In contrast to Vygotsky, Reiman explains that Piaget viewed knowledge construction as a process of individual adaptation. When faced with new information, an individual can choose to either dismiss or engage it. If one chooses to engage and the new information is similar to existing information, it is said to be assimilated. If the new information in some way extends or enriches existing information, it is viewed as being accommodated into existing cognitive structures. If new information is complex and challenging, it causes a state of disequilibrium, which can feel uncomfortable and even stressful. This discomfort is resolved through a process of equilibration that requires changes in cognitive structures.

How do Vygotsky and Piaget's theories apply to reflection and teacher learning? Reiman (1999) suggests that when teachers take on new and more complex roles or contexts of practice, disequilibrium occurs. Disequilibrium presents an opportunity for cognitive growth which, he argues, is well supported by a capable other. The capable other determines the individual learner's zone of proximal development and the scaffolds for promoting growth. He explains,

Table 4.4   Thoughts About Suspension and Listening in Dialogue

The point of engaging in dialogue is to exchange ideas, opinions, and observations. The purpose according to David Bohm (1989), in his book *On Dialogue*, is to create meaning from the flow of conversation. Dialogue is not analyzing, picking a side, or winning an argument. It is ongoing, involves the sharing of views, and means having a learning conversation with someone or a group of people.

One of the first requirements of dialogue is to suspend judgment. To do so we must notice our own thinking. Garmston and Wellman (1999) refer to suspension as "the essential internal skill of dialogue" (p. 54) and explain that "to suspend means to set aside our perceptions, our feelings, or judgments and our impulses for a time and listen to and monitor carefully our own internal experience and what comes up from within the group" (p. 54). Suspension allows us to be open to others' views. Like the Zen master who overflowed the cup of the student, you must empty your cup (or mind) before more can be put into the vessel. Suspension is a way of emptying the cup.

John Dewey (1933), in his book *How to Think*, wrote about suspending judgment as a prerequisite to good thinking. We used to say to people, "be non-judgmental." This was problematic. How do you be "non" something? We now say, set aside judgment or suspend judgment while in dialogue. It does not mean giving up your opinions. It does mean choosing to temporarily put your views aside and be open to the views of someone else.

We like what John Carse (1986) says in his book *Finite and Infinite Games*. A finite game is like Monopoly, Sorry!, and gin rummy. The goal of a finite game is to win. When you win, the game is over. In an infinite game, the goal of the game is to continue the game. We like to think of dialogue as an infinite game, one in which the conversation continues over time and supports extending and deepening our understanding and our learning.

To engage in dialogue requires acceptance of another person's point of view without responding in dismissal, disgust, or disengagement. Others can have opinions that are true for them. We can be aware of how other points of view create emotions in us. It is our responsibility to manage our own emotions. Keeping our breathing rates slow and deep can keep us from getting riled and from losing our ability to suspend. If we do not understand, we can choose to inquire with the genuine purpose of understanding, *not* as an opportunity to challenge, tell, or teach. We can simply check it out, by asking questions, paraphrasing, or clarifying for understanding.

To have an exchange of ideas, we must listen. Be fully present and listen. Sometimes in workshops we ask, "What percentage of time are you listening, and what percentage of time are you waiting?" Many times people are waiting to get a word in or are composing their own ideas rather than truly listening. Madeline Burley-Allen (1995), in her book *The Forgotten Art of Listening*, says that in communicating we spend 9 percent of our time writing, 16 percent reading, 35 percent speaking, and 40 percent listening. So, where in the curriculum do we teach listening?

As challenging as it is to suspend and to truly listen, when we do suspend, we have found it enhances our understanding and our learning in ways that would not otherwise have been possible. It is a gift we can give ourselves, as well as those with whom we engage.

The instructor, hoping to guide reflection, must skillfully match and mismatch . . . responses according to the unique needs of the [learner]. . . . Matching means "starting where the learner is." Conversely, "mismatching" implies providing additional challenge. . . . The challenge for the instructor is knowing when to support (match) and when to challenge (mismatch). (p. 7)

Reiman refers to the process of matching and mismatching as *guided reflection*. He identifies seven categories of guidance that are differentially provided by a mentor (capable other) depending on the feelings, thinking, and behavior demonstrated by a mentee. The mentor response categories are as follows: accepting feelings, praising or encouraging, acknowledging and clarifying ideas, prompting inquiry, providing information, giving directions, and addressing problems. Some of these responses are considered matching responses, in that their function is to affirm and encourage. Others are considered mismatching, in that their function is to challenge. Here is an example. If a mentee is expressing self-doubt in a new situation, a mentor might choose a matching response of praise and encouragement, recognizing the impact of feelings on the ability to reflect. If a mentee is viewing a situation from only one viewpoint, a mentor may choose a mismatching response, such as prompting inquiry, to foster more divergent thinking.

Reiman is careful to emphasize that the reflection framework is just that, a framework, not a prescription. It can guide a mentor's choice of responses but is informed by variables within and around mentees in their respective practice contexts. Reflection partners, as well as mentors, can learn when and how to support or to challenge, such that reflection is enhanced.

Reiman (1999) synthesized the findings of numerous quantitative studies involving preservice teachers who were engaged in new teaching roles and who, in the process, were required to use dialogue journals. The reflection framework was used to guide the instructor responses to student entries in the journals. The preservice teachers also were expected to use the framework to guide reflection with their peers (other preservice teachers). The result was "greater gains in cognitive-structural growth across conceptual, moral, and ego domains" (p. 16). The requirement that teachers apply the framework with peers was indicated to be an important variable:

This element of the intervention studies appears to be a key aspect of the guided reflection process because it encourages the novice or experienced educator to empathize, clarify, and raise more complex professional and personal issues with his or her colleague or tutee. The role taking experience, by itself, would not guarantee social perspective taking. (p. 14)

What are some implications of Reiman's theoretical discussion and practice applications of the guided reflection framework? First, given substantial variability among teachers, the zone of proximal development concept is useful to guide teacher reflection. Second, a flexible framework that offers various means of matching and mismatching teacher responses further supports differentiated support for individual reflection. Third, the use of interactive dialogue as teachers engage in new roles has the potential to "awaken and rouse to life functions which are in a stage of maturing, which lie in the zone of proximal development" (Vygotsky, 1956, p. 273, as quoted by Reiman, 1999, p. 17). Finally, Reiman suggests that the state of disequilibrium should be recognized as integral to the process of teacher reflection, learning, and development.

Coaching

The previous discussion underscores the significant role of another person in reflective practice, especially someone skilled at listening and asking questions to expand thinking. In educational contexts, such a person is often referred to as a *coach*. Schön (1987) speaks about the role and intent of coaching:

> The student cannot be taught what he needs to know, but he can be coached; he has to see on his own behalf and in his own way the relations between means and methods employed and results achieved. Nobody else can see for him, and he can't see just by being "told," although the right kind of telling may guide his seeing and thus help him see what he needs to see. (p. 14)

Also in support of coaching is recognition that knowledge construction is enhanced when learners are engaged in authentic, meaningful, and complex problems of practice (as opposed to being engaged in isolated contexts and made-up problems). Coaching, done in authentic contexts, mitigates the problem of knowledge and skill transfer.

Many published studies focus on promoting reflective thought in the context of hierarchical relationships, such as a novice being guided by an expert teacher. Reflective practice in the context of horizontal relationships, however, is equally—and sometimes more—powerful. Food service personnel can coach teachers; secretaries can coach principals. Coaching does not have to be just about professional staff. Coaching often occurs in horizontal relationships. Much evidence exists to support the claim that both partners learn, regardless of whether the relationship is horizontal or vertical or bottom-up. Ash and Levitt (2003), for example, demonstrated that teacher learning increases when teachers use formative assessment practices with students. They studied the trajectory of teacher change. First teachers listened to students, observed students, or examined student work to identify current levels of understanding. Then they identified discrepancies between current and desired levels of student understanding. Next, the teachers reflected on their own practices (subject area expertise, pedagogical knowledge) to determine ways for scaffolding student learning to the next reasonable target. Each step of the trajectory requires complex cognitive engagement (i.e., learning) on the part of the teacher. Teachers reported improving their capacity to listen to students and to move students to higher levels of thought and understanding. It could be argued that Ash and Levitt's trajectory explains a process of learning for any individual involved deliberate reflective practices with partners.

The practice of coaching, generally viewed in nonhierarchal ways, has increased in schools. There has been an explosion of coaching initiatives, including peer coaching, cognitive coaching, leadership coaching, and school coaching. Here we articulate some basic tenets about coaching and urge you to consult the cited texts to further your knowledge and to support your practice of coaching. The topic itself requires book-length coverage (and much practice).

Coaching grew from a realization that traditional approaches to staff development, such as isolated workshops, were largely ineffective means of changing practice (Showers & Joyce, 1996). Whatever excitement or possibilities might have been created during a workshop were lost unless after participants returned to school there was regular follow-up focused on continuously supporting implementation of new practices (Joyce & Showers, 2002). Coaching is predicated on adult learning principles that emphasize the need for development to be relevant to and embedded in practice, supported by collaboration among peers, and approached as a continuous and intentional process. (Recall the discussion in Chapter 2 on adult learning principles.)

According to Joyce and Showers (2002), when the intent is transfer of knowledge and skills into daily practice (which, in education, would almost always be the case), the results of peer coaching far surpass workshops or even demonstrations. Further, the authors emphasize the importance of schoolwide commitments to coaching, including the involvement of administrators. In their work, they require the following supports from schools:

- "Commitment to practice/use whatever change the faculty has decided to implement"
- Faculty and staff assistance and support of one another "in the change process, including shared planning of instructional objectives and development of materials and lessons"
- "Collection of data, both on the implementation of their planned change and on student effects relevant to the school's identified target for student growth" (Joyce & Showers, 2002, p. 88)

From years of practice and research, Joyce and Showers also conclude that feedback should be omitted from the coaching process because when viewed as providing feedback, interactions tend to fall into supervisory (hierarchal) structures. We qualify their assertion to suggest that certain types of feedback are useful. As Sanford (1995) explains, useful feedback results only when two conditions are met. First, feedback must be perceived as judgment-free data, and second, interactions around feedback must be perceived as judgment-free inquiry. In other words, constructive feedback is not evaluative.

Another feature of Joyce and Showers's peer coaching involves the person serving as coach being the person doing the teaching, and the person being coached to be the person doing the observing. Rarely do teachers have opportunities to observe colleagues teach for the sole purpose of learning. There is much to be learned from such reflection opportunities.

Robbins (2004) describes peer coaching as an umbrella category that can involve many types of interactions, ranging from coteaching, to unit planning, to videotape analysis, to action research. Common to all peer coaching, however, is a focus on the teacher as learner. According to Robbins,

> Peer coaching is a confidential process in which two or more professional colleagues work together to reflect on current practices; expand, refine, and build new skills; share ideas; teach one another; conduct classroom research; or solve problems in the workplace. (p. 164)

Additional information, examples, and training materials are indexed in Robbins's chapter in the NSDC (National Staff Development Council) resource *Powerful Designs for Staff Learning* (mentioned in Chapter 2), which includes access to user-friendly content on a CD-ROM.

In the best of all practice worlds, reflection and learning practices, such as peer coaching, would be embraced on a schoolwide basis, as reinforced by Joyce and Showers. Practice in an imperfect world suggests that successive approximations are better than no approximation at all. So although we, too, encourage and support schoolwide development, we also applaud smaller efforts aimed at continuous development and renewal of professional practice. Reflection with partners is a valid and powerful means of achieving this aim.

Before moving on to consider the examples of partner reflection offered in the next section, you may wish to refresh your memory about the questioning, responding, reframing, and dialogue sections in Chapter 2 (pp. 42–45) for specific strategies that promote inquiry and thinking. The reflection frameworks offered throughout Chapter 3 might also be useful.

REFLECTIVE PRACTICE WITH PARTNERS: EXAMPLES FROM PRACTICE

Partner reflection may be one of the most commonly used supports for continuous learning. It holds much potential for increasing diverse thinking and fostering meaningful change in practice—in a relaxed context that is more easily scheduled into our daily lives than when more people are involved. We now share both formal and informal ways to reflect with partners.

Reflective Voice Mail Bridges the Time Crunch

Voice mail was probably not envisioned as a mechanism for reflective practice, but for two authors of this book it became a crucial channel for ongoing partner reflection. As is common with many educators, we found it exceedingly difficult to allocate time to meet regularly in person. Voice mail emerged as a productive and convenient communication and reflection link, because it can be accessed at any time to record or review messages. Over time, its use expanded beyond simple project updates to sharing more lengthy perceptions, insights, and questions. Because the voice-mail modality is solely auditory, we were keenly aware of the intonation, affect, and emotional overtones. Because there is no need to respond immediately, we could listen with the intent of understanding first and responding later. The wait time in between messages allowed us think in a more coherent and creative manner about our shared work.

Cognitive Coaching: Three Examples

Cognitive coaching is a way to expand the thinking capacity of individuals so they create their own best ways to address issues. Cognitive coaching has a much sharper focus on building capacity for problem solving than does peer coaching. The five–states-of-mind framework is core to cognitive coaching and includes the capacity-building domains of efficacy, flexibility, craftsmanship, consciousness, and interdependence (see Costa & Garmston, 2002, and Chapter 3, pp. 89–90). When someone chooses to be coached, the coach poses thoughtfully constructed questions to elicit that person's thinking. This framework can be flexibly used to construct the questions and offer responses. Here are some example questions (also shared in Chapter 2 and in Resource 4.A as a reflection protocol) for reflective thinking on a lesson:

- How do you think the lesson went? What happened that caused it to go that way?
- When you think about what you had planned and what actually happened, what were the similarities and what were the differences?

- As you think about the results you got, what were some of the ways you designed the lesson to cause that to happen?
- When you reflect back, what would you do differently next time you teach this lesson?
- As you consider this lesson, what outcomes do you want to have happen again?
- What are some of the professional goals that you are working on in your practice?
- What resources are available as you work toward your professional goals?

The following sections offer three examples of a principal coaching a variety of staff members.

Coaching for Interdisciplinary Instruction

One summer day, a biology teacher and an English teacher came into the office to talk to the assistant principal about team teaching. They wanted the same students during first and second hour so they could do some two-hour instructional blocks. This was a very traditional school, organized around a six-period day. Because the administrator had coached both of the them individually, he knew they were excellent teachers. Both were also very global thinkers. Attending to details was not their strength.

After the teachers talked about their plan, the principal assumed a coaching role and inquired about specific aspects of implementation; that is, he asked them to reflect forward on their anticipated work together. He asked questions such as, What are you going to do the first week of class? What are some of the common themes across your disciplines—for example, how is conflict evident in living systems and evident in written words? The teachers had a great idea and they knew the results they wanted for students, but they had not yet figured out how to get started. Throughout the summer, the principal and teachers met every couple of weeks for a brief coaching session. The teachers created a more specific instructional plan, and classes were scheduled back-to-back so the students would be together for two periods.

The principal and teachers met four times during the first trimester. Coaching questions included, How are you integrating the two content areas? How are you learning about teaming together? What roles do each of you assume? How do you know you are making a difference for the kids? In what ways do you see the students making connections between biology and English? How are your relationships with your other colleagues? At the end of the first trimester, the principal asked them about the outcomes of their interdisciplinary venture. The English teacher said he was now teaching composition using the scientific method, and the biology teacher said he was now teaching science using journaling. Sometimes magic happens when you are able to facilitate putting people together and you let learning happen.

Coaching to Reflect Back, Then Forward

One day, a world language teacher asked the principal for an hour of his time. She said, "You always give me great ideas." He was surprised, especially because he speaks only English. He was trying to remember any idea he had suggested and asked, "What idea have I given you?" After pausing, she said, "Well, all I know is that I come out of our talks with more ideas." The principal relaxed, knowing that he needed to ask reflective questions, not give ideas. Coaching supports others to come up with their own best ways.

The principal inquired about the year that had just finished. How did the results compare with what the teacher had thought would happen? What influenced those results? What might make sense to work on next year? These types of questions provided an opportunity for the teacher to reflect backward, inward, and forward. It is important to emphasize again that the principal facilitated the reflection process by asking questions to help the teacher clarify her own thinking. In this situation, the coach's role was to ask questions that supported the teacher taking risks, generating new ideas, and reflecting on her practice.

Coaching to Promote Problem Solving

In a junior high school, a course in coaching for reflective thought was being offered to the staff. The principal, who was the instructor, held an informational meeting before school started. The principal was enthusiastic when he heard that the head custodian was interested in attending. They knew each other from another building, so trust was already established. The principal asked the custodian why he signed up for coaching. The custodian said he had a lot of trouble controlling his temper (which the principal already knew, and he valued him as a good worker) and he wanted to be seen by staff as a problem solver rather than someone who reacted to problems by becoming angry and yelling.

The principal and the custodian engaged in a coaching relationship for the entire year. They met formally about once each month. Informally, they interacted daily as principal and custodian around facility-related issues. These informal interactions helped to build a positive, trusting relationship. Some of the issues addressed in the formal sessions included "What are options for responding to teachers who want everything *now?*" "How might requests for action from the principal's office be presented?" "When there are multiple priorities for immediate action, what are some of the factors that need to be considered?" The principal as coach also followed up on previous issues and asked, What happened? What worked? What didn't? Have there been any new challenges? Any surprises? At the end of the year, the custodian said that teachers treated him differently because he had volunteered to be coached. He thought that the teachers respected him more and that they knew he was there to learn and improve, just as the teachers were. He did not say that his own self-respect had increased in the process, but this was evident in his actions and interactions. Relationships improved. Staff members remarked to the principal that the custodian was more helpful and congenial. Students felt noticeably better about him, too. The custodian accomplished a great deal that year by having the courage to reflect on his behavior, consider alternatives, and choose different actions.

Nurturing Reflective Capacity Beginning With Induction

In a growing third-ring suburban school district, there is a strong value in building and sustaining reflective capacity within the staff. Beginning with the initial interview, prospective teachers get a hint of expectations for reflection by questions intended to elicit reflection. For example, "When reflecting on your job performance, what are main factors you consider?"

Once hired, teachers are required to participate in a two-day New Teacher Support Program where the seed for continuous growth and reflection is carefully and firmly planted. Each new teacher receives one of two resources. First-year teachers are given Harry and Rosemary Wong's (1998) *The First Days of School.* Teachers with one or more years of experience are given Jon Saphier and Robert Gower's (1997) *The Skillful Teacher: Building Your Teaching Skills.* Portions of these resources are revisited throughout the year by principals and district office personnel as one means of inviting reflection and growth for new staff.

The teachers are also introduced to Charlotte Danielson's (1996) work, *Enhancing Professional Practice: A Framework for Teaching.* The principals use this framework or a similar model not just as an evaluation tool, but also as a means to invite reflective conversations with the teachers about instructional choices and student learning. Principals are not interested only in how students behave, but in how they learn and how learning is assessed.

Systematic efforts to support reflective practice continue throughout the year with individualized cognitive coaching, small group mini-forums, and a full-day workshop. Each of these induction components is described below.

Individualized Cognitive Coaching

The cognitive coaching component involves a minimum of one scheduled observation and coaching session between the teacher and a district coach who is not in a supervisory position. In preparation for the session, teachers complete a form that describes the student learning goals, evidence that would indicate reaching those goals, strategies or learning activities for engaging students, the teacher's personal learning focus for the lesson, and data the teacher would like the coach to collect when observed. (A copy of this new teacher cognitive coaching preconference form is located in Resource 4.B.)

We have learned that it is important to invite reflection not only around the lesson development, but also around a personal learning goal aimed at enhancing professional effectiveness. We have noticed that many teachers, including experienced ones, struggle with identifying a personal learning goal. If they are really stuck, we ask them to reference the *Skillful Teacher* resource and tag an area for personal development. The coach will then gather data for the teacher around his or her personal learning goal. The data that is collected is shared after the teacher has first reflected about the instructional decisions that were made prior to the lesson and how those decisions affected student learning. At the end of the postconference, the coach shares the data in a *matter-of-fact* (nonevaluative) way and invites the teacher to make observations and assessments on what the data mean. Only the coach and the teacher meet together for the postconference. This gives the teacher a safe space in which to reflect, apart from the formal evaluation done by the principal. The teacher then meets with his or her principal after the reflecting conference is over. (This meeting is described later in this example.)

Mini-Forums

Mini-forums are held every other month at the end of the school day for about 90 minutes. They are designed to provide a safety net for staff and a space for reflective dialogue. Although the structure is flexible to allow conversation about common issues that arise among the new teachers, there are predetermined topics, such as curriculum maps and secure outcomes, professional learning communities, cognitive coaching, and differentiated instruction. Of the seven forums, the first, middle, and last bring together all teachers who are new to the district. The intent is to convey the message that all K–12 teachers must work together to best serve the interests of students. Mixing staff also creates the potential for better understanding and appreciation of varied roles and responsibilities. In the other four meetings, elementary and secondary teachers convene separately to delve more deeply into level-related topics.

December Workshop

All new teachers participate in a one-day December workshop that explores cognitive coaching, Ladder of Inference, single-loop and double-loop learning, perception and how it affects attention, and trust. The purpose of the workshop is to expose staff to ways that we tend to limit ourselves as learners and to emphasize the need for continuous growth and examination of professional practices in order to effectively support learning for all students. After the December workshop, each teacher participates in a reflective conference that is embedded in the second observation by the school principal. As described earlier, the teacher meets with the principal after engaging in the reflective conference with the coach.

Principals report that since implementation of the new teacher support program, teachers are better able to articulate the strengths and limitations of their instruction and the learning that occurred during the lesson. An unanticipated outcome of the coaching process has been increased reflection by the principals as they converse with coaches about the learning that is occurring in the classrooms. Each of these conversations invites a deeper and clearer picture of what represents authentic student learning. Principal observations and feedback now have a richer context for "learning" in the classroom. It is not unusual to hear principals talk about the pacing of a lesson or how attention was intentionally structured to focus the learning.

As Oliver Wendell Holmes said, "A mind that is stretched by a new experience can never go back to its old dimensions." In Big Lake, we are committed to intentionally developing reflective capacities not only in new teachers but in all staff. Supervision and coaching can find a home together if roles and expectations are clearly understood and respected by everyone. *Contributed by Jim Roussin, Director of Teaching and Learning, Big Lake Schools, Minnesota*

Principal-Teacher Interactive Journaling

A principal colleague engaged in interactive journaling with some of the teachers in his school. Some of the teachers exchanged journals every 2 weeks, some once a month. After a few days, the journals were returned. Most important, the dialogue was ongoing and could occur outside of face-to-face meetings, which were always difficult to schedule. For teachers who are more reflective or introverted, this approach to journaling with a partner allows more time to craft questions or consider responses than in real-time, face-to-face interactions. Communicating through journals also may be more comfortable for some people than in-person meetings.

Reflective Practice in Paraprofessional Development and Teaming

Paraprofessionals frequently provide direct instruction to special education students, often with little or no preparation. In addition, paraprofessional training and supervision is now a common responsibility of many specialist teachers. The following example describes the efforts of one special educator to develop paraprofessionals to be reflective in their work with students.

Evergreen is an urban high school with 1,850 students, 30 of whom have physical disabilities and are supported by 3 special educators and 11 paraprofessionals. The students attend general education classes and a special education support class. Their programs are individualized because of their complex needs and multiple services. The special education teacher implemented a job-embedded paraprofessional development plan that included reflection to enhance the knowledge and skills for supporting students and to create a culture in which inquiry and reflection were the norm, not the exception. She wanted paraprofessionals to (1) learn specific strategies for supporting individual students in their respective classroom contexts; (2) develop a sense of being team members who share responsibility for overall program effectiveness; and (3) embed the program vision and philosophy throughout the whole school day.

The core focus of the job-embedded paraprofessional development plan was student learning. The special educator met individually with each paraprofessional to discuss individual students, share student information and effective instructional strategies, and reflect on what was working well, what wasn't, and why. As specific training needs were identified, she arranged for appropriate staff members (e.g., occupational therapists) to meet with the paraprofessionals to teach the information and skills. Reflective questions were continually woven into everyday conversations so that the paraprofessionals developed a set of shared values and goals that served as a foundation for making decisions about practice. Acknowledging the paraprofessionals' needs and showing respect for their input were significant influences in developing a new team culture built on trust. Small-group meetings were held to discuss general instructional and support issues as well as specific student issues, as appropriate. One small-group structure, called "Kid of the Day," allowed any teacher or paraprofessional to initiate a meeting if there was an issue or concern about a student that needed to be discussed by the team. To create time for these meetings, team members covered each other's assignments for short periods. The special educator also scheduled meetings with all of the paraprofessionals every 2 to 3 weeks. In addition to presenting individual topics, she facilitated discussions on the assumptions that the paraprofessionals held about students and student learning, on roles and responsibilities, and on what showing respect for students and staff looks like.

As raising questions and learning together became the norm rather than the exception, the paraprofessionals asked more targeted questions about students, provided feedback on student programs, and shared ideas on how to work effectively with students. They facilitated student involvement and self-advocacy rather than simply "doing it" for the students. Modeling by the paraprofessional helped the general educators learn how to work with individual students. Some paraprofessionals also became involved in schoolwide initiatives.

Schoolwide Dyads and Triads

A middle school principal, who was committed to coaching as a way to increase reflection, took a risk and asked the teachers in his building to form triads for the school year. His objective was for these small teams to talk about learning, teaching, students, and education. During workshop week, the staff members chose partners. In the beginning, most groups simply got together and tried to engage in learning conversations. Some just went through the motions of reflective practice. At the end of the school year, the principal asked whether the staff members would be willing to continue these conversations. One staff member declined, and everyone else said they would—as long as one change occurred. They explained that in the beginning, because they were unsure of what was going to happen, they partnered with their friends. The next year, they wanted to change reflection partners so that each triad would include different grade levels and disciplines. The staff members felt they would learn more by having conversations with people from different perspectives rather than with their friends. High praise goes to that staff; learning requires trust. By the end of the year, they were willing to take greater risks to learn more. This example illustrates the interweaving of trust (Chapter 2), courage (Chapter 3), communication, and time.

Weekly Reviews

As teachers begin to work more closely with one another in the design, delivery, and evaluation of instruction for students, they need more time together to plan and reflect. In many schools with diverse student populations, increasing numbers of general educators, special educators, and second-language teachers are coteaching for some parts of the school day or week, frequently during language arts or math blocks of time. In order to teach together, they must come to know all the students, recognize and use their respective strengths as teachers, and plan for instruction together. In our work with teacher teams, Thursdays consistently emerge as the best day to meet, because the present week can be reviewed and planning for the next week can begin. At one school, the principal and staff decided to leave every Thursday afternoon open, meaning that no other meetings could be scheduled after school on Thursdays. Early in the school year, meetings of instructional partners usually are consumed by planning units and lessons, determining coteaching roles, and generally getting organized. Over time, the focus shifts to reflecting on individual students who are struggling, work samples from many students, and classroom performance as a whole, which results in regular grouping and regrouping of students. In other words, the emphasis and depth of the reflection evolves as the coteaching relationship and experiences evolve. Regular reflection and dialogue can result in the discovery of new solutions and in ongoing differentiation of instruction to meet varied student needs.

Science Teachers Initiate Conversations for Student Success

At an urban high school, two science teachers involved in a schoolwide project designed to focus on literacy reflected regularly during their lunch period. They did not share common students or a common prep, but they did share an office. One teacher taught general science to ninth-grade students; the other teacher, biology to 10th graders. During their lunch periods, they discussed students, ways of embedding new literacy strategies, pertinent schoolwide issues, and science activities. They also identified concerns about grading practices in the science department, which prompted them to initiate conversations with other members of the department. Key questions were discussed, such as, Why are so many students failing 10th-grade biology? What could be done to help these students? How could we help teachers to prepare ninth graders for the content in upper-level classes? As an indicator of their value, these department conversations have continued. *Submitted by Barb Vallejo, Literacy Coach, Saint Paul Public Schools, Minnesota*

Listening Practice

As collaborative ways of working and learning become more common and expected, intentional efforts to develop listening skills can greatly enhance reflection and communication. We describe here a listening activity developed by a colleague to help people experience and be mindful of what it is like to be heard as well as what it is like to be listened to. This experience is unique for many people. The activity is organized by forming dyads, with one person designated as the listener and the other as the speaker; or triads, with a listener, a speaker, and an observer. The speaker talks about a particular topic for 3 minutes. During this time, the listener just listens and does not talk. If used, the observer watches both the speaker and listener. At the end of 3 minutes, participants reflect on how it felt to be in their respective roles. They then switch roles.

Participants usually comment that speaking without being interrupted and listening without speaking is a highly unusual experience. And they report that 3 minutes is a long time! Speakers frequently express appreciation for the time to slow down their thinking. They do not have to worry that a pause in their speaking will result in a loss of their speaking role. Sometimes, speakers are uncomfortable because they are used to being interrupted or receiving verbal affirmations. Listeners frequently comment on feeling relaxed, because they are not expected to respond immediately. They feel they can listen more deeply because they are not trying to figure out what to say or waiting for a pause to add their perspective. Whatever the views, participants gain insight about uninterrupted listening and speaking and what a gift they can be, even if done only for a few minutes.

Consider carefully the topics for this listening activity. Hot topics can reduce thinking by listeners and speakers. Emotion can take over the process. In one school, for example, there was controversy about pull-out special education services. Teachers tended to feel strongly one way or the other. Large-group discussions had not been productive. The listening activity was used in two stages. First, partners took turns listening when the topic was of little consequence (e.g., a favorite family tradition). Afterward, they processed how that interaction felt and what each was thinking. Second, partners took turns listening to how the other felt about pull-out services and why. Afterward, they processed this listening session, as well. Finally, the whole group processed their learning from both sessions, considering content and process through questions such as, How did your listening and speaking differ in the different sessions? What accounted for the differences? What could help listening when the topics are more emotionally charged? Collectively, what did we learn about how people view pull-out services? What might be some productive next steps?

REFLECTIVE PRACTICE WITH PARTNERS: MORE IDEAS TO CONSIDER

Many of the ideas shared in Chapter 3 for individual reflection are also well suited for use with partners. For example, reflecting on teaching portfolios and professional readings can be enhanced with another person supporting inquiry. Exchanging teacher narratives can provide insight into the thinking and practice of others, which prompts thinking about ourselves. In the next chapter, videotaping, book clubs, and teacher dialogues are described as ways to reflect and can also work well for partners. Here we offer a menu of ideas for reflective practice with partners. As you read, consider ideas you might find useful to enhance your practice.

Dialogue Journals/Interactive Journals

As with the first edition of this book, dialogue journals, also referred to as interactive journals, are considered an effective means of aiding the process of reflective thinking. The process usually begins with one person making an individual journal entry and then sharing it with another person, who shares his or her thoughts and makes inquiries to expand thinking (Keating, 1993). Essentially, this is inquiry and learning through writing instead of conversation. In the process, relationships are also formed between participants. Supporting this means of reflection are the questioning, responding, and reframing strategies described in Chapter 2 (pp. 42–55).

There are many studies of dialogue or interactive journals in the literature, primarily in the context of preservice teacher education. In most of these accounts, feedback was provided to preservice teachers by experienced educators (e.g., cooperating teachers or university supervisors). This approach concurs with discussion earlier in this chapter about the value and support realized when experienced professionals intentionally guide those who are newer to practice. Following are highlights from four studies in which dialogue or interactive journals were used to expand the thinking and practice of preservice teacher education students.

Using a Reflection Typology in Journaling

Two teacher educators, one of English and one of social studies, focused on which strategies would improve reflective journaling by preservice teachers (Spalding & Wilson, 2002). Both teacher educators explicitly taught differences between narrative and reflective writing, introduced Valli's (1997) reflection typology (referenced in Table 1.1 on p. 7), and required students to submit weekly journal reflections on a topic of their choice. Both also provided feedback that included positive comments, questions to elicit thinking and elaboration, and personal comments about their own thoughts and views. One of the instructors hand wrote feedback in the margins of the journals and regularly noted the initials R (reflection in/on action), P (personalistic), D (deliberative), or C (critical) to indicate the type of reflection (according to Valli's construct) represented in the entries. Sometimes this instructor also requested that students mark letters designating types of reflection. The other instructor used e-mail and encouraged creativity in journal writing by modeling strategies such as metaphor or poetry. She did not mark the type of reflection in the entries as did the first instructor. Results indicated that early in the process, journal entries were primarily descriptive of events. Feedback from the instructors prompted students to become more deliberative in their reflections—identifying what seemed to work, what did not, and why—and generative of ideas for improvement. Students said that feedback was extremely important. It indicated instructor interest and assisted the students in becoming more reflective. Introducing students to the Valli instruction typology was also viewed as useful for understanding that reflective thinking takes different forms and serves different functions. Also important, follow-up with students after they became teachers indicated continued use of reflection as a means of assessing their teaching.

Master Teachers and Interns Paired Up for Journaling

In another approach to dialogue journals, master teachers were paired with intern teachers, and both engaged in a daily dialogue journal process with a prompt to "write about issues and experiences in the classroom" (Christensen, Wilson, Sunal, Blalock, St. Clair-Shingleton, & Warren, 2004). The master teacher and intern in each pair wrote in the same journal. Significant differences were noted in what the master teacher and intern paid attention to in the class. Interns' comments focused on classroom management and discipline, made more global assessments about success and failure, expressed feelings ("I feel . . ."), and sought to elicit feedback, especially seeking approval (they wanted feedback). The master teachers' entries held professional language and insight, and focused more specifically on content, pedagogy, and students. Master teachers also entered queries for interns and responses to interns' queries to shift the thinking toward teaching and learning.

Mini-Inquiries

In the context of a Professional Development School, Perry and Power (2004) employed several strategies intended to develop inquiring teachers, including a curriculum class focused on inquiry, an inquiry project in which interns developed questions and collected data, small-group observations of mentor teachers, and mini-inquiries, which were based on the work of Harste and Leland (1999). Of particular interest was Perry and Powers's use of mini-inquiries as "quick investigations of issues that get raised through professional readings, conversations or occurrences in classrooms" (p. 131). Sample questions were as follows: How do mentor teachers keep their classrooms running smoothly? What is appropriate technology of specific grade levels? How do teachers accommodate for special needs? Some inquiries were intentionally aligned with the time of year, such as, How do teachers begin the year? See Table 4.5 for an example of a mini-inquiry used at the beginning of the school year. In preparing responses, interns made note of their observations, interviewed teachers, and read various materials. Importantly, the "mini-inquiries provided a mechanism for the interns to question their mentors about teaching practices and goals, to delve into the mentor's reasoning behind their practices, and in doing so expand their own view of teaching" (p. 131).

Structured Reflection Logs

Finally, we offer an example of how special education teacher educators used structured reflective logs to better prepare preservice general education students for inclusive school and classroom settings (Kolar & Dickson, 2002). The authors offered examples of questions, question sets, scenarios, and video reflections to which the preservice teachers were expected to respond. One sample question set is provided here:

> Reflect on your experiences with individuals with disabilities. What experiences have you had with individuals with disabilities? This could be in elementary school, middle school, high school, or college. It could be with someone in your family or a friend. How have your experiences with people with disabilities influenced your understanding of them? How have your experiences influenced your expectations for working with students with disabilities in your classroom? (p. 396)

The preservice teachers viewed the reflective logs positively as tools for reflecting on their own experiences with individuals with disabilities, for expressing and formulating their thoughts and opinions about teaching students with disabilities, for making connections between prior experiences and the course content, and for developing a resource of ideas that could be valuable future teaching. Not surprisingly, time was viewed as a constraint. As indicated previously, structured reflection through journaling

Table 4.5   Sample Mini-Inquiry for Teacher Interns (Perry & Power, 2004)

Mini-Inquiry 1

How do teachers begin the year?

The early days of every school year offer new and experienced teachers exciting opportunities and challenges. The beginning of the year is hectic, at times over-whelming, *and* crucial to setting the tone and day-to-day routines for the year.

In this first Mini-Inquiry, please interview your mentor prior to the first day of school to find out what he or she does the first few days of school and why. The following questions to help you gather data have been created by mentors and former interns:

1. What lifelong values, skills, and attitudes do you hope your students will take away from your class this year, and why?

2. What are examples of activities you do early in the year to support those goals?

3. How do you create classroom rules, and why? How do you manage behavior problems, and why? How do you communicate that to your students?

4. How far ahead do you plan early in the year?

5. Do your plans for this year differ from previous years'? How and why?

6. How do you encourage risk taking and independence in students early in the year? Please give examples.

In addition, while working in your mentor's classroom the first two days this fall, observe your mentor while reflecting on your interview.

SOURCE: Reprinted with permission from C. M. Perry & B. M. Power (2004). Finding the truths in teacher preparation field experiences. *Teacher Educator Quarterly, 31*(2), 125–36.

seems well suited to foster critical reflection on issues of race and culture; so, too, is the case on issues involving students with disabilities.

Many of these examples relate to preservice teacher education, a context in which journaling and reflection can be, and often is, required. Regardless, the structures, interactions, and feedback offered through the interactive journaling did foster reflective thought and, in some cases, influenced practice. Even though practicing educators might reasonably question the feasibility of dialogic or interactive journaling, it may be a viable reflection strategy in teams or schools in which a culture of collaborative learning has been cultivated. It could also prove invaluable for early-career teachers as a part of their induction and mentoring process. Certainly the strategy offers much potential if the time were to be claimed.

Online Directed Journaling

Described for a cohort of advanced-practice nurses engaged in community health clinical experiences, online directed journaling allowed the nurses to learn with and from one another as they practiced in different settings (Daroszewski, Kinser, & Lloyd, 2004). The specific intent was to foster discussion, mentoring, critical thinking, and socialization throughout the entire clinical experience.

All of the nurses had 24-hour access to a Web site discussion board and were expected to post at least one in-depth journal entry each week. In addition, they were expected to comment on at least two entries posted by other nurses. The clinical experience extended across 20 weeks. Five topics were posted at the beginning of the 20-week period. Students could select which of the five topics they would respond to during each 5-week period. This allowed flexibility to choose topics that were particularly relevant to each nurse in a given week. Table 4.6 lists the topics, many of which would have direct application to educators, as well.

Evaluation of the online journaling experience showed strong positive views, with an average rating of 4.7 on a 5 (high) scale. Comments were also positive, with participants indicating that online journaling was user-friendly and fostered learning from the experiences and perspectives of other nurses. Overall, moving journaling from an individual to a shared reflection and learning modality was viewed as extremely valuable.

This reflective practice strategy holds great potential for educators, as well, within and across sites and school districts. First-year teachers or principals might be well supported as a cohort through use of online shared journaling. Teachers implementing a new curriculum (e.g., science teachers across a school district) or principals launching a new governance structure could benefit from an easy-to-access way of reflecting and communicating with colleagues. Ease of engagement, 24-hour access, prompts to elicit thinking, and simple guidelines (each person provides one entry and responds to one entry) seem to be key features for success.

Reflective Interviews

Again, most noted in the teacher preparation literature, but applicable for practicing teachers, as well, is the use of interviews to prompt reflective thought about practice. In studies by both Pultorak (1996) and Dinkelman (2000), preservice teachers left alone to reflect gravitated almost exclusively to technical and practical dimensions of their practice. Guided by an interview, however, they engaged around critical dimensions, especially with practice.

In the Pultorak study, preservice teachers engaged in multiple forms of reflection at several intervals across a 16-week period. The nature of the reflections varied with each form. Journaling every other day yielded

Table 4.6   Sample Topics for Online Directed Journaling by Advanced Nursing Students (Daroszewski, Kinser, & Lloyd, 2004)

Weeks	Topics
FIRST QUARTER Weeks 1 to 5	1. Practice philosophy of the preceptor
	2. Components, players, and roles of the political environment of the clinical site
	3. Barriers to advanced practice at the clinical site
	4. A legal issue encountered
	5. An ethical issue encountered
Weeks 6 to 10	1. Tools for practice and how they are used
	2. Problem in the targeted population not being addressed
	3. Resources to address the problem
	4. Process to secure the resources
	5. Physical and emotional effects of practice
SECOND QUARTER Weeks 11 to 15	1. Preceptor role in decisions
	2. Preceptor role in policy development
	3. Types of data collected at the clinical site
	4. Data collection system
	5. Data not being collected that would be important to collect
Weeks 16 to 20	1. Challenge to implementation of selected intervention
	2. Preparation process for intervention implementation
	3. Easiest part of the intervention implementation
	4. Something unexpected that occurred
	5. Change in implementation design or implementation for the future

SOURCE: Reprinted with permission from E. B. Daroszewski, A. G. Kinser, & S. L. Lloyd (2004). Online directed journaling in community health advanced practice nursing clinical education. *Educational Innovations, 43*(4), 175–80.

entries that were predominantly technical and practical in nature, although between a quarter and half of the comments tapped critical dimensions. Journaling every other week about overall teaching experiences of the past couple of weeks yielded entries that were almost exclusively technical in nature, as did journaling after observing other teachers.

When engaged in reflective interviews, however, critical reflection abilities increased substantially over time, with just 4 percent of the students able to critically reflect at the beginning of the semester, but 43 percent by midsemester and 77 percent by the end of the semester.

When the preservice teachers in the Dinkelman (2000) study were asked to identify the strongest influences on their reflections, journaling and being interviewed were ranked the highest, followed by observations, although observations did not elicit much critical reflection. Following are the questions used in the reflective interviews conducted in the Pultorak (1996) study. Note that the first six questions are oriented toward reflection on technical dimensions of practice; the next two toward practical reflection; and the last two more toward critical reflection.

- What were essential strengths of the lesson?
- What, if anything, would you change about the lesson?
- Do you think the lesson was successful? Why?
- Which conditions were important to the outcome?
- What, if any, unanticipated learning outcomes resulted from the lesson?
- What did you think about student behaviors?
- Can you think of another way you might have taught this lesson?
- Can you think of other alternative pedagogical approaches to teaching this lesson that might improve the learning process?
- How would you justify the importance of the content covered to a parent, administrator, and/or student?
- Did any moral or ethical concerns occur as a result of the lesson? (Pultorak, 1996, p. 285)

Structured Dialogue

Pugach and Johnson (1990) conducted a study on the use of a structured dialogue process with general-education classroom teachers to promote reflection on how to more effectively support students with learning and behavior challenges in their classrooms. The goal was to increase the repertoire of effective interventions in the classroom and decrease referrals to special education. The teachers were provided with training about effective interventions and were then coached to engage in self-inquiry about actual classroom challenges involving students with learning and behavior challenges. Teachers were coached through the following four-step process: (1) reframing the problem through clarifying questions; (2) summarizing insights from the reframing process, including the identification of patterns of behavior exhibited by the student and specific variables over which the teacher has control; (3) generating potential actions and predicting the outcomes of each; and (4) developing a plan to evaluate the proposed change. What were the outcomes? When compared with a control group of teachers, those who participated in the structure dialogue significantly increased their tolerance of student behavior, shifted their attention from student-centered to teacher-centered problem orientation, and increased their confidence in dealing with classroom situations.

Framing Experiences From Practice Using Stories

Learning from practice, at the preservice or inservice or ongoing service levels, requires learning to think critically about the meaning of real-world experiences. Schall (1995) presented a set of questions used to assist preservice human services personnel in focusing and thinking critically about experiences in the field before presenting them to others for shared reflection:

- What prompts you to tell the story?
- What's the moral of your story?
- What's the specific point you are trying to convey?
- What is the generalized lesson of the story you or others might abstract?
- How could you generalize this lesson and test it?

According to Schall, "This focusing process allows students to begin to make meaning from the 'mess' of their experience at work. The appeal of this approach is its relative simplicity. It does not depend on a master teacher or require only gifted senior level learners" (1995, p. 214).

Reflection Structures to Foster Equity

Elliott and Schiff (2001) emphasize the importance of providing educators with opportunities to safely share their feelings about equity issues and of intentionally embedding reflection about equity into typical educational practices, ranging from lesson plan design to curriculum reviews, from personal to organizational practices. They propose structures and guidelines for sharing experiences and feelings about equity issues, as well as for fostering reflection and learning about equity-related practices. The authors explain that "change in attitudes and beliefs occur as people are listened to and allowed to tell their own stories" (p. 40).

Guidelines offered to help to ensure safety and respect include allowing each participant equal time; assuring confidentiality; and not allowing criticism, interruptions, analyses, or advice-giving. *Dyads* are considered relatively safe structures within which two people can take turns listening to each other about topics, such as the effect of school on one's confidence as a learner, the kinds of assets and gifts acquired from one's culture, or strategies that have proven helpful in creating bridges and alliances across racial lines. *Support groups* are suggested as a structure that works well for educators to talk about their experiences with bias. A third structure is referred to as *personal experience panels*; in these, three to five individuals take a few minutes each to talk about their experiences with a particular equity situation in curricular or extracurricular activities (e.g., math expectations, competitive or cooperative instructional practices, school-sponsored dances and athletics, or testing). After panel members share their thoughts, a facilitator can raise general questions about the focal topic to the entire group, not just the panel members.

Practices that may be engaged in individually or with others include examination of instructional practices; informal assessments; scoring rubrics; student work; and test results and curricular choices to determine the presence of bias or culturally appropriate designs, strategies, and materials. Elliott and Schiff offer a set of questions on which to reflect when reviewing curriculum:

- Are a variety of examples from various socioeconomic groups included?
- Are examples relevant to all socioeconomic groups?
- Do problem-solving strategies reflect cultural values other than the dominant culture?
- Are females, minorities, and people with disabilities shown in a variety of settings and environments and engaging in a variety of behaviors, not those associated with stereotypes?
- Are representations of status and power distributed equally and fairly across diverse population groups?
- Do representations in curriculum material convey messages that differences are valuable?
- Are the messages accurate? (2001, p. 42)

The authors also suggest use of action research as a structure that allows teachers to ask questions of particular concern to themselves, such as, "Is my teaching culturally responsive? Are my attitudes and expectations responsive to cultural differences? Am I consistent, equitable, and individualized with each student and his/her needs?" (p. 42).

In closing, the authors remind us, "Everyone in America is influenced by societal messages that communicate biases related to race, ethnicity, gender, and economic status. No one escapes the negative influences of media and political institutions, one of which is the public school" (p. 42). So, too, are the public schools places in which reflection on practice through an equity lens, followed by commitments and actions for improvement, can and must make a real difference in the lives of today's young people and the generations that will follow.

Observational Learning

Highly effective educators are often good observers. Taggart and Wilson (1998) explain,

Observation is a skill that practitioners must possess to develop insights needed to make wise decisions. Observations should be ongoing, systematic, and developed to the point that a focus can be established, notes taken, and actions explored in a relatively short amount of time with high effectiveness. Inferences and judgments are not components of the observation process, which makes the observation skills difficult for many practitioners. (p. 58)

Observing peers is one way to learn more about students and teaching. Systematic observations with a written documentation of events can serve as the basis for reflection with partners. Written documentation can take the form of a running record, a checklist, or an observational recording form easily used in the flow of instructional routines. In the paradigm of reflective practice, facts (description) are shared; interpretation is a collaborative responsibility.

Gitlin (1999) offers an example of four teachers who took turns observing one another teach. Observations were followed by monthly dialogue. Participation was voluntary and teacher-directed. The teachers set the agenda for learning. They valued this approach because it

allows questions and priorities of reform to emerge from the teacher dialogue, [and] emphasizes the need for teachers to raise critical concerns about each other's practice, including the taken-for-granted aims, goals, and intentions that inform their work . . . [it] helps to identify tensions between one's teaching philosophy and practice. (p. 638)

As a result of this learning experience, teachers reported that reflection had become more central in their teaching lives. "Now we talk constantly about what is really important in terms of teaching. . . . This project has [made me] realize that probably one of the best resources of knowledge are the people you work with" (Gitlin, 1999, p. 641).

Classroom Coaching

An interesting twist on typical approaches to teacher observations was introduced as classroom coaching by Black, Molseed, and Sayler (2003). Instead of having teachers be observed just teaching their own students or observing another teacher teaching their own students, this approach allowed classroom teachers to observe their own students being taught by a different teacher. In this case, the different teachers were visiting teachers from a nearby university center. (The visiting teachers, however, could be other teachers in the same school or district.) The classroom teacher and coaches together watched and then discussed videotapes of classroom instruction. Next, the classroom teacher taught his or her own class. Then, each of the visiting teachers taught the classroom teacher's class on subsequent days while the classroom teacher sat in the back of the room observing. Debriefing addressed a range of interests, including curriculum, instructional strategies, student engagement and behavior, interactions, and overall classroom climate. The classroom teachers reported great insights from being able to observe and reflect on their own students in their own classrooms. Not only did they observe varied instructional styles but also observed how their students engaged with other teachers. This type of coaching model aligns with features advocated by Joyce and Showers (2002), described earlier in this chapter.

Action Research

One of the most widely recognized and researched ways to systematically reflect on and improve practice is action research. Action research is defined as "a disciplined process of inquiry conducted by and for those taking the action. The primary reason for engaging in action research is to assist the actor in improving and refining his or her actions" (Sagor, 2000, p. 3). Teachers are central in the action research process. Action research is a structured way to promote reflection on practice and contribute to the overall development of a professional-learning culture in schools. Sagor (2000) describes a seven-step action-research process that "becomes an endless cycle for the inquiring teacher" (p. 3). The seven steps are (a) selecting a focus, (b) clarifying theories, (c) identifying research questions, (d) collecting data, (e) analyzing data, (f) reporting results, and (g) taking informed action. This process is similar to other reflection frameworks offered in this book. Important differences, however, are the emphases on formalizing research questions and systematically collecting and analyzing student data.

In recent years, conducting action research on a schoolwide basis has been emphasized (Calhoun, 1994). A primary reason for this emphasis is recognition that action research in isolated areas of a school has little or no effect on overall student performance in the school. Action research, therefore, should also be considered as a way to promote reflection and learning in small groups or teams (Chapter 5) and schoolwide (Chapter 6). Interested readers can refer to any of the easily available action research resources (see, for example, Glanz, 1998, 1999; Glickman, 1995; Lerner, 1997; McLean, 1995; Sagor, 1992, 2000; Stringer, 1996; Taggart & Wilson, 1998).

GETTING STARTED WITH REFLECTIVE PRACTICE PARTNERS

Reflection with a partner is a gift you can give to yourself as well as to a partner. Most of us are driven to learn and improve, and a trusted partner can support our growth. In addition to the benefit of improvements in practice, a relationship is formed that is a valuable resource and support in many aspects of your work life. As you walk down the hallways, into a faculty meeting, or through the workroom, you carry with you the assurance that at least one person knows and cares about you, your practice, and your desire to continuously improve. You are not alone. By reflecting with partners, you can move from a congenial level of interaction to a more substantial and collaborative interaction, in which commitments to improvement are shared.

As cited by Maggio (1992), Anaïs Nin names the potential that exists within friendships when writing that "Each friend represents a world in us, a world possibly not born until they arrive, and it is only by this meeting that a new world is born" (p. 129). Nin's words may serve as inspiration for reflective practice with others. Some of our greatest insights have emerged from the relative safety of reflection with partners. So, too, have some of our most valued and long-term friendships that provide not only support but also challenge to our thinking and learning processes. How, through our interactions with our reflective practice partners, might new ways of thinking, doing, and being be born?

To guide your thinking about moving forward with reflection as partners, we invite you to contemplate the following questions. (Refer to Resource 4.C for a modified set of these questions.)

- What are my biggest questions about my teaching or leadership practice? What do I want to learn more about?
- Why am I drawn to reflecting with a partner or two?
- Who can support and enrich my learning? Who would bring a different perspective that would enrich my learning? Who would be interested in contributing to my growth as an educator?
- What type of environment is conducive to listening, exploring, and thinking?
- How often would I like to, or how often would it be reasonable to, get together?
- What would make our reflection time a real treat (e.g., coffee and good food)?
- What type of reflection framework, strategy, or protocol would support our learning together?

Using the Chapter Reflection Page (Figure 4.2), you can jot down what you recall as big ideas, insights, questions, and targets for future action. You may also want to write down something you wish to reflect on with a partner and a particular person with whom you might follow up to begin the process.

Figure 4.2 Chapter Reflection Page

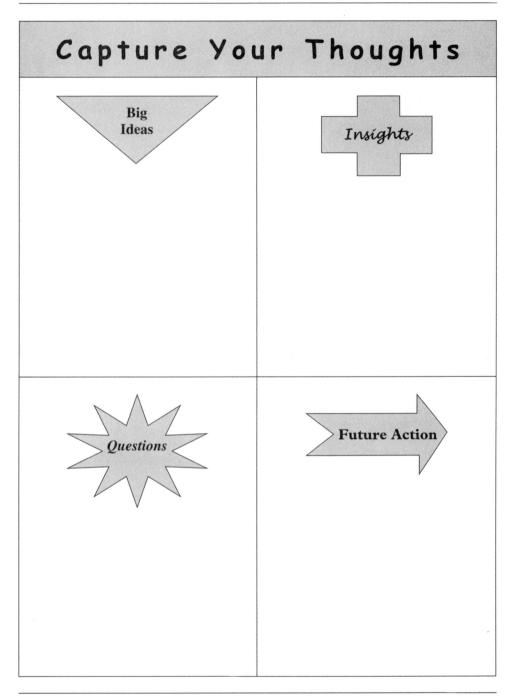

5

Reflective Practice in Small Groups and Teams

Teamwork is often like the weather—everyone talks about it, but often nobody does anything about it. It is seldom achieved by intellectualizing, but is rather the practical application of attitude, common goals, and experience working together. It is a learned art.

—Twyman L. Towery (1995, p. 18)
The Wisdom of Wolves

Clearly, there are a significant number of small groups and teams meeting in schools. Teamwork and collaboration are much-lauded features in education. It is probably not an overstatement to suggest that many educators are on meeting overload. When a new committee is proposed or mandated, a groan can be heard from the staff. How valuable are these meetings? Do the outcomes make a difference for student learning? Does a sense of renewal and recommitment among group members result? Which meetings really matter? Although meeting in groups and teams is commonplace, reflection and learning in these situations are not.

Face-to-face meeting time is perhaps the most valuable learning resource in schools. We argue that the vast majority of this time should be spent reflecting and learning together in ways that lead to actions which positively impact school renewal and student learning. Given the increasing diversity, complexity, and pace in the field of education, learning together to increase effectiveness in "the swamp" of practice (see Schon in Chapter 1) is a necessity. "Reflective practice is vital for the swamp. It enables people to be present and it helps them and their organizations make meaning from what are generally complex, multidimensional experiences" (Schall, 1995, p. 208). External knowledge and resources go only so far to support educational practice. Groups of educators frequently have tasks that are open-ended and complex, and that require collaborative inquiry to come up with new understandings, interventions, and plans appropriate to local contexts of practice. Educators must "work together to construct knowledge rather than to discover objective truths" (Cranton, 1996, p. 27) as a primary way of advancing practice. "Teamwork is itself both a process and a principle [of adult learning]" (Vella, 1994, p. 19).

In a study comparing teamed and nonteamed middle school teachers, Pounder (1999) found that teamed teachers (i.e., those whose jobs had a shared work-group emphasis) reported significantly higher levels of knowledge about students, skill variety in their work, helpfulness and effectiveness within their work group, teaching efficacy, professional commitment, and overall satisfaction and growth. Survey data from students in both schools indicated that students in the teamed school were more satisfied with their relationships with other students and with safety and student discipline. They were less satisfied, however, with the nature and amount of schoolwork. Students were more likely to be held accountable to high and shared expectations by teachers who worked collaboratively. Reflecting on the overall findings from the study, Pounder suggested that "the most encouraging of these results may be the increased knowledge that teamed teachers seem to gain about students" (p. 338). The design of effective instruction begins with understanding the abilities, interests, challenges, and learning strengths of individual students. While learning together in teams or groups, educators can increase their understanding of students, and this understanding may serve as a foundation for their curricular, instructional, and educational practices.

The journey toward reflection and learning in groups and teams is not an easy one. "Teamwork cannot be taken for granted. . . . people must learn how to work together efficiently" (Vella, 1994, p. 20). One of the greatest challenges is the establishment of trust. Contrary to the adage claiming safety in numbers, Osterman and Kottkamp (1993) remind us,

> Reflective practice in a group setting is a high risk process . . . In most organizations, problems are viewed as a sign of weakness . . . to break this conspiracy of silence requires new organizational norms. To engage in the reflective process, individuals need

to believe that discussions of problems will not be interpreted as incompetence or weakness. (44–45)

Despite the inherent risks and challenges involved in expanding reflective practice to groups or teams, there are good reasons to venture forth into this domain. Recall from Chapter 1 the potential gains that can be realized at the group or team level of the Reflective Practice Spiral. In groups, more resources (e.g., experience, knowledge, energy) are available. And as participants grow in their collegiality, optimism about making significant improvements grows, as well. With more people there is more potential for school renewal and also more attention that needs to be paid to fostering collaborative reflective interactions. Productive learning does not "just happen" in groups of children or adults. Design and planning are important.

In this chapter, we expand on the "how-to" reflective practice information presented in previous chapters to focus on the context of groups and teams. In the considerations section we provide a lot of detail about group design and facilitation. We do this for three reasons. First, managing group learning is much more complex than individual or partner learning. More design work is required to elicit constructive participation by all members. Second, we anticipate that many of our readers spend a lot of time working with groups of educators. We wish to directly support your work in this regard. Third, research indicates that clear expectations and structures increase the likelihood that reflection, learning, and useful outcomes will actually result from group interactions. Supovitz (2002), for example, found that teachers involved in a large four-year teaming initiative liked to collaborate and that positive changes in school culture had occurred. There was, however, little or no change in instructional practice. He concluded,

> The communities that develop are often not communities engaged in instructional improvement. For teacher communities to focus on instructional improvement, . . . communities need organizational structures, cultures of instructional exploration, and ongoing professional learning opportunities to support sustained inquiries into improving teaching and learning. (p. 1591)

As with the other chapters, considerations are followed by examples, ideas, and suggestions for getting started with reflective practice in small groups. We encourage you to pause, reflect, and jot down notes as you work your way through this chapter. We intentionally provided lengthy descriptions in some of the examples so that you could see the inherent messiness of the work and also reflect on possibilities for advancing reflective practices in your work. We also invite you to reflect on the examples to note not only the *how-tos* but also the *whys*. Recall, from Chapter 2, Peter Block's reframing of *how* questions to *what* and *why* questions. *Why* questions get at the purposes which underline all the doing. If

Figure 5.1   Theory of Action for Reflective Practice

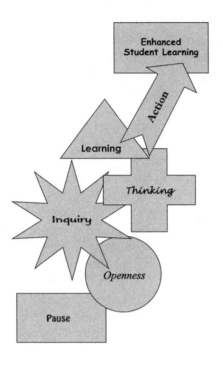

there is no meaningful *why*, then the *hows* do not matter much. We should continuously ask ourselves why we are doing these things and why we are doing these things in these ways. Finally, we offer the Reflective Practice Theory of Action (Figure 5.1), once again. The elements apply equally well to group reflective practices as they did to individual and partner reflection.

One additional preliminary note regarding this chapter concerns use of the term *professional learning communities,* or PLCs, as they are commonly called. Since the first edition of this book, there has been a proliferation of groups referred to as PLCs. In some cases, PLCs are, in fact, communities of educators in which professional learning occurs with an explicit focus on student learning. In some cases, however, *PLC* has become a replacement term for "team meeting," "department meeting," or another group in which learning may or may not be the focus. In this chapter we have chosen to continue using the terms *small group* or *team.* In addition, because the PLC movement initially emerged in the context of schoolwide improvement efforts, we address PLCs more specifically in Chapter 6.

SPECIAL CONSIDERATIONS FOR REFLECTIVE PRACTICE IN SMALL GROUPS AND TEAMS

Many educators have become skeptical, if not resistant, about being part of small groups, teams, and especially committees! Honestly, many have good reasons for their negative views. Through experience, they have learned that working in groups is often frustrating, energy draining, and unproductive. In short, it has been a waste of their time. The likelihood of negative prior experiences makes it both more difficult and more important that efforts to promote reflection and learning in groups be carefully designed and facilitated for success. A period of unlearning precedes new learning. In other words, reluctant members must move through the stage of "prove to me that it is going to be different this time" before they will choose to expend energy and risk participation in group reflection and learning.

In this section, special considerations for designing reflective practices in small groups and teams are discussed. Our intent is to address the question, "What is known about promoting group interactions among educators so that learning and productive outcomes result?" We offer a short-course response. Many excellent resources respond to this question more fully (see, for example, Garmston & Wellman, 1999; Hare, 1994; Johnson & Johnson, 1999; Straus, 2002; Thousand & Villa, 2000). Addressed in previous chapters was the centrality of purpose. Educators are more likely to engage in reflective group work if the purpose has meaning for them and is likely to make a difference for students. Described here are additional considerations, including the nature of group development, group member roles, and group processes that support reflection and learning. Also shared are strategies for allocating time for group reflection and learning. A list of all the considerations is provided in Table 5.1 for easy reference. As you review this information, keep in mind there are no absolutes for design, only an array of possibilities and considerations on which to continuously reflect to determine appropriate applications in specific contexts. Each group develops its own ways of being.

What Can Be Expected in Terms of Group Development Over Time?

One significant influence on reflection and learning in groups is the nature of how groups develop over time. In the classic work of Tuckman (1965), four phases of group development were identified: forming, storming, norming, and performing (Figure 5.2). In the *forming* phase, groups experience relative niceness among members. Members begin to learn about one another and the task at hand. Typically, interactions are courteous and cautious, if not superficial. This is a period of checking each

Table 5.1   Considerations for Reflective Practice in Small Groups and Teams

Group Development Over Time
    Forming
    Storming
    Norming
    Performing

Group Size and Group Composition
    Same view or different view?
    Heterogeneity or homogeneity?
    Voluntary or mandated?
    Existing or reconfigured groups?

Group Member Roles
    (see Table 5.2)

Structures and Processes to Support Group Reflection and Learning
    Planning the group process
    Opening the group process
        Introductions
        Overview and Review
        Warm-up Activities
        Group Norms and Expectations
    Engaging the Core Agenda
    Closing the Group Process

Allocating Time for Reflection and Learning Together
    Freed-up Time
    Purchased Time
    Common Time
    Restructured or Rescheduled Time
    Better-Used Time

other out. How do individuals relate to the group's purpose and members? How safe is it here? What is our potential for doing real work? Can I learn anything from this experience? Do I have a contribution to make? Will this be worth my time and energy?

As group members come to know one another, begin to understand more about their charge, and try to figure out how to proceed together, a period of *storming* ensues. How does the specific work of the group become defined? What are the best ways to proceed? What is important to each group member? How are different perspectives heard and responded to? What are the sources of conflict, and which ones need to be addressed? Who participates, who doesn't, and why? It is during this storming phase of group development that many groups fall apart. Even if group members continue to attend meetings, they may psychologically disengage or, worse, choose to behave in counterproductive ways. To move forward, group

Figure 5.2   Phases of Group Development (Tuckman, 1965)

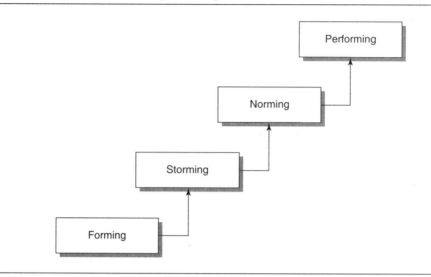

members must learn how to interact with one another respectfully and how to engage in effective group processes, such as problem or task clarification, conflict management, decision making, and action planning. Sometimes it is necessary to engage a facilitator to guide the group and teach effective processes, especially in the early stages of norming and storming or when hot issues are the focus, or when there is a low level of trust or collaboration experience in the group.

If the group successfully navigates the storming phase, they move into a period of relative calm and clarity referred to as *norming*. This is when members have clarified their task and have figured out how it will be addressed by the group. Members know one another better. Individual strengths (e.g., organization, humor, focus) and preferences (e.g., room arrangements, learning supports, food) have been sorted out and used to the advantage of the group. Most important, learning now will have been experienced by group members, at least in the domain of effective group process. Ultimately, this learning results in greater efficiency. Keep in mind, groups and teams experience a learning curve just as individuals do. Efficiency and high performance come after learning how to work together. It is at this point that groups reach the *performing* phase.

Without an awareness of group development phases, members can interpret storming as a sign of ineffectiveness and incompatibility, instead of as an inevitable part of the messiness of becoming a functioning group. Reframed in a personal context, most of us can relate well to this process. Recall times in your life when you and another person (e.g., sibling, roommate, partner, stepparent) took up shared residence. Remember the period of adjustment? At first it may go smoothly, each person trying to be accommodating, learning about each other in new ways, observing different ways of doing things, noticing different degrees of tolerance for disorder. Then, it gets harder to remain graceful in managing the differences. With good communication, though, you eventually learn and decide how to manage differences and to share responsibilities. Finally, norms, expectations, compromises, agreements, and strategies are mutually figured out. The possibilities for living or working together well can be realized. Working well in groups involves a similar process of getting to know one another as individuals and learning how to work together as you engage around shared goals.

How Do Group Size and Group Composition Influence Teamwork?

Group Size

Envision a third-grade team of five people and a fourth-grade team of nine. Considering just the variable of size, which group is more likely to have full participation, and why? An optimal group size for working and learning together is considered to be four to six people (Johnson & Johnson, 1999). This size offers varied perspectives and skills while still allowing, if not expecting, participation by all members. Somewhat larger groups frequently are necessary in schools and can function well if relationships are developed and processes are well designed and implemented (Hare, 1994; Thousand & Villa, 2000). When groups are large, individual participation can still be achieved by breaking into smaller groups. For example, in a group of 15, participants might be asked to form subgroups of five people with the expectation of sharing the subgroup's perspectives with the entire group. In general, groups need to be big enough to offer a variety of perspectives and to have sufficient resources for learning and for accomplishing the work. They should be small enough or made small enough to promote trust and participation.

Group Composition

Group effectiveness is significantly influenced by who specifically is part of a group. One consideration is the *same-versus-different view dimension*. You can have a very congenial group of like-minded folks, but this does not necessarily assure effectiveness. In general, you want all relevant perspectives, including diverse perspectives, to be part of the conversation. Without those views, plans can be doomed to fail even before they are conceived, either because of insufficient perspective or knowledge to come up with a workable plan, or because those not included have the power and influence to sabotage results.

Another consideration in determining group composition is the *heterogeneity-versus-homogeneity dimension* related to characteristics such as gender, age, race, amount and type of experience, and disciplinary or content-area background. Heterogeneity in groups has the potential to enhance learning, given the enriched pool of information, perspectives, and skills. Teams formed to explore integrated service models, for example, should involve general educators, special educators, and second-language teachers. Groups formed to determine space use in a school should include teachers from across content areas and grade levels. Committees formed to provide leadership and oversight for staff development should include teachers and administrators representing the many and varied school and district constituents. Another reason to promote heterogeneous group composition is to intentionally foster connections among people who rarely see one another. Recall the web of relationships (Figure 1.3 on p. 26) and the benefits that can be realized when a rich network of relationships extends throughout a school.

Having just promoted the value of heterogeneity, we now point out that a relatively homogeneous group composition is at times appropriate and productive. For example, early in the process of becoming more reflective, educators may feel more comfortable examining their practices with colleagues whom they know well and who have similar experiences and perspectives. This allows skill development and practice in a relatively safe environment. Another example might involve the review of science curricula for possible adoption. This task reasonably falls to science teachers. The degree of homogeneity and heterogeneity within a group depends, in part, on the purpose of the group. The key is to specifically consider this factor and be intentional about involving the right mix of participants.

Another consideration is the *voluntary-versus-mandated dimension.* The value of voluntary or self-organized learning groups is easily understood. Initiation, interest, and self-direction foster learning, ownership, and commitment. Mandated assignments are a reminder of the hierarchical organization of schools and are often resented. Unprofessional behavior sometimes results. At "prison inservices" (mandated), for example, you can count on about a third of participants being mad when they walk into the room. Vella (1994) urges that people be allowed to choose "their own teams as often as possible, especially when the learning task is complex and difficult" (p. 18). When choice is not possible, recognize that the only type of participation that can be mandated is physical presence. Genuine engagement of the mind and heart comes only from the inside. With a mandate in place, it is even more important to intentionally design the group process to promote active engagement. Sometimes acknowledging the mandate and inviting participation anyway can lessen the negative effects of mandates.

One final consideration related to group composition is the *existing-versus-reconfigured dimension.* Depending on the purpose of the group and the people who should be involved, existing groups could be used, existing groups could be reconfigured, or new groups might be convened.

After groups have been together for a while, two threats to effectiveness can emerge: groupthink and group expectations (Fullan, 2001b). Groupthink is evident when nothing new is going on—no new learning, no new generation of ideas, no different perspectives, no inquiry. Such groups fall into predictable, often unproductive, patterns of engagement. Group expectations are the unspoken assumptions about how people behave and interact in a particular group context. Over time, expectations become constraints. Members assume expected roles and offer anticipated responses. Attempts to change or adjust these expectations are often punished or ignored, resulting in groups becoming stuck. Change is needed but rarely initiated. Going along to get along sometimes keeps us from confronting issues. It is easier to ride the horse in the direction it is going, even if that direction is off-course.

New people or new combinations of people can have the effect of unfreezing thinking, routines, and expectations. Newly configured groups provide an opportunity to set new expectations, to consider new roles and patterns of participation, to establish a culture of learning and inquiry, and to form new relationships before unproductive norms take hold and the refreezing process sets in. New people bring new potential and energy that can be put to good use with an intentional design to support learning and reflection. When existing groups have ceased to be functional, changing group composition, in addition to changing expectations and structures for interactions, can go a long way toward improving effectiveness.

What Are the Group-Member Roles?

Group-Member Roles

Sharing responsibility for group learning and working enhances effectiveness. The most important role is that of *engaged participant*, a role for which each group member is responsible (Garmston & Wellman, 1997, 1999). In the absence of engaged participation by group members, nothing much is accomplished. "In strong groups, engaged participants monitor their personal adherence to meeting standards . . . [and also] monitor the group's adherence to standards" (p. 82). Other roles that are frequently assigned and sometimes rotated among group members include facilitator, recorder, timekeeper, and observer. Some group members may also have role authority or knowledge authority (Garmston & Wellman, 1997, 1999). Examples of someone with role authority are a principal who is a group member with a teacher from her building, or a curriculum director who participates as a member of a group of subject-area teacher leaders. By nature of their positions, the principal and curriculum director have authority over other members and responsibility for outcomes. A group member with knowledge authority has a high level of expertise about the content focus of the group. A group member with role authority

Table 5.2   Group Member Roles

Participant

- Listens well
- Contributes own perspective
- Assists process, movement of group
- Demonstrates awareness of self and others
- Seeks information, clarification, and other perspectives
- Monitors own and group behavior

Facilitator

- Clarifies purpose, task, process
- Guides process to assure participation
- Monitors and adjusts process as needed
- Remains neutral about topic and outcome
- Solicits summary and clarification about follow-up

Recorder

- Listens well, stays alert, and remains neutral
- Records main ideas using participants' words
- Seeks clarification and correction of record
- Summarizes and checks for accuracy

Timekeeper

- Monitors passing of time
- Alerts group about time limits
- Inquires about group's desire to alter/extend time limits

Observer

- Formally or informally monitors group process and interaction
- Provides feedback about observations for group reflection

Content authority

- Contributes knowledge and experienced perspective about content or task focus

Role authority

- Provides oversight, support, and coordination regarding resources, decisions, and follow-through

SOURCE: Adapted from R. Garmston & B. Wellman (1999); J. S. Thousand & R. Villa (2000); and J. York-Barr, R. Kronberg, & M. B. Doyle (1996).

has a high level of knowledge about policies, mandates, budgets, and other structures that may affect the group's work and decisions. Drawing from the work of several authors (e.g., Garmston & Wellman, 1997, 1999; Thousand & Villa, 2000; York-Barr, Kronberg, & Doyle, 1996), responsibilities for group member roles are listed in Table 5.2.

Facilitator Role

The role of facilitator requires special consideration in the design of group reflection and learning. Osterman and Kottkamp (1993) explain that frequently, "reflective practice requires a facilitator, someone who helps to begin the process and assumes responsibility for ensuring the participants' safety" (p. 46). Three primary goals of the facilitator are facilitation of task accomplishment, development of group skills and processes, and overall development of the group (Garmston & Wellman, 1999). It is often the case that individuals assigned responsibility for facilitating groups do not fully understand the significance of the facilitator role. It is not unusual for assigned facilitators to see their role as moving through an agenda, sometimes with expedience. This is, after all, likely to reflect their experience in groups.

Killion and Simmons (1992) make important distinctions between a training perspective and a facilitation perspective when working with groups. Trainers (sometimes referred to as *presenters*) are responsible for providing specific information and material to participants, for supporting the development of predetermined skills, and for accomplishing explicit outcomes. In contrast, facilitators are responsible for guiding groups through processes to discover their own insights and outcomes. Tasks within facilitated groups are usually more open, requiring group members to listen, learn, and figure things out together. The facilitator supports the work of the group by skillfully designing and implementing effective group processes. Training is an outside-in process. Facilitation is an inside-out process.

So what makes a good facilitator? First and foremost, effective facilitators must be trusted by members of the group. A trusting relationship between facilitator and group participants has to exist or emerge (Osterman & Kottkamp, 2004; Vella, 1994). If members do not know a facilitator personally, trust must be established through interactions. Much is communicated by how the facilitator presents him- or herself, how role expectations are communicated, and how the facilitator engages with members—individually and collectively. Significantly, facilitators must be viewed as outcome-neutral, meaning they do not have a vested interest in a particular group outcome. If the facilitator is not viewed as outcome-neutral, members are likely to feel manipulated and distrustful of the process. In addition to members trusting the facilitator, the facilitator must trust the group to come up with its own best outcomes. Facilitators must trust that the intentionally designed processes, skillfully implemented, will guide the group in realizing its own best outcomes. Recognizing that underlying beliefs and values influence behaviors, Osterman and Kottkamp (2004) explain,

> To serve as an effective facilitator, actions have to be grounded in
> a certain set of beliefs, beliefs that reflect a deep commitment to

Figure 5.3   Reflective Practice Facilitator Position Description

Position Available:
Facilitator for Reflective Practice
WANTED

A person who is inherently curious; someone who doesn't have all the answers and isn't afraid to admit it; someone who is confident enough in his or her ability to accept challenges in a nondefensive manner; someone who is secure enough to make his or her thinking public and therefore subject to discussion; someone who is a good listener; someone who likes other people and trusts them to make the right decisions if given the opportunity; someone who is able to see things from another's perspective and is sensitive to the needs and feelings of others; someone who is able to relax and lean back and let others assume the responsibility of their own learning. Some experience desirable but not as important as the ability to learn from mistakes.

SOURCE: Reprinted by permission from K. F. Osterman & R. B. Kottkamp (1993). *Reflective practice for educators: Improving schooling through professional development*, p. 64. Copyright © 1993. Reprinted by permission of Corwin Press.

the potential for human change and development. These beliefs about professional development constitute a "credo for reflective practice."

- Everyone needs professional growth opportunities
- All professionals want to improve
- All professionals can learn
- All professionals are capable of assuming responsibility for their own professional growth and development
- People need and want information about their performance
- Collaboration enriches professional development

True feelings are conveyed in very subtle ways that are difficult to disguise. Unless the facilitator has a deep commitment to these beliefs about professional development—or at least can suspend doubt—she or he will be unable to disguise real feelings. The facilitator has to be a person who not only espouses this educational philosophy but also models it. (pp. 72–79)

Osterman and Kottkamp also present a want ad (Figure 5.3) for a reflective practice facilitator that eloquently captures the characteristics of individuals well suited for that role.

Given the primary importance of trust between the facilitator and group members, as well as among group members themselves, "The facilitator must be skilled at developing an environment in which the participants feel comfortable enough to contribute actively (safety) and an environment in which they have the opportunity to participate (equity)" (Osterman & Kottkamp, 1993, p. 63). How can you get a read on the degree of safety felt by participants? The energy level is a good indicator. Look for visible signs that people are interested and "awake," such as verbal participation, alert body posture, and nonverbal cues that suggest interest (or lack of). Also be aware of what Vella (1994) refers to as "fatal plops" that endanger group safety:

> The fatal plop [is] when an adult learner says something in a group, only to have the words hit the floor with a resounding "plop," without affirmation, without even recognition that she has spoken, with the teacher proceeding as if nothing had been said—[this] is a great way to destroy safety. (p. 8)

She goes on to explain that the fatal plop destroys safety not only for the one person but also for everyone in the group. As an individual, then, a facilitator must demonstrate capacities for fostering trust (described previously in Chapter 2, pp. 35–40): be present, be open, listen, seek understanding, assume mutuality, honor the person, and honor the process.

In the process of facilitating a group, effective facilitators engage in a lot of thinking about their thinking (i.e., metacognition). This form of reflection-in-action is one of the most difficult types of reflection. However, these in–the-moment reflections prompt immediate adjustments in process needed to keep the group climate safe and the group processes effective. In this way, facilitating is very much like teaching. Astute teachers know when they are connecting with individuals and with groups of students and when they are not. When they are not connecting, they make immediate adjustments in practice to reengage attention and participation. The same is true of effective facilitators. Garmston and Wellman (1999, p. 90) identify five metacognitive capabilities that foster the capacity for reflection-in-action:

- To know one's intention and choose congruent behaviors
- To set aside unproductive patterns of listening, responding, and inquiry
- To know when to assert and when to integrate
- To know and support the group's purposes, topics, processes, and development
- To emotionally disassociate from events in order to make strategic decisions about process

Effective facilitators must also be skilled at promoting thinking through questioning and responding. They must be particularly adept at facilitating dialogue, given its powerful effect on adult learning (Vella, 1994). Thinking, questioning, responding, reframing, and engaging in dialogue are capacities for not only the facilitator but also group members. Finally, an effective facilitator guides groups through constructive dialogue, viewing issues and events from different perspectives, generating ideas, solving problems, managing and learning from conflict, and making decisions.

Who facilitates? When deciding specifically who might facilitate group learning and process, the purpose of the group and characteristics of the individual are both important considerations. Perhaps the most important consideration is whom the group will allow to serve as facilitator. Who can stay focused on the process and participation without getting stuck in the content or dynamics? We often encourage teachers to facilitate groups other than those with which they are primarily associated. For example, a second-grade teacher may facilitate the fifth-grade team meeting. We also encourage teachers to facilitate in pairs. When facilitation is shared, one person can observe the process and participants while the other guides the process. Teamed facilitators can take turns in each role. Another advantage is shared reflection after the group adjourns: What worked? What did not work? Why? What might be some next steps?

In many situations, a member of a group or some other person from within the school is assigned responsibility for running meetings, groups, or teams. Sometimes, an external person is used. Advantages and disadvantages of use of internal and external facilitators are listed in Table 5.3. Internal facilitators are usually more readily available, and they bring a better understanding of the context. As a facilitator, however, they may have difficulty remaining neutral (even when they are committed to being so). Further, they are not free to be a group participant and to share their substantive views. Straus (2002), in his book *How to Make Collaboration Work,* states, "If you are a leader, manager, or chair of a group or organization, you should seriously consider not running your own meetings . . . I believe it's a conflict of interest for a leader to run a meeting when he or she has a large stake in the subject matter" (pp. 118–119). External facilitators bring a more objective perspective and may also bring more expertise as a facilitator. They offer the distinct advantage of allowing insiders to participate fully as group members. When group members have little experience, knowledge, or capacity for effective group learning or when group members do not interact well, external facilitators can often shape more effective interactions using well-designed and tightly structured processes. On the downside, external facilitators are often more costly and less convenient in terms of scheduling and communication.

Individuals with role and knowledge authority also present particular advantages and disadvantages as facilitators. Individuals with role authority may have the advantage of information regarding budget, policy, and a more comprehensive systems perspective. They have the potential disadvantage of confusing their role as facilitator and their role as boss.

Table 5.3   Potential Advantages and Disadvantages of Internal Versus External Facilitators

	Potential Advantages	*Potential Disadvantages*
Internal facilitator	Knowledge of context can support facilitation design	Knowledge of context can result in bias
	Opportunity to foster or expand relationships internally	Personal or professional interest in the outcome
	Aware of group outcomes and needs	Role confusion for facilitator and participants
	Builds internal capacity for facilitation	May have less facilitation expertise than an external person
		Cannot act as a participant, resulting in lost perspective or vote
External facilitator	Little knowledge of context, better able to remain neutral	Little knowledge of context, less able to consider relevant context variables in facilitation design
	Expertise in facilitation and group-process skills	Must establish credibility with group
		May be less convenient or efficient in terms of scheduling, time, and communication
		May incur more costs

Another disadvantage is that group members may be concerned about repercussions which can diminish participation by group members. Individuals with knowledge authority can bring valuable information and perspective to a group but may also have difficulty moving outside of their expert role to facilitate new reflection and learning by group members. Knowing there is an expert in their midst, some members may be less likely to raise questions or share views, for fear of being wrong or perceived as not very knowledgeable. Conversely, some may be more likely to ask questions and use group time to request specific assistance. Either way, group participation and learning can be inhibited. In some instances, however, knowledge authority may be an important facilitator characteristic. For example, when adopting a new science curriculum, groups may be well guided by an outsider who has knowledge authority and who is a strong facilitator. Knowledge authority fosters credibility and can diminish resistance, blocking, or sabotage during implementation. In such cases, it is important for the person to clarify when she is serving as facilitator and when she is stepping in to offer knowledge-specific perspectives.

Similarly, when facilitators emerge from within groups, they must be clear about when they are in the role of facilitator and when they are in the role of participant. This clarity helps group members understand the difference and minimizes the likelihood of them feeling manipulated because someone leads the process who has a vested interest in the actions and outcomes. When it is necessary or appropriate to be in the role of participant, facilitators formally step out of that role. They inform the group that they are taking off the "hat" of facilitator temporarily, to contribute their perspective as a group member. They then share their perspective and provide the opportunity for others to interact with them while still in the group-member role. Afterward, they return to the role of facilitator. It is difficult to facilitate when one is also a group member. It requires a high level of awareness about one's thinking, assumptions, biases, desires, and roles. After groups move to a point of learning and working together well, a formal facilitator role becomes less important or can be easily rotated among group members.

What Structures and Processes Support Group Reflection and Learning?

As suggested previously, it cannot be assumed that individuals know how to interact effectively in the context of a group (Will, 1997), even when they reflect well as individuals. Groups present a much more complex context and require an expanded repertoire of skills and processes. Specific group structures and processes assist in creating the conditions that promote participation, thinking, learning, and working together. Early in a group's development, careful attention to design and facilitation are especially important. In a major study of what contributes to the effectiveness of different kinds of groups, Hackman (1991) identified a significant principle he refers to as *self-fueling spirals,* meaning that over time, the rich get richer and the poor get poorer. He observed that if groups got off to a good start, they tended to perform better over time. Conversely, if they did not get off to a good start, they tended to perform poorly over time. How, then, can the likelihood of a good start be maximized?

There must be an intentional design to create a safe and productive learning environment. In considering safety, however, recall from the previous chapter that learning, particularly learning that involves reframing, involves periods of discomfort. "Safety does not obviate the natural challenge of learning new concepts, skills, or attitudes. Safety does not take away from the hard work of learning" (Vella, 1994, p. 6). Considerations related to the structures and processes for learning in groups are presented sequentially below: planning for groups, opening the group process, engaging in the core agenda, and closing the group process. A sample agenda that illustrates specific attention to group process design is offered as the first example from practice, *Intentional Session Design to Foster Learning,* on page 174 (Figure 5.7) of this chapter.

Planning the Group Process

Planning for groups (design work) is a form of reflection-for-action. While keeping in mind the desired outcomes for the group session, designers need to think through how to bring the group to a common focus, to promote a safe and participatory climate, and to facilitate effective interactions. In new groups, large groups, and groups facing known challenges (e.g., conflicted issues or difficult interpersonal dynamics), a tighter process is often advantageous. Adherence to an agenda decreases the likelihood of unproductive interactions. However, an agenda that is too tight or a process that is too controlled can result in diminished or superficial participation. Some groups, especially those that are self-organized, rarely need a formal agenda or carefully sequenced process. The group's purpose and participants influence the specific design for group interaction significantly. The examples provided later in this chapter show different structures that align with the characteristics of different groups. Magestro and Stanford-Blair (2000) outline a planning template for staff development that occurs in groups. A slightly modified version of their template is outlined here:

- *Identify the purpose and objectives* of the meeting: What do you want participants to learn and be able to do as a result of this activity?
- *Select the resources* you plan to use as a basis for the activity. Include both content resources (e.g., journal articles, books, videos, inquiry kits) and process resources (e.g., overhead transparencies, flip charts).
- *Prepare an agenda* that fits the time frame. Include an activator (i.e., an activity to elicit prior knowledge, beliefs, or attitudes), brief input (usually information from the content resources), interaction (opportunities for participants to reflect on, engage with, and respond to the input), and summarizer (individual or group activity to bring attention to important aspects of the learning and that specifies personal commitments for follow-up).
- *Specify revisit or follow-up activities,* such as peer planning or coaching.

Consider carefully the location, time, physical-space arrangement, and refreshments. Convenience, comfort, and quality are sometimes competing dimensions to consider. The most convenient location is usually at the school site. If the meeting location is off-site, there are the deterrents of travel time and directions. Some people will choose not to attend. Meeting off-site, however, offers some quality advantages, such as the potential for being served good food and drink (e.g., at a coffee shop), meeting in a room designed for adult learning (e.g., seated comfortably in adult-sized chairs around tables as opposed to meeting in child-sized desks and chairs), and settling in to an environment that supports thinking (e.g., a pleasant room with windows and a peaceful view). Most important, meeting off-site greatly diminishes the inevitable distractions (e.g., people coming and going, bells, unexpected student issues). Early in a group formation and learning process, it can be very beneficial to arrange for off-site meetings and to allocate larger periods of time so that participants are comfortable, are free of distractions, and have sufficient time and space to move into a reflective mode.

Finding common times to meet is a major challenge. Specific strategies are offered later in this chapter (Table 5.4). In addition, one of the examples from practice, *Time for Team-Learning Task Force,* describes a site-based task-force process focused on scheduling time for teams to meet. Before and after school are often convenient times but pose quality constraints. Before school, participants can be distracted by the impending start of the instructional day. After school, participants can be either drained or wound up. Time in the middle of the day has both problems. Release time provides the best quality advantage, as long as students do not incur instructional disadvantages. Depending on the nature of the task, half-day meeting blocks are desirable and sometimes can be arranged using internal coverage. When meetings are held before, during, or immediately after the instructional day, an activity should be planned that assists members' transition from the fast-paced instructional day to more reflective learning time.

The physical arrangement of the meeting area also affects reflection and learning. In general, a circle arrangement is desirable so participants can easily see one another. Another reason for choosing a circle is captured eloquently in the words of a Sioux elder (Lame Deer & Erdoes, 1994), presented in Figure 5.4. Circles diminish a power orientation. There is no one sitting at the head or the foot of the table. The desired interaction is among members of the group, not between group members and a facilitator, for example. If the group is to use paper or other materials, participants can be comfortably arranged around tables that are large enough to hold the materials and allow room to work but are small enough for everyone to feel connected (Vella, 1994). If presenting, active facilitation, or public recording is expected, a U-shape works well. The key design features are comfort, openness, and participants oriented toward each other.

Finally, planning for refreshments, even if just cool, fresh water or hot water with tea and coffee bags, indicates a degree of caring for the physical needs of participants. Ongoing groups frequently rotate responsibilities for refreshments. Sometimes, this responsibility takes care of itself when groups decide to meet at conveniently located restaurants.

Opening the Group Process

The way in which a group or meeting begins communicates to participants the degree of safety, respect, preparation, and perceived importance of the time planned together. Participants should be welcomed as they

Figure 5.4   Symbolism of Circle From Sioux Elder Perspective (Lame Deer & Erdoes, 1994)

A reading from John
Lame Deer, a Sioux Elder

We Indians live in a world of symbols and
images where the spiritual and commonplace are one.
To you symbols are just words, spoken or written in a book.
To us they are a part of nature, part of ourselves—the earth, the sun,
the wind, and the rain, stones, trees, animals, even little insects like ants and
grasshoppers. We try to understand them not with the head but with the heart,
and we need no more than a hint to give us the meaning …

To our way of thinking the Indians' symbol is the circle, the hoop. Nature wants
things to be round. The bodies of human beings and animals have no corners.
With us the circle stands for the togetherness of people who sit with one another
around the campfire, relatives and friends united in peace while the pipe passes
from hand to hand. The camps in which every tipi had its place was also a ring.
The tipi was a ring in which people sat in a circle and all families in the
village were in turn circles within a larger circle, part of the larger hoop
which was the seven campfires of the Sioux, representing one nation.

The nation was only part of the universe, in itself circular
and made of earth, which is round, of the sun, which is
round, of the stars, which are found. The moon, the
horizon, the rainbow--the circles within circles,
with no beginning and no end.

SOURCE: Reprinted by permission from J. Lame Deer & R. Erdoes (1994). *Lame Deer, seeker of visions* (pp. 108, 110–111). New York: Washington Square.

arrive, greeted by name if possible, and invited to help themselves to refreshments. This begins the process of acknowledgment, communicates caring, and assists with the psychological transition from where the participants just were to where they now are—soon to be engaged participants in a group reflection and learning process. Here are some other guidelines for initiating the group:

Introductions: Make sure participants get to know one another by name and position. It is also helpful if each participant states his or her relationship to the topic at hand. These introductions offer background information and perspective that assists members in understanding one another. Use nametags if necessary, or write names on chart paper in the order in which participants are seated.

Overview and Review: Reference an agenda (either posted or on handouts) and introduce the purpose of the meeting—both the *big* purpose (i.e., the long-term goal of the group) and the more focused purpose of the current meeting. Provide an overview of the activities, time frames, process, and desired outcomes. Ask for input and solicit questions. Assign group roles as appropriate. In subsequent meetings, review the process and outcomes of the previous meeting. These activities clarify purpose and orient the group to the present.

Warm-Up Activities: There are two types of warm-up activities often used in group work, relationship-building and on-ramp activities. Relationship-building activities are useful early in the formation of a group, especially one that will meet on an ongoing basis. These activities should be safe but personal (Will, 1997). For example, ask participants to share a little-known fact about themselves, describe a favorite family ritual, inform the group about where they were born, or find out who travels the farthest to get to school every day. This process provides an opportunity for participants to practice disclosure in a safe way (they determine what to share and what not to share) and offers another way to know each person in the group, which assists with remembering names. What participants choose to share varies greatly. One teacher shared that as a young child, she tried to teach her pet fish to walk. Another was afraid of elevators. This disclosure prompted a number of participants to join her in using the stairs (job-embedded exercise!). A young teacher shared that just a few years ago, when he was in the best physical shape ever, he had a stroke. Each of these disclosures expands the understanding and connections among group members. Through stories of humorous events or personal challenges, individuals become connected in ways other than just work. This builds the relationships, which strengthens commitments to group purpose, participants, and process. One way to keep these types of connecting activities going is to rotate responsibility for leading an icebreaking activity at the beginning of each session. This also fosters shared responsibility for group development.

On-ramp activities assist participants with getting oriented to the group task or purpose. To help reframe meetings as opportunities for learning, for example, a brief reflection activity might be inserted. We have a handout with reflective practice quotes and invite participants to read the quotes and share a quote that struck them as meaningful. (One such handout is located in Resource 5.A and may be copied for professional learning purposes). You might also use Figure 5.1 (Theory of Action for Reflective Practice) to prompt thinking, or share a story or an abstract from a recent research article—each with carefully constructed questions to prompt reflection and conversation. These activities serve the function of bringing the thoughts and energy of group members into the present.

Group Norms and Expectations: Paying attention to norms and expectations at every session serves as a reminder of behaviors and dispositions that facilitate learning and working together. We frequently begin group sessions with the verbal or visual reminder that "we are all in the same room, but not in the same place" (anonymous, as quoted by Garmston & Wellman, 1997, p. 29). This serves to acknowledge differences among individuals and to support an expectation that different perspectives will be shared. Norms and expectations can be provided or generated, or a combination of both. They should be posted in clear view. For starters, you could offer the personal capacities for reflection described in Chapter 2 (pp. 35–55). We also suggest the seven norms of collaborative work developed by Bill Baker and formally articulated in the work of Garmston and Wellman (1997, 1999). "When the seven norms of collaborative work become an established part of group life and group work, cohesion, energy, and commitment to shared work and to the group increase dramatically" (Garmston & Wellman, 1999, p. 37). Figure 5.5 shows these norms, along with visual reminders about dialogue, discussion, and suspension as tools for individual and group use. This depiction, which we call the *tabletop norms,* has been formatted as a handout in the Resources (Resource 5.B) and can be sized for insertion in 5-by-7-inch self-standing acrylic picture frames to be placed on tables within the group. To be effective, norms and expectations must be regularly and intentionally revisited. One way to accomplish this is to invite group members to identify norms on which to focus at the start of each meeting.

Engaging in the Core Agenda

Developing effective ways to reflect and learn in a group requires consciousness about group processes, as well as group expectations, tasks, and outcomes. Again, we refer you to Figure 5.7 for a sample agenda that specifies both content and process. In addition to planned processes (such as those on the sample agenda), engaging in the core part of a meeting requires unplanned processes informed by reflection-in-action. As the group begins to move through the agenda, participation is monitored. Initially, group members who serve in formal roles (e.g., facilitator, recorder, or observer) may be more active in monitoring functions. Over time, it is expected that all participants help to monitor group effectiveness and make or suggest modifications to enhance functioning. Adhering to the seven norms of collaborative work or another agreed-upon interaction framework also enhances effectiveness. It is also helpful for groups to be explicit about the type of processes they are engaging in, such as idea generating, conflict resolution, problem solving, or action planning.

Figure 5.5   Tabletop Collaborative Group Norms

Dialogue

Discussion

Suspension

Pause

Paraphrase

Presume positive intentions

Probe for specificity

Pursue balance inquiry/advocacy

Put ideas on the table

Pay attention to self and others

SOURCE: Adapted with permission from R. Garmston & B. Wellman (1997). *The Adaptive School: A Sourcebook for Developing Collaborative Groups.* Norwood, MA: Christopher-Gordon.

Distinguishing between dialogue and discussion is also important, because each form of conversation involves different types of thinking and participation. Sometimes participation is increased by breaking larger groups into smaller groups. In sum, processes for engaging in the core agenda are designed beforehand but often require adjustments, sometimes big adjustments, along the way.

Closing the Group Process

Specific attention to ending a group session affirms the importance of the effort. "People need to feel that the work of the group is meaningful if they are to take such activities seriously in the future" (Will, 1997, p. 37). Closing a session is a form of reflection-on-action that addresses both the content and process of the session. Content closing involves reviewing the session purpose, highlighting insights or outcomes, specifying follow-up, and projecting the purpose for future sessions. Debriefing the process involves reflection on how effectively the group learned and worked together. We suggest three options for group reflection and closure: posing general questions, using reflection frameworks, and responding to group-process checklists. Each of these options can take the form of whole-group; or small-group, then whole-group; or individual, then whole-group processing. General questions might include a focus on the content (for example, "What were the most significant insights or outcomes of today's gathering?") and a focus on process (for example, "What were strengths in terms of our overall group process and what might be some things to work on next time?"). Metaphors and synectics also work well for closing and are described later in this chapter. A variety of reflection frameworks that can target both content and process are shown in Figure 5.6. Used most effectively, they would first involve asking participants to spend a few moments reflecting individually or with a partner before sharing with the whole group. Groups also can use checklists or surveys of specific group and individual behaviors as a way to reflect on their effectiveness. See Garmston and Wellman (1999) for a checklist that focuses on the seven norms of collaborative work. See also Thousand and Villa (2000) for a survey titled "Are We Really a Team?" and other tools used to prompt reflection and learning about the group process.

Regardless of the specific method of reflection chosen, group capacity is enhanced when individuals and the group as a whole reflect on their contributions, learning, and outcomes. Consider again that "adults do not learn from experience, they learn from processing experience" (Garmston & Wellman, 1997, p. 1, inspired by Judy Arin-Krupp).

How Can Time Be Allocated for Learning Together?

Time is our most valuable, nonrenewable resource. Educators must make wise decisions about how time is best used in schools. School renewal and improvement efforts that occur on the fringes of the school day or school year are unlikely to become embedded dimensions of school culture (Speck, 2002). This means that embedding professional learning in the school day and throughout the school year must be a priority. Time has been consistently identified as an essential structural condition within organizations to support both individual and collective learning (Donahoe, 1993; Louis, 1992; Raywid, 1993; U.S. Department of Education, 1996; Watts & Castle, 1993). "If student achievement is to improve, then teachers need time to learn, practice, implement, observe and reflect" (Specke, 2002, p. 17). Although having time does not guarantee effective reflection and collaboration, not having time precludes even the possibility. Unless schools intentionally schedule collaborative time for professional learning, the dominant culture of isolated teacher work will continue (Adelman, 1998). Schein (2004) states that there is probably no more important factor in the analysis

Figure 5.6   Sample of Closing Reflection Protocols

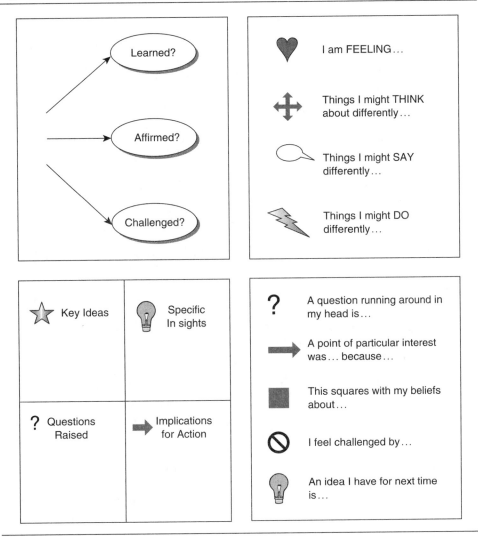

Original source unknown.

of an organization's culture than how it allocates and uses time. The pace of events, the rhythms of the building, the sequence in which things are done, and meeting agendas are all signs of what an organization or team values. "The perspective most needed . . . is that of time as a resource that can be shaped and reshaped to meet educational needs, rather than as a straitjacket into which teaching and learning have to be stuffed" (U.S. Department of Education, 1996, p. 11).

Allocating time for collaborative learning has become a high priority for many schools across the country. A decision that such time is important

Table 5.4   Time for Reflection and Learning: Strategies and Examples

Strategy for Finding Time	What Is It?	What Have Schools Done?
Freed-up Time	Temporary blocks of time were created for teachers through the use of substitutes, volunteers, or creative use of staff.	• Hired substitutes to release groups of teachers to meet every other week. • Scheduled special performances or assemblies so grade-level teams are free to meet during this time. • Arranged for a licensed staff member without regular classroom assignments to cover a classroom so that the classroom teacher has time to observe a peer teaching or to meet with a team member. • Created a reflection pool: teachers volunteered to give up their prep time to cover a colleague's class, allowing the colleague time for reflection. In exchange, the freed-up colleague then placed his or her name in the pool and covered another colleague's class.
Purchased Time	Schools found creative ways to find and fund professional time, including use of early retirees, foundation funding, or contractual compensation. These strategies can be temporary, transitional, or institutionalized by building it into contracts.	• Negotiated teacher contracts that lengthen the teachers' day by one hour after students leave, creating time for teachers to meet. • Schools on year-round schedules dedicated two to three paid days during intersessions for teacher meetings and staff development. • Offered compensatory pay for summer meeting and learning together. Teachers stayed later one day a week to meet in reflective practice groups in exchange for being able to leave at the same time as students on another day. • Negotiated two hours a month for each special education paraprofessional to engage in team meetings and/or building staff development.
Common Time	Schools developed team or grade-level schedules to create a common planning period or lunch period.	• Created brown-bag lunch groups that met once a week to reflect on their practice. In schools with a 90-minute block schedule, 60 minutes of one planning period were dedicated to reflection on student learning, 30 to daily business. • Targeted an available period of time, such as a common prep period, for embedding staff development into the day.

Strategy for Finding Time	What Is It?	What Have Schools Done?
Restructured or Rescheduled Time	Schools formally altered the school calendar or teaching schedule on a permanent basis.	• Specialists (e.g., art, music, gym) developed a series of half-day programs to periodically free up each grade-level team to meet. • Banked time by arranging for students to attend school several extra minutes on four days a week and to be released early on the fifth day, creating a block of time for teachers to meet during the school day. • Created a longer block of time by scheduling grade-level common planning periods or special events immediately before or after a team's lunch period. Then rotated the schedules so all grades had one extended lunch period every two weeks. • Teachers met in individual study groups after school throughout the school year in exchange for not having to attend a scheduled staff development day. • Organized community service opportunities for all students for one-half day a week to create a block of time for teachers to meet. • Once a week, teachers arrived early at school and students started later, to create a block of time for teachers to meet.
Better-Used Time	Staff examined current practices to see how schools are using the time they currently have to meet. When we meet, what do we meet about? Is our meeting time aligned with what we want to create and accomplish? How can we best focus our time together on instruction and professional development?	• Refocused weekly faculty meetings so that school business was discussed once a month and reflective practice groups met the other three weeks to focus on students, curriculum, instruction, assessment, and other teaching and learning topics. • Used alternative communication formats (e.g., memos, e-mail, voice mail) to dedicate more faculty meeting time to issues and discussions requiring broad input. • Explored ways in which technology could be used to develop collegial networks within and across buildings (e.g., e-mail, online discussion groups).

SOURCE: Framework from Watts & Castle (1993) and also used by North Central Regional Educational Laboratory (1994).

must be followed up with efforts to make it happen. After clarifying specific reasons for meeting, decisions must be made about who needs to meet together, how often meetings should be held, and when and where to meet. As a general rule, when scheduling team time, blocks should be designated that allow at least 45 uninterrupted minutes, preferably an hour or more. Shorter blocks of time make it difficult for teachers to shift from *doing* mode to reflective and learning mode. Watts and Castle (1993) identified five strategies that schools have used to create time for teachers to meet and learn together: freeing up temporary blocks of time, purchasing additional time, using common planning time, restructuring individual school or district schedules, and carefully examining how staff members are using the time they currently have available. In Table 5.4 each of these strategies is described, along with specific examples from actual schools and districts.

Scheduling regular meeting times significantly in advance, preferably for an entire school year, and marking these times on a school calendar elevates such meetings to priority status so staff can resist pressure to schedule other meetings during these times. Even when time to meet is not a schoolwide value or norm, grade-level, subject-area, and special-services teams can consider these strategies to create regular meeting times. In the following section of this chapter, one of the examples from practice involves a task force of teachers who studied various ways to schedule collaborative meeting time, then examined their school's schedule to figure out how to build in such regularly scheduled time. Some of the steps in their process may be useful as you consider how to allocate time for team learning in your school.

REFLECTIVE PRACTICE IN SMALL GROUPS AND TEAMS: EXAMPLES FROM PRACTICE

Because of the many teams, committees, and ad hoc and governance groups in schools, embedding reflective practices within these structures could result in significant advances in educational practice. In this section, we describe numerous examples from work that is occurring in Minnesota. We begin by highlighting intentional decisions in the design of group learning. This is followed by examples from elementary, middle, and high school educators who engage in reflective practices as a part of addressing relevant issues in their respective practice settings. As you read these examples, we invite you to reflect on the following questions:

- In what ways have learning opportunities been intentionally designed?
- How do planning and design promote participation by group members?

- How is reflection used to promote learning and monitor the group process and progress?
- What is the role of the facilitator? How do facilitators initiate and guide group learning and process? What are some examples of facilitators reflecting in and on action?
- What particular example do I want to remember and ponder further? Why?

Intentional Design of a Book Study Group

Careful attention to the design of group, committee, or team sessions increases the likelihood of clarity, efficiency and effectiveness. It also communicates respect for participants' time and an expectation for focused engagement. Just as writing a specific lesson plan for student instruction may positively impact student learning, writing a specific plan for facilitating adult meetings aims to positively impact the learning process for adults. Shown in Figure 5.7 is a learning group agenda designed to support a group of mentor teachers interested in learning about ways to increase the capacity of teachers in the district to reach and teach economically disadvantaged students. They chose to study the book *Star Teachers of Children in Poverty* (Haberman, 1995). Notice the agenda's specificity of purpose, outcomes, content, and process. As educators experience the results of well-designed learning sessions, they may be more apt to pay specific attention to the content and process design of groups they facilitate. A blank protocol of this agenda format is located in Resource 5.C and may be copied for professional learning purposes. *Contributed by Jennifer Kunze, Bloomington Public Schools, Minnesota.*

Middle School Teachers Facilitate Learning With Peers

Two middle school teachers invited their colleagues to form a collaborative group to learn more about research-based instructional strategies. They chose the book *Classroom Instruction That Works: Research-Based Strategies for Increasing Student Achievement* (Marzano, Pickering, & Pollock, 2001) to guide their learning. The teacher leaders articulated the following objectives: to practice using norms of collaborative work during group interactions; to read about research-based instructional strategies; to implement one research-based strategy in the classroom and share that experience with group members; and to identify strengths and applications for all the instructional strategies studied. Six teacher colleagues representing each of the core areas (math, social studies, science, and language arts) decided to join them.

The teachers who led this effort developed a schedule by which one instructional strategy was the focus of each learning session. A unique feature of this study process was that in addition to reading about the

Figure 5.7   Sample Learning Group Agenda

Learning Group Plan: Session #1	
PURPOSE: The overall purpose of the book study is to begin the process of explicitly addressing teacher capacity to reach and teach economically disadvantaged students. Participants will study the views, characteristics, and practices of successful teachers of such students as presented by Martin Haberman in his book, *Star Teachers of Children in Poverty.*	SCHEDULE OF MEETINGS: Session 1: 2/24, 8-9:30 Session 2: 3/3, 8-9:30 Session 3: 3/14, 10-11:30 Session 4: 3/27, 8-9:30

OUTCOMES: Participants will be able to . . .
1) Identify and apply the Norms of Collaborative Work (from Garmston & Wellman).
2) Use dialogue to collaboratively learn about the potential effects of poverty on learning and teaching.
3) Compare and contrast characteristics of successful and unsuccessful teachers of children in poverty.
4) Appraise how learning from this study process can be used to strengthen our district mentor program.

CONTENT		PROCESS
1. Purpose, outcomes, expectations. Overall and today.	O P E N I N G	1. Inform and ask for additional ideas.
2. Norms of Collaborative Work		2. Introduce each norm, reference handout. Group: invite participants to identify norms our group usually does well and those we could work on. Individually: ask each participant to identify for him- or herself a norm or two to focus on today.
3. Ways of Talking (dialogue, discussion, choice points)		3. Present summary using handout as guide. Ask participants which means of conversation is likely to be most productive given the purpose of this group. Explain how dialogue fosters understanding and learning. Emphasize choice point.
4. Opener: Freewrite #1	C O R E	4. Ask participants to individually freewrite in response to the following question: In what ways do you see poverty influencing teaching and learning? Round robin debrief.
5. Dialogue: KW(L) starter		5. To initiate, pose the following questions to the whole group: a) What do we know about children of poverty in our school district? (incidence, location, strengths, concerns) b) What do we know about teacher effectiveness with children of poverty in our school district? c) What do we need/want to learn more about effective teaching and learning for students who live in poverty?
6. Pre-reading of book		6. Individual: ask participants to silently read the forward, preface, and introduction: highlighting key words and phrases, areas of interest; checking items that raise questions. Group: invite comments about interests and questions.
7. Closing shared reflection	C L O S I N G	7. Round robin response to the following questions: Why should we as mentors learn more about poverty and teaching? How might this impact our work?
8. Prep for next session		8. Read chapters 1 and 2. Complete the "shape" reading reflection form.

instructional strategies, participants were each expected to select one instructional strategy and practice using it with their students before the group was scheduled to talk about it. The teachers viewed this as a form of action research.

To help set the standard for effective group interactions, the teacher leaders introduced norms of collaborative work (Garmston & Wellman, 1999, described earlier in this chapter) and explained distinctions between discussion and dialogue. They also suggested that their colleagues use the 4-Step Reflection Process (described in Chapter 3) to prepare what each would share about their respective instructional strategies and to guide the overall learning process for each group session. (Recall that the 4-Step Process included the following reflection prompts: what happened? [description]; why? [analysis and interpretation]; so what? [overall meaning]; and now what? [implications for action].)

During the last collaborative group session, the teacher leaders asked participants to evaluate the group learning experience by responding to the following questions:

- *Content questions:* Was the book selected relevant to what you want to accomplish in the classroom? Did you have adequate time to practice and reflect on the strategy you selected? How will what you learned be useful to you? In what ways will you be able to apply what you learned?
- *Process questions:* Was the collaborative group format helpful to your learning? If yes, how? Was the group facilitator well prepared? Were the goals and objectives clearly specified when you began?
- *Context questions:* Was the meeting room setting conducive to learning? Did you get the type of treats that you really wanted to eat?

In reflecting on the sessions and on the responses to the evaluation, the teacher leaders concluded that participants were mostly positive about the learning process, the action research, and using the Marzano et al. (2001) book. Participants indicated feeling proud that they were already using many of the instructional strategies in their daily lessons. Participants also indicated that allocating time to meet within the school day was positive and important.

Reflecting on their roles as learning facilitators, the teacher leader pair shared that initially, responsibility for leading a peer group felt a little scary. Sometimes they felt pressure to put on a "dog and pony show." They created a mental picture, however, that helped support them in their new roles as facilitators. They envisioned serving as a *guide*. They felt that no one expects a guide to entertain along a journey or even to know exactly which routes will be taken. They envisioned the role of a guide as assuming responsibility for gathering and reflecting on collective wisdom and then for determining specific paths to take. These teachers decided they could do that. Overall, in assuming roles as facilitators and participants, the teacher leaders felt that taking time out of their busy schedules to study collaboratively was worthwhile and that they grew as facilitators. Most gratifying of all for them was participants indicating having grown as teachers. *Contributed by Sarah Holm and Gary Aylward, Richfield Public Schools, Minnesota.*

Time for Team-Learning Task Force at Plains Elementary

Plains Elementary School, a K–6 urban school with 650 students, was developing collaborative instructional models to support its diverse student population. Recognizing that time to meet is a key factor for successful collaboration, a task force was formed with the charge of finding time for teams to meet. Task force members reflected on readings about scheduling options. They examined current school schedules and considered the impact of various options. They also solicited feedback from other Plains faculty throughout the process.

The task force participants were a representative group of 10 teachers, including teachers from primary and intermediate grades, special education, English language learning (ELL), fine arts, and the teachers' union, as well as two teachers with prior experience developing schoolwide schedules. The principal, as an ad hoc member, was kept abreast of task force progress. Representative membership was intended to ensure that schoolwide perspectives were heard and that task force recommendations would be well conceived and well received.

Early on, half- or full-day meetings were held off-site (but nearby) to keep participants focused and to eliminate interruptions. Initial meetings were scheduled three to four weeks apart to allow time for participants to reflect on the options, questions, and directions that resulted from the meetings. This schedule also allowed participants to obtain feedback from staff not involved in the meetings. When the task force process shifted from learning and brainstorming to decision making and planning, the meetings were scheduled closer together to sustain momentum for accomplishing their task. A brief summary of the task force process follows.

Meeting 1: Reflecting on Beliefs, Practices, and Research. Participants reviewed research about why team meeting time was important and how other schools had created blocks of time for teachers to meet and learn together. Through dialogue, participants considered how the various time strategies might apply in their school. The process was intentionally kept open to consider a variety of options. No decisions were made.

Meeting 2: Identifying Principles for Decision Making. Typical of most complex learning, there were points of confusion and tension. In particular, as task force participants considered how time to meet might work into the school schedule, they recognized that before figuring out a schedule, they had to determine how teams would be configured. Some were uncomfortable with this expanded dimension of their work. To move forward, task force members decided on two principles to guide decision making:

(a) program coherence and consistency for students and, as much as possible, for staff; and (b) regular meeting times for grade-level instructional teams to reflect on curricular, instructional, and student performance issues.

Meeting 3: Updating the Principal. Task force members updated the principal by sharing posters that summarized work of the previous meetings. It became apparent to all that despite the challenges, substantial progress had been made. The principal agreed with the principles and encouraged the group to continue.

Meetings 4–6: Developing Specific Schedule Options. Using paper cutouts of all staff members (color coded by position), task force members spent a day brainstorming ways staff might be reorganized into grade-level teams composed of classroom teachers, specialists, and assistants. The cutouts were arranged and rearranged amid much conversation of advantages and disadvantages of different configurations. The purposes of the activity were to identify who needed time to meet and then brainstorm scheduling options that supported both short weekly and long monthly blocks of time for team reflection and planning. Two short follow-up meetings (meetings 5 and 6) were held to fine-tune the two scheduling options.

Meetings With the Rest of the Staff: Soliciting Feedback. Task force members decided to meet separately with each grade-level team to summarize the task force process, share the decision-making principles, propose two scheduling options, and solicit feedback. The task force facilitator and selected members led these meetings. No decisions were made.

Making Final Recommendations. After gathering and reflecting on the feedback from the grade-level teams, task force members made two recommendations. First, they recommended that general education and special services teachers be formally reconfigured into grade-level instructional teams. These teams would meet once each week during a common prep period. Second, they recommended a schoolwide schedule with monthly "double preps." This meant that once a month, students in each grade would attend two consecutive prep periods, thereby freeing up grade-level teams to meet for an additional 100-minute block of time. The principal and the faculty accepted both recommendations with implementation to begin the following school year.

Design elements of this task force process included multiple perspectives, feedback loops with broader constituents, reflection on both external and internal knowledge, engagement over an extended period of time, decision making grounded in student-centered learning principles, and intentionally crafted task force sessions. The result was a thoughtfully constructed and well-supported set of outcomes that ultimately will enrich both staff and student learning.

Reading Reflection Groups at Washington High School

The focus on reading intensified at Washington High School when passing the state's basic standards test became a graduation requirement. At Washington, many teachers believed that reading was a special education issue, not a schoolwide issue. Several special education teachers asserted that student success in reading was not *owned* by one department and that if such a view persisted, the school would not be successful in reaching its reading goals for students. These special educators led the reframing of poor reading proficiency, from "this is a special education problem" to "this is a schoolwide issue." Working with site administrators and several other teachers, the special educators created a three-year plan by which all teachers would be expected to participate in an intensive reading-instruction program focused on embedding literacy strategies in all subject-area classes. Reflective practices were central to the design of the plan.

During the first year, an intensive reading program was offered during the summer by a local education cooperative. By design, follow-up for this learning took the form of voluntary biweekly participation in a reading reflection group facilitated at Washington by a site special educator. Staff members who attended the summer session, as well as those who did not, were invited to participate in the reading reflection group. Between 15 and 20 teachers from a variety of subject areas regularly joined the reading reflection group, which met on Friday mornings before school. Each session focused on participant-identified reading-related topics or issues. Teachers were encouraged to share lessons, to foster learning from one another. The diverse participant backgrounds sparked broad application and rich learning for everyone.

The special educator who served as facilitator intentionally designed the group sessions to foster relationships and learning. First, she made it fun. She believed the staff members needed to find the experience both enjoyable and valuable or they would not return to the early-morning sessions. Second, she provided food at each meeting, another way to show caring and to foster connection. Third, she purposefully modeled reflection and inquiry throughout the conversations. Subtly, this introduced questioning and alternative thinking into the group's culture. Fourth, she arranged to have every session begin with a short reading activity and included other teachers in this session opening. A math teacher, for example, offered a short lesson on Latin roots and how he applied this information in his classes. This elicited dialogue about how reading instruction might be embedded into subject-area curriculum and classes.

Over the course of the first year, several significant and positive changes became evident. New relationships formed among teachers across departments and grade levels because the initiative was school-wide. Many teachers were regularly embedding reading strategies into their subject-area instructional practices because of their increased knowledge, idea sharing, and supported use of reading strategies. In the spring of the first year, evidence of student progress in reading led the principal to ask the special educators to develop a similar process for math.

New Ways of Thinking About
Space Allocation at Newbury High School

Allocating space at Newbury High School was a volatile topic. Historically, administrators made decisions about space, and many staff did not trust their decision-making process. Some teachers were known to effectively maneuver for better space. It was no coincidence that new teachers were the "floaters" who taught in several rooms. Further, space allocation was based on short-term needs instead of long-term department and school needs; this resulted in a predictable cycle of putting up walls one year and tearing them down the next.

One teacher at Newbury was particularly bothered by this annual cycle and sought to design a more inclusive and equitable process. She proposed that a volunteer committee study schoolwide space issues and make specific recommendations to department chairpersons. The chairpersons would then make final decisions. Her proposal was accepted and a committee was formed, including an assistant principal, 13 staff who volunteered from a variety of departments, and key individuals specifically invited to participate (e.g., custodian, athletic director, police liaison). Described below are the major components of the committee's process.

Developing Committee Norms and Expectations

Committee members agreed on general expectations: interactions would be respectful, all members would be heard, and reflection and learning would be an essential part of the process. To achieve this, they adopted the seven norms of collaborative work (Garmston & Wellman, 1999; also see Figure 5.5, p. 167). The norms were reviewed and monitored, especially during tense conversations. Differences between dialogue and discussion were described, and ways to engage in both forms of conversation were reviewed. A ritual, referred to as Rumor of the Week, was established that invited members to share rumors they had heard about the committee's work. This kept the committee in touch with staff perceptions and also created opportunities to teach and model direct yet respectful ways to dispel rumors. As a result, trust in the committee members and the committee process developed.

Clarifying Values for Decision Making

All teachers at Washington were surveyed to identify values on which space-utilization decisions should be made. Using the survey results, department chairs facilitated conversations with their members to rank-order the values. Space committee members then compiled this feedback and identified four values for decision making: (a) use of space for instruction had priority over use of space for noninstructional purposes; (b) every teacher should teach in space that is conducive to student learning; (c) special consideration should be given to classes with unique instructional needs (e.g., art, science); and (d) teachers who taught five classes a day should have one classroom for the whole day.

Determining Short- and Long-Term Space Needs

Committee members intentionally designed a process to press teachers into thinking beyond their own realm of practice to consider space needs of all staff. Using an open-ended survey, each staff member was asked to describe his or her space needs, including how the space would be used. These results were compiled to focus conversations within departments about their short- and long-term space needs. Next, the committee took a walking tour of the school to refresh their memory about the physical layout and specific facilities so they had current knowledge of space for making decisions.

Engaging in Dialogue

As they moved into dialogue, committee members were given (a) the values for decision making; (b) each department's short- and long-term needs; (c) the master schedule, including details about staffing assignments; (d) a map of the building; and (e) a database of current room usage. Members then proceeded to talk about space use, room by room, floor by floor, and period by period. They made an effort to ensure understanding about why specific uses were suggested, as well as the inherent trade-offs with different options. They created a color-coded map that visually displayed all staff or program changes. The facilitator continually archived information to document the decision trail for future reference.

Presenting Recommendations

After extensive dialogue, a space allocation plan and accompanying rationale for each decision were presented to the administration and department chairs. The plan was reviewed. The committee was asked to revisit a few issues that had been raised by staff. Ultimately, the plan was unanimously approved. Afterward, the facilitator solicited input from the committee members and the department chairs about the decision-making process. No changes were recommended. The committee process of studying the issues, soliciting input and feedback, clearly articulating values for decision making, and providing a rationale for each decision became accepted practices for space allocation. Even though all staff members did not agree with every decision, they trusted the process and honored the outcome.

Reflecting on the Space Allocation Process

Committee members learned to think organizationally as they examined issues that affected the work of all staff and students. In doing so, they learned more about what other staff members do and how their work contributes to the high school as a whole. New relationships were established that supported movement away from self-interest and "turf culture." Committee members learned to develop, organize, and participate in a fair and ethical process in which dialogue was a valued means of interaction. Agreed-upon public norms and values fostered adherence to effective and professional interactions.

REFLECTIVE PRACTICE IN SMALL GROUPS AND TEAMS: MORE IDEAS TO CONSIDER

Some of the examples and ideas for reflecting on your own (Chapter 3) and with partners (Chapter 4) have applications for groups, as well. Mapping, reframing, reflection scripts, and action research are such examples. The following section includes additional ideas for fostering reflection to improve practice in the context of small groups and teams. Many of the ideas and strategies overlap. The learning processes most strongly featured throughout these examples include reflection through dialogue with colleagues and other forms of inquiry, such as reframing and asking questions. Some examples come from our experiences; others are from colleagues or the literature. Readers are encouraged to seek original sources for additional information.

Reflective Planning for Differentiated Instruction

Given the increasing variety of students in today's classrooms, teachers are becoming more and more adept at differentiating instruction to effectively match student learning interests, styles, and abilities. Kronberg and York-Barr (1998) developed a framework to guide individual teachers and teacher teams in a reflective planning process for differentiating teaching and learning opportunities in specific courses or curricular units. The seven-step framework, along with a sampling of questions to prompt thinking about each step, is presented in Table 5.5 and is also avail-

Table 5.5   Reflective Planning Framework for Differentiating Instruction

- Step 1: Identify key concepts, standards, guiding principles or essential questions, and desired outcomes.
  Sample reflective question: *What do I want students to know (e.g., concepts, facts, vocabulary words) and understand (e.g., generalizations, links with prior knowledge or experiences) at the end of this unit?*

- Step 2: Differentiate levels of student understanding.
  Sample reflective questions: *Given the core concepts, relevant applications, key generalizations, and critical skills that I want all students to learn, how can I extend the knowledge and skills for those students ready to move further? How can I ensure that students needing a more basic level also receive enriching opportunities to learn about the key concepts?*

- Step 3: Determine which skills are important for the students to learn, review, and apply.
  Sample reflective questions: *What do I want students to be able to do at the end of this unit? What new skills will students need to learn for this unit? What opportunities are present for students to review and apply skills they have already learned?*

- Step 4: If relevant to your particular context, identify which district objectives and/or state standards might interface with the unit or topical area.
  Sample reflective questions: *In context of the intended learning from this unit, how can I blend district objectives and/or state standards?*

- Step 5: Given the range of student needs, abilities, strengths, and experiences, determine how students can best learn about the identified concepts, principles, or essential questions.
  Sample reflective questions: *What activities can be used that will maximize student strengths, interests, abilities, and experiences? What do students already know about this topic? What additional support needs will some of the students have? How can the activities best accommodate those additional support needs? How best can I group students for the activities in this unit?*

- Step 6: Select product options that will encourage students to apply their learning from the unit as well as integrating the knowledge and skills from the unit with previous knowledge and experiences.
  Sample reflective questions: *What kinds of products will allow students to demonstrate what they have learned relative to the key concepts, principles or questions? What products would show integration and application? How can individual student strengths be used to guide demonstrations? How might student choice be incorporated into product selection? In what ways can students best share what they have learned?*

- Step 7: Select formative and summative assessment approaches that can be used throughout the unit to provide helpful feedback to both students and staff.
  Sample reflective questions: *How can I best assess what students already know about the topic? What kinds of feedback do I want throughout the unit to help me determine the effectiveness of the lessons and activities? How can I best design assessment tools that will be sensitive to varied levels of student proficiency? How can I actively involve students in self-assessment?* (p. 34).

SOURCE: Adapted with permission from R. Kronberg & J. York-Barr. (1998). *Differentiated teaching and learning in heterogeneous classrooms.* Minneapolis: University of Minnesota, Institute on Community Integration.

able as Resource 5.D. For more information and examples about this differentiation framework, go to www.ici.umn.edu and search for *Differentiated Teaching and Learning.*

Reflective Protocols for Collaborative Examination of Student Work

Looking at student work has always been a part of a teacher's work. Typically this work has been done in isolation. As benefits of collaborative reflective practice and standards for student learning have increased, so, too, has interest in examining student work with colleagues in order to probe more deeply the work students do and to consider implications for instruction.

Examining student work requires inquiry. Teachers ask questions about practice, about students, and about student work—rather than seeking to just reinforce what they already know. Teachers bring student work to colleagues for shared reflection and insight that can lead to new instructional approaches, better ways to assess learning, and identification of gaps in the curriculum. Often, the work of students reveals positive growth resulting from specific teaching practices. By examining work together, collegial support develops, as well.

Examining student work is best done in four- to eight-person teams but is also valuable in mentor–new teacher partnerships. Usually a team meets during regularly scheduled or predetermined times, such as team meetings, monthly staff meetings, or staff development days. Such teams often are configured around a common grade level or subject area, although valuable insight is offered when teams cross grade levels or subject areas. In one school, for example, cross-grade-level configurations combined general educators, special educators, ELL teachers, and other specialists , resulting in schoolwide understanding of the district math curriculum that previously had not been collectively understood or consistently implemented. Teachers came to realize how their work with students impacted math learning experiences across all grades.

At the heart of examining student work is a protocol that articulates a step-by-step collaborative process for eliciting reflection about student work and the clues therein about student understanding, assessment, and instructional practices. There are distinct advantages in adhering to a structured protocol. Clear expectations create a sense of safety which fosters greater reflection and sharing. Multiple viewpoints are intentionally solicited. And student work is probed more deeply than might typically occur.

Numerous protocols have been developed for examining student work. We introduce two here. The Standards in Practice Protocol, developed by Ruth Mitchell of the Education Trust (http://www2.edtrust.org), begins with teachers examining a specific assignment to determine the demands of the task and how well it aligns with district or state standards. Teachers then share and score student work, analyzing scoring differences among group members, which leads to greater consensus over time. Also fostered are substantial discussions about the quality of an assessment or about the ways in which different instructional approaches produce different levels of achievement. This protocol works especially well for common assessments used by multiple teachers but also can be used for improving an individual teacher's assessment of a key learning goal.

The Collaborative Assessment Protocol, developed by Steve Seidel of Project Zero at Harvard University (http://www.pz.harvard.edu), is a good choice for guiding thinking about common goals within a school or district, such as writing across the grades or throughout subject-area courses. It works well when each teacher brings three to six pieces of work around a common assessment, skill area, or concept. The student learning goal is the frame of reference for examining the work. This protocol is highly driven by evidence or data. Team members look at the work for "evidence" of student strengths, misunderstandings, or errors. Use of this protocol invites multiple teachers to bring work each time and works well to track student progress across a school year.

A protocol for examining student work that was based on the work of these authors but developed specifically for use in the Student Work Initiative at the Intermediate District 287 PREP Center, Plymouth, Minnesota, is located in Table 5.6 and is also available as Resource 5.E at the end of this book. More information about the two protocols described here, and others, is available from the Looking At Student Work Collaborative (www.lasw .org) and the District 287 PREP Center (www.prepcenter.org).

Regardless of the protocol used, it is important to not just "do a protocol" but to have focused, in-depth, reflective conversations about teaching and learning and how teachers can capture strong results in the work of students. In their work, students tell us what they are learning. It is the evidence they leave behind for teachers to ponder, as would an archaeologist analyzing artifacts from a site. What clues are students leaving about what educators intend them to learn? The process of examining student work helps educators extract important messages to affirm success in teaching and learning and to identify strategies for continuous improvement by both students and teachers. *Contributed by Nancy A. Nutting of Minneapolis Minnesota, and Cindy Stevenson of the Lakeville Public Schools, Minnesota.*

Photographs to Prompt Sharing, Understanding, and Critical Reflection

A team of middle school teachers developed an "urgent curiosity" about the intersection of their teaching practices and six students considered at risk for being lost within the education system or, worse, for leaving school (Kroeger et al., 2004). They developed an action research project that employed two strategies, open-ended interviews and Photovoice (Wang & Burris, 1997), in an attempt to understand their students better and develop stronger

Table 5.6   Protocol for Collaboratively Examining Student Work

1. Get started and Study the Student Work (15 minutes)
   - Group members identify the learning goal correlated with the student work.
   - Group members individually look at student work and make notes about the strengths and weaknesses evident in the work.

2. Describe the work: what do you see? (20 minutes)
   - Group members describe what they see in the work.
     a) What are the specific skills and understandings evident in the work?
     b) What don't students know as evidenced in or missing from the work?

3. Identify next steps for instruction (20 minutes)
   - Everyone is invited to share ideas for the next instructional steps to improve achievement toward and beyond lesson objective:
     a) How have group members approached these skills and concepts in the past? What instructional strategies did they focus on since last session?
     b) How can group members build on the skills/concepts evidenced in the work?
     c) What will each member of the group do within his/her instructional setting to improve learning in this area?
     d) What ideas does this generate for the group or school?

4. Reflect on the experience and identify next steps for staff development (5 minutes)
   - Group discusses how the protocol process is working.
   - Group identifies any needed professional development or resources.
   - Group schedules next review of student work and determines the learning goal on which to focus and the type of work to bring.

SOURCE: Developed by Nancy Nutting, consultant from Minneapolis, Minnesota, and Cindy Stevenson of the Lakeville Public Schools, Minnesota.

bonds. Here we focus on the use of Photovoice, which involves taking photographs to document various aspects of one's life and using the photographs to prompt sharing stories about one's life.

The six students were provided disposable cameras and asked to "take pictures that depicted their lives as learners" (Kroeger et al., p. 51). Once the photos were developed, the students selected and titled them to be placed in an album. Before the photographs, conversations were largely teacher-directed. Students were reluctant participants. Once the photographs became part of the conversations, the balance of interaction shifted dramatically. "[Students] eagerly shared their photographs and the stories that accompanied them. On the basis of the photo prompts, students—individually and as a group—interpreted, explained, and even re-explained the meaning and context of the photographs" (p. 51). The enthusiasm was palpable.

A subject commonly photographed by students was animals and pets. Initially this student interest was noted only casually by the teachers. Over time, the teachers came to recognize and value this as a topic of significant importance to the students. When asked why animals were important, one student shared, "You can tell [animals] anything, and they won't tell anyone else behind your back" (Kroeger et al., p. 53). Another explained, "They are like friends, and you can actually talk to them and stuff" (p. 53). In offering these responses, the teachers recognized themes of trust and confidentiality as issues of significance to the students.

Listening to students tell their stories revealed more about their real interests and also about their experiences and reflections about school. The teachers developed a heightened awareness about how most of school is explicitly conceived and directed by teachers. Student voices are rarely heard, valued, or acted upon. This understanding prompted more in-depth reflection around Paulo Freire's view that the recurring themes of education should come from the experiences and perspectives of the individuals being oppressed.

Through use of the photographs and the related storytelling, the teachers learned more about each student as a whole person and more about the students' experiences and perceptions of school, which fostered stronger personal connections between the students and the teachers. More knowledge of the students supported greater differentiation and options in instructional situations. Another outcome was more positive relationships with parents of these children. One teacher explained, "As Photovoice proceeded, Eric began to report to his mother that his teachers actually wanted him in school. By the end of the year she [the mother] had become part of the team" (Kroeger et al., p. 56). It is truly remarkable how the genuine concern led to inquiry by a teaching team that resulted in trying a different way to connect with students and that did, indeed, foster learning and action for the benefit of students. The team of middle school teachers offered the following final thoughts:

> When, as teachers, we reach that place where we no longer understand the struggling student, when we hear ourselves saying, I've tried everything—or worse—nothing is working, it is then that we need to take a step back and listen. We listen to the student. We listen to the environment. We listen to ourselves and then we reflect on our practice. While the simple act of reflection does not guarantee critical insight, it is the place to begin. (Kroeger et al., 2004, p. 56)

What types of possibilities for learning may grow from efforts such as this, when students and adults engage in inquiry together? What else might we learn from the children? In what ways are we already listening to children in our current work? In what ways can we do better?

Metaphors and Synectics

Metaphors (also described in Chapter 3) offer a way to give meaning to an experience or object symbolically. "Metaphor is a transfer of meaning from one object to another on the basis of perceived similarity" (Taggart & Wilson, 1998, p. 188). Hagstrom, Hubbard, Hurtig, Mortola, Ostrow, and White (2000) used metaphor to write about their experiences as teachers. They completed the sentence stem "Teaching is like . . ." with responses that included the ocean, making bread, and geology. Then they wrote short essays to further explain their metaphor choice. Shared use of metaphors enriched their individual and collective understanding of life as a teacher. This process "resulted in some of the most joyful and most thought provoking writing we have ever done" (p. 25).

A specific type of metaphor, referred to as *synectics,* can be an effective and fun way to close a group session by eliciting higher-level thinking and application. One way to do this is to invite each small group to write down four nouns—for example, "cat, chocolate, bicycle, bus." Then ask that they select one of the nouns to complete the following sentence: X is like X because . . . Here are two examples: (a) Dialogue is like chocolate, because it is rich, you share it with people who are close to you, and you want it to last a long time; (b) Coteaching is like riding a bicycle, because it takes two strong wheels working together to get anywhere.

A final idea for use of metaphor in groups is to capture both current and desired future states. For example, during initiation into reflective practice, a team of teachers was asked to identify a metaphor for how reflection felt very early in the learning process and how they hoped it would feel by the end of the year. Here is a sample response: "Reflective practice now feels like an elephant because it is big, heavy, bulky, and slow. In the spring, I hope it will feel like a monkey—flexible, flowing, responsive, and moving between different levels."

Talking Cards

Talking Cards is a strategy for obtaining full but anonymous participation in a group context. Each member is provided with index cards and the same color felt-tip pen or marker. A question is posed to the group, and members write their responses on index cards (one idea or response per card). All the index cards are then collected and laid out for group members to see and sort the cards into clusters or themes to make sense of all the ideas shared. The group then labels each cluster. This results in a comprehensive presentation of group members' collective perspectives that can be used to understand issues and make well-informed decisions.

We use this strategy regularly with groups of teachers. For example, we used a variation of this process to help teams of general educators, special educators, and English-language teachers reflect on their first few months of team teaching. First they were asked, "If you were to explain your team teaching approach to another school, what features would you point out?" Their descriptions were outlined on poster paper, posted, and explained to the other teams.

Second, each teacher was asked to respond to four questions, individually and anonymously, using a different-colored index card for each question. This prompted perspective sharing about how well the team teaching was working or not. The questions were as follows:

- What have been the advantages of team teaching for students? (green cards)
- What have been the disadvantages of team teaching for students? (pink cards)
- What have been the advantages of team teaching for the adults? (yellow cards)
- What have been the disadvantages of team teaching for the adults? (blue cards)

The teachers could contribute as many responses as they wanted for each question. They simply wrote each response on an individual card. When all the teachers finished writing, the cards were collected, sorted by color, displayed on the table or floor, and sorted into clusters. The clusters were then labeled. For example, cluster labels that were related to advantages for students included "modeling from peers" and "closer relationships with classmates." Cluster labels for adult team-member advantages included "learning ideas from other teachers" and "feeling more connected to team members."

Last, each group inquired about what this means, the so-what and now-what aspects of the reflection process. Questions included, "What is our overall assessment of how things have been going? What strengths do we want to maximize? How might we reduce the disadvantages? What might be our next steps for improving how we teach and learn together?" The card responses can also be typed to provide a record for more reflection at a later point. The conversation that occurs in the sorting, clustering, and inquiry aspects of this process is invaluable. This is when the individual and collective group learning occurs.

Six Hats

Recall from Chapter 2 the description of ways to reframe experiences. Six Hats is another reframing tool that assists groups in thinking about how to move forward. Proposed by de Bono (1970), this process requires groups to consider the implications of potential actions or interventions from six different perspectives. For example, a schoolwide teacher planning team posed the following question to themselves: "If we were to propose a bolder focus on reflective practice in our high school, what should we be thinking about in terms of implementation supports and potential issues?" The principal led the reflective conversation by actually wearing six different-colored hats (i.e., frames) in guiding the group's thinking about each perspective. Following is a sampling of the responses that emerged when considering each "hat":

- The white hat symbolizes data: What does research say about reflective practice? How effective has it been, and in what circumstances? How much does it cost to implement?
- The yellow hat symbolizes sunshine: There will be a better appreciation of differences. This will boost staff morale! Students will benefit from improved instruction. Problem-solving and perspective-taking skills will increase.
- The black hat symbolizes caution: This will be a hard idea to sell. The staff will see it as another fad. The site council will want to see the budgetary implications. People who think they are doing well may be disillusioned; they may even leave. It is going to take a lot of time and resources to get it off the ground.
- The red hat symbolizes emotion: Some of the teachers are going to panic; others will see it as touchy-feely nonsense. People will feel so much more connected to one another. I am excited about all the possibilities.
- The green hat symbolizes growth: We will all learn so much. I will become a better teacher, maybe even a better person. This will be a challenge, but I could use some new ways of thinking about meaningful assessment. Reflecting on our teaching with other staff members will result in a wider array of instructional strategies.
- The blue hat symbolizes process: We will have to put together information to share with the staff and site council. What team of teachers could examine the schedule to figure out when groups could meet? A kickoff during workshop week could get us off to a good start next school year. There will need to be a lead team to keep this on the front burner.

By engaging in conversation from each of the different perspectives, the group was able to anticipate needs and responses of staff. This process supported their reflection-for-action and resulted in a plan for moving forward. In debriefing the six-hats process, participants shared insights about the type of perspective they typically bring to a conversation. Some recognized they quickly assume a cautious or data-based way of thinking. Others respond positively, because they home in on the growth potential. Still others move immediately to planning a process for getting things done. These personal insights were constructive, in that each member could see strengths in the varied perspectives and recognize that variation reflected individual diversity. Individual and shared understanding were increased by this reframing exercise.

EXPLORE Alternative Viewpoints

Pierce and Kalkman (2003) present EXPLORE, a directed reflection strategy they use to increase students' recognition and understanding of their own and others' views and to then seek alternative and external views. Here is their description of the strategy:

- *Examine* opinions. Initially, students are presented with a controversial statement and are asked to commit themselves to a position relative to that issue.
- Create *pairs*. People who agree with the statement raise their right hands, while people who disagree raise their left hands. Class members stand and walk up to someone with whom they can grasp opposite hands.
- *Listen.* Each member of a pair takes a turn explaining his or her position. The other member is instructed to listen effectively enough to be able to summarize what was just stated so that the speaker can agree that the summary was accurate.
- *Organize.* When both people's positions have been heard accurately, they organize the information into a compare/contrast matrix.
- *Research.* Each member of the pair conducts research to determine what the literature says about the conditions under which either approach to the issue could be correct.
- *Evaluation.* Members of each pair share their findings and agree on research-based statements. (Pierce & Kalkman, 2003, p. 129)

This strategy or specific steps within this strategy could be easily adopted for use in practice settings, such as departmental or schoolwide considerations of existing practices or proposed initiatives. Instead of members of each of the many pairs engaging in the organization, research, and evaluation steps independently, this could be done collaboratively in groups. Further, there would be practice situations in which decisions would need to be made about a common direction for proceeding. Understanding alternative views and considering external information (e.g., research) would serve as part of the dialogue in which all members engage prior to moving forward into decision making. Regardless of the specific decision made, this type of approach ensures recognition and consideration of multiple perspectives.

Self-Organized Teacher Support Groups

In the reflective practice literature, there is support for self-organized learning groups. Rich (1992) reports on voluntary teacher groups that were self-organized to meet teacher needs for support around curriculum and instruction. This specific effort grew from teacher frustration with the manner in which a district-sponsored all-day workshop was conducted. One stated,

We needed time to talk about how the program might look in practice. The curriculum was readable and we knew the theory, but we wanted to talk to other teachers about what to do with the new materials and about how to manage the program. We were also concerned about balancing the program to address skills and children's needs. (p. 33)

Two teachers asked others who shared this frustration to join with them in planning their own professional-development program. Two weeks later, seven teachers went to the first meeting at one teacher's home. They decided to meet monthly and to include discussion of professional reading and sharing of classroom practices and learning. Responsibility for choosing and distributing articles was rotated. Participants were also encouraged to bring a friend.

Over the years, the group developed a newsletter that compiled their learning about effective classroom practice, shared their learning at faculty meetings, and presented workshops to other interested teachers. As the group grew, subgroups were formed to keep the size manageable, but participants continued to meet as a whole group every couple of months. Eventually, there were voluntary teacher-support groups in every section of the city.

Teacher Dialogues

Arnold (1995) describes teacher dialogues that were used to reflect on instructional practice. The dialogues were held at least twice each month during the school day and included four to five teachers and a leader. Initially, the leader assumed primary responsibility for facilitating conversation by posing reflective questions. Topics for reflection varied depending on teacher interests and needs, such as discussing application of state-curricular frameworks. Research was frequently reviewed in the dialogues, as well. On some occasions, teachers arranged to observe one another teaching, which enriched the subsequent dialogues. The dialogues were viewed as a successful approach to learning when teachers

(a) feel comfortable enough to reveal problems in their own instructional program and seek solutions from the groups; (b) bring in ideas they found to be especially successful with their class and urge others to try them; (c) volunteer to share new research; (d) invite the group to see a lesson in their class; and (e) . . . [find that a] need for the leader decreases because of the group's increased capacity for leadership. (p. 35)

Four factors to consider in the development of teacher dialogues were offered: scheduling of time during the school day; use of reflective questions to focus on instructional practice and student learning; selection of a knowledgeable and skillful facilitative leader who is a good teacher; and evaluation of the effectiveness of the dialogues, including an oral reflection at the end of each session.

Video Clubs

Videotapes provide an "objective record of what actually took place" in a specific instructional context (Wallace, 1991, p. 8, as cited in Bailey, Curtis, & Nunan, 1998, p. 553). Sherin (2000) explains that video clubs "are opportunities for teachers to review their classroom interactions in ways that are different from their standard daily practices" (p. 36). Groups of four teachers gather monthly to watch and then converse about short (10-minute) segments of videotaped teaching. The purpose is to specifically examine and reflect on instructional practice, *not* to evaluate. Use of video allows teachers to narrow their view of classroom interactions. Unlike being in the act of teaching, the teacher does not have to attend to the entire group. Individual or small groups of students can be observed more carefully. Teachers can also observe how they responded, then consider why they responded in that way and consider alternatives. A significant finding was that "teachers reported not only increased understanding when reflecting on video, but also paying more attention to student responses during instruction" (Sherin, 2000, p. 37). In a study of 87 in-service and preservice teachers, 87 percent stated that "seeing themselves on videotape had made them aware of habits and mannerisms that they were now trying to change" (Wallace, 1979, p. 13). This result indicates that reflection-on-action subsequently increased reflection-in-action.

Teacher Book Clubs

Goldberg and Pesko (2000) initiated teacher book clubs, based on a belief that literacy instruction would improve if teachers themselves were involved in reading and reflecting on literature. The selections were plea-sure reading, not professional reading. This recreated an opportunity to personalize the experience of literature and better understand the range of reading styles and reading responses of students. "We read and discuss literature, analyze our personal preferences for reading, reflect on class-room practices, and modify classroom practices on the basis of what we have learned" (p. 39).

Reflection Roundtables

We began the use of reflection roundtables as a way of gathering medium-sized groups of teachers within our partnership schools to engage in conversations about a variety of issues and topics. Early in our work with one school, we needed a schoolwide perspective about how general and special educators worked together, the strengths and challenges in their present way of providing services to students with disabilities, and the areas or ideas for improvement that would make a difference for students. We did not want to hear from only a handful of teachers or a few lead teams. We also did not want to interact with the entire faculty at once. We wanted the interaction to be a reflection and learning opportunity for all those involved. We held a series of three roundtable conversations; each had a mix of eight to 12 teachers and lasted about 90 minutes. These round-tables increased our understanding and the understanding of all the teachers engaged in the conversation. It also was the start of trust and rela-tionship building. The reflection roundtable continued to be used as a way to solicit input, feedback, and, ultimately, decision making about new directions for service provision.

Another use of reflection roundtables occurred in a school that had successfully piloted a general educator and special educator coteaching model of instruction during language arts and math. In the spring of the pilot year, the entire faculty needed to be involved in a conversation about implementation and outcomes of the coteaching model. A series of round-table conversations was held with small groups of teachers, this time homogeneously grouped. We sat around small tables and asked partici-pants what they wanted to know about the pilot. We shared what the coteaching looked like in each of the pilot classrooms, what the teachers thought about it, and how the students had responded. We were careful to disclose a balanced view of the process and outcomes. Participants asked questions and expressed concerns and special considerations. The cumula-tive learning and perspectives offered during the roundtable conversa-tions were then (anonymously) shared during an extended faculty meeting. The faculty talked further in small groups during the meeting and, ultimately, made the decision to expand coteaching in specific ways and with specific cautions.

Reflection roundtables have been an effective means of sharing, learning, understanding, and relationship building that ultimately sup-port decision making. They offer opportunities for dialogue before moving toward decision making. They have been effective because of the relatively small group size, intentional group composition (heterogeneous or homo-geneous depending on purpose), high degrees of participation, initial focus on reflection and inquiry through dialogue, and multiple gatherings and conversations before decision making.

Think Tank Structure

A group of five elementary teachers and three university professors developed a discourse community that they referred to as a Think Tank, which focused on learning more about how children acquire new vocabu-lary (Henry et al., 1999). They met for dinner every six to eight weeks throughout a school year to reflect on their experiencing and thinking about promoting vocabulary with students. "Through dialogue, the members of this group shared their expertise over time, building a common voice and a common knowledge base" (p. 258). Five expectations emerged as important in their group learning: safety built on trust, dialogue as a means of learning, collaboration among equals, personal commitment, and time together. They identified several functions of their interactions: description, analysis, expansion, summarizing, and defining. Outcomes indicated enhanced knowledge related to the content focus (vocabulary learning in students) and the reflection and learning process.

Interactive Reflective Teaching Seminars

Seminars that included preservice teachers, cooperating teachers and principals, and college faculty members provided a means for interactive reflection on teaching practice (Diss, Buckley, & Pfau, 1992). "Reflective teaching is an introspective process of examining one's own teaching behavior" (p. 28). The focus of reflection was the instructional decision-making process of the teachers to gain insight about decision making in action. "Reflective teachers identified the strengths and weaknesses of their instructional decisions through inquiry, observations, peer interaction, and analysis to improve classroom decision making" (p. 28). The interactive seminars occurred four times in a semester. In addition to attending the seminars, preservice teachers observed experienced teachers for a total of 16 hours over the course of a semester. Prior to the observations, they identified specific questions about teaching that guided their observations. In the words of the authors,

> participants' reactions to the program were extremely favorable. Teachers reported that the seminars contributed to their professional growth by: (a) increasing their awareness of the need to think critically and creatively about decision making; (b) broadening their teaching repertoires; (c) providing confirmation of their effective teaching methods; and (d) reinforcing the value of ongoing reflective teaching. (Diss et. al., 1992, p. 30)

Teachers rarely talk together about their practice, which made the interactive design of the program especially valuable. Also valued was the mix of preservice and experienced teachers.

Guided Storytelling to Prompt Reflection for Action

The Professional Development School (PDS) context offers rich opportunities for reflection and learning, not only for preservice teachers but for experienced teachers and university faculty, as well. Greater proximity and collaboration in this context can also give rise to more conflicts. Such was the case in a PDS described by Cooner and Tochterman (2004). One specific area of conflict involved discrepancies between the views of curriculum and teaching advocated by university faculty and those experienced by student teachers in the PDS practice setting. Instead of allowing the conflict to result in severed ties, a decision was made to productively and collaboratively engage the conflict.

University faculty and PDS teachers formed a steering committee intended "to repair practice through collaboration, examination, and development of theory" (Cooner & Tochterman, 2004, p. 186). Modeled after the Joint Storytelling Project of the National Education Association Ground (Wallace, 1996), guided storytelling was used as a way to share experiences and views and to prompt reflection, dialogue and collaboratively determined action. The authors explain, "In the process of telling and re-telling the stories, teachers reflect on their experiences and learn new and different lessons from them each time. Therefore, story telling combined with the process of reflection can be educative" (p. 185).

Guided by a facilitator and honoring established ground rules, teachers told their personal stories about the curriculum conflict. After all stories were shared, everyone engaged in dialogue about the stories and identified themes. Emerging from the reflection and dialogue prompted by the stories was a more collaborative partnership that resulted in changes in university courses and in professional teaching practices in the school. PDS teachers became more involved in teaching university classes, initially assisting with small groups and then assuming more active coteaching roles. They also began experimenting with new practices in their classrooms at the PDS.

Guided storytelling was an effective way to understand varied perspectives, to prompt inquiry, and to foster new insights and learning. Genuine partnerships were established in which explicit connections were made between practice in authentic school settings and theory and research. Significantly, new practices were cocreated and put into use.

It is encouraging to know of efforts that seek to connect educators who bring different viewpoints and experiences "to the table" to grapple with issues around "swamp" knowledge and "high hard ground" knowledge (recall Schön's work in Chapter 2) in hopes of ultimately developing (or, as in this case, cocreating) strengthened practices that positively impact students.

GETTING STARTED WITH REFLECTIVE PRACTICE IN SMALL GROUPS AND TEAMS

We opened this chapter suggesting that many educators are on meeting overload, then offered a lengthy review of key considerations in working together as a team, and ended the chapter with numerous examples of small groups and teams engaged in meaningful reflective learning experiences. As a way to further understand the place of face-to-face meeting time in schools, we ask graduate students in a collaboration course to create a list of groups (e.g., teams, committees, PLCs) that meet in their respective schools. We then ask them to estimate the amount of time spent in meetings and to identify groups that seem to be effective. Their findings are reliably disappointing and enlightening—disappointing because few groups meet about teaching and learning and because very little learning occurs for group members. and enlightening because of the clarity that emerges about the need to shift priorities in how face-to-face time is utilized in schools. We would like to suggest that the first priority for educators spending time together should be reflection and learning focused on students and instruction. As you reflect on how meeting time might be best utilized in your school, consider the following questions. (Refer to Resource 5.F for a modified set of these questions that can be copied and used for professional learning purposes.)

- What is the purpose of the group? What is the focus for learning? What are the desired outcomes? Which students are likely to benefit from the learning that occurs within this group of educators? How conflicted is the focus of the group?
- How structured will the group process need to be to address the given purpose? Is there a specific time frame that must be honored? What kind of design will best promote participation, learning, and positive outcomes?
- Should an existing group or team of individuals convene? Should additional individuals be included? Does a new group need to be configured?
- Who should be part of the group? Who has an important perspective to share? Who will be expected to follow through with the outcomes?
- How big should the group be? If a large number of people are involved, how can their participation be promoted? When might we need to consider breaking into smaller groups?
- Do we need to assign specific group roles? Should they be rotated? Who will assume lead roles in the group? Might two teachers share responsibility for organizing, communicating, and preparing? Is a facilitator needed? If so, who might that be?
- Do the group members know one another well? If they do not, how should we explicitly focus on developing relationships and trust?
- What experiences do group members have with reflection and learning? How intentional do we need to be about development of individual and group capacities for reflecting, learning, and working together?

- How will we determine the effectiveness of the group process? What content and process reflection strategies might we use?
- What were some of your favorite examples from this chapter, and why? Which stories and strategies offered the most hope for you in your current setting? What ideas were you most challenged by?

The Chapter Reflection Page (Figure 5.8) can be used to jot down your thoughts in response to these questions. You may also want to make notes, drawings, or mind maps about the learning and insights that were most significant for you as you read this chapter.

When reflecting in groups or teams, the potential emerges to influence more broadly the educational practices within and throughout the school. This potential significantly increases when multiple groups and teams embed reflective practices in their work and when efforts expand to include the vast majority of individuals and groups in a school. The sustainability of groups depends on four factors: a meaningful and continuing purpose; positive and productive working relationships; the opportunity for learning, growth, and contribution; and the outcomes realized by students. These factors provide a framework for evaluating the effectiveness, or likelihood of effectiveness, in schools. We invite you to keep these factors in mind as you read Chapter 6, which more carefully examines issues of expanded and sustainable schoolwide reflective practice.

Figure 5.8   Chapter Reflection Page

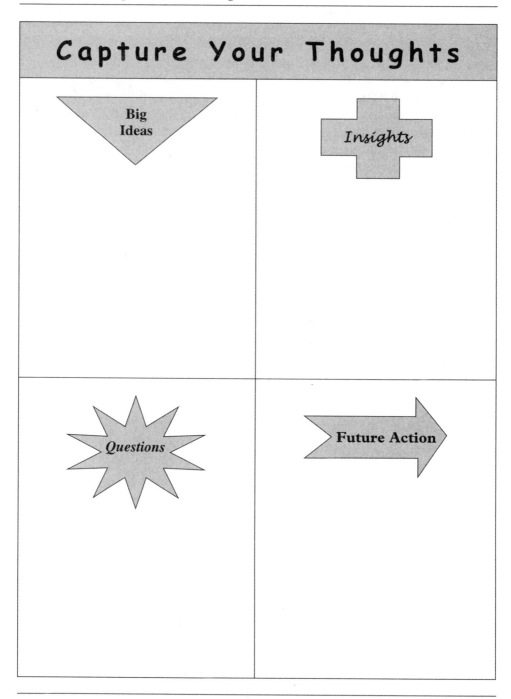

6

Schoolwide Reflective Practice

Reflective organizations are places where people can bring themselves fully to work. Being fully present at work is a remarkable and powerful experience, all the more so if one contrasts it experientially with its opposite, disconnection or alienation.

—Ellen Schall (1995, p. 207), *Learning to Love the Swamp*

A principal who was new to a building arrived at a faculty meeting several weeks into the school year and announced, "Please get your coats and meet me in the parking lot." Somewhat perplexed, the faculty complied with this request. As soon as everyone reconvened in the parking lot, the principal explained that in his short time in the building, he had noticed that the *real* meetings among faculty occurred in the parking lot. He wanted to have a real meeting, one in which faculty members actively participated in a process of sharing, listening, inquiring, and learning. How do we get more real meetings occurring in schools? How do we shift the focus of face-to-face time, at faculty meetings and elsewhere, to opportunities for learning. What topics of interaction would inspire ongoing reflection and inquiry on a schoolwide basis? What conditions would promote honest, open exchanges among staff members? Who leads the process? Where do you start?

Costa and Kallick (2000b) suggest that "every school's goal should be to habituate reflection throughout the organization—individually and collectively, with teachers, students, and the school community" (p. 60). Indeed, the greatest potential for reflective practice to renew schools lies with the collective thinking, inquiry, understanding, and action that can result from schoolwide engagement around a compelling purpose and an inspiring vision. Facilitating reflective practices at the organizational level, however, is much more complex than at the individual, partner, or small-group levels.

Organizational learning is more complex and dynamic than a mere magnification of individual learning. The level of complexity increases tremendously when we go from a single individual to a large collection of diverse individuals. Issues of motivation and reward, for instance, which are an integral part of human learning, become doubly complicated within organizations. Although the meaning of the term *learning* remains essentially the same as in the individual case, the learning process is fundamentally different at the organizational level (Kim, 1993, p. 40).

What would schoolwide reflective practice look like? What would you see and hear that would suggest the presence of authentic inquiry about practice? If you could take off the roof of a school to get a full (bird's-eye) view of how and where groups of people reflect and learn together, what would you hope to see? What might they be conversing about? School-wide reflective practice does not mean that everyone is reflecting on the same thing in the same way at the same time. At times, entire faculties participate in collective, schoolwide initiatives. At other times, reflective practices are embedded in a variety of professional learning activities throughout the school. Envision lots of groups learning throughout a school, some of them ongoing, others formed around specific tasks and then disbanded when their work is completed. What matters most is that all staff members are involved in some type of learning or shared-work initiative that relates to schoolwide priorities or performance goals, in addition to continuing their own individual reflection and learning aimed at improving their professional practice. As reflection increases, errors decrease (Argyris, 1977): more thought means better decisions. Consider the cumulative positive effects if such error detection and correction were to happen on a schoolwide basis.

Here are some examples of what schoolwide reflective practice could look like. An entire school staff might be involved in study groups on a common topic, such as reading in the content areas or performance assessment. Interdisciplinary groups might form to exchange disciplinary perspectives to create a set of integrated student outcomes that would be addressed within each discipline. Teachers from one subject area might join to create common assessments for use across all sections of designated courses. Cross-grade-level teams might explore best practices for effective student transitions between grades. A schoolwide curriculum adoption might initially require teachers from across grade levels to meet to determine where and how state standards are located within the curriculum.

The ultimate goal of schoolwide reflective practices is continuous improvement of organizational, team, and individual practices in order to increase student learning. Increased student learning requires coherence and continuity in the educational experience for students, which requires strong connections among educators throughout the school. Coherence results when resources are allocated to align staff, schedules, and materials in support of "a common instructional framework [that] guides curriculum, teaching, assessment, and learning climate. The framework combines specific expectations for student learning, with specific strategies and materials to guide teaching and assessment" (Newmann, Smith, Allensworth, & Bryk, 2001, p. 299). Some students, particularly those who tend to be marginalized from mainstream school opportunities, experience high degrees of fragmentation, disconnection, and depersonalization. Such students are placed at risk for psychological and, eventually, physical disengagement.

For this reason we tell teachers, "If the adults are separate, the kids will be separate." Teachers must form strong relationships, not only with students, but with each other, throughout the school and across typical structures and groupings, so that coherence and social support are realized. The relationships among educators serve as the pathways through which information and resources flow throughout the school. Strong collegial relationships are the means by which teachers can connect students to the learning, personnel, and social resources available in the wider school community. Coherence and continuity can be achieved as the web of relationships forms among teachers and extends to include and support students. As the connections become dense and the strands become strong, all students are more likely to access a meaningful, connected, well–supported, high-quality educational experience. Only when each and every student is provided a high-quality program can the purpose of public education be realized. Within a connected, caring, and competent community of educators, no student will fall through open spaces in the web. Increasing the amount, diversity, and strength of relationships requires intentional focus by the formal and informal leaders in a school. Margaret Wheatley (1992) explains that relationships, not formal roles or positions, are the means by which the collective power of an organization is realized.

In this chapter, we describe considerations for reflective practice that come into play especially at the schoolwide level. As suggested earlier, success at the organizational level is more complicated and requires more intentional focus on design. Our Theory of Reflective Practice (Figure 6.1) applies at this organizational level of practice, as it did at the group, partner, and individual levels. Orchestrating the pausing, inquiry, thinking,

Figure 6.1   Theory of Action for Reflective Practice

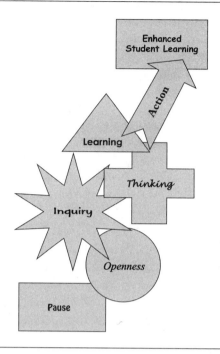

learning, and action in some collective fashion, however, presents many more challenges and many more opportunities. Later in this chapter we describe the experience of numerous schools in which reflective practices were embedded in schoolwide improvement efforts. We also share some smaller-scale but still schoolwide examples, along with additional strategies and ideas for fostering schoolwide reflective practices. Finally we offer a comprehensive set of questions to prompt thinking and planning for getting started with schoolwide reflective practices.

SPECIAL CONSIDERATIONS FOR SCHOOLWIDE REFLECTIVE PRACTICES

There is no one right way to employ reflective practices on a school-wide basis. In fact, the inherent messiness of designing for schoolwide reflective practices could easily overwhelm one with possibilities, as well as complexity. The "ready-fire-aim" approach advocated by Fullan (2001b) indicates that a certain amount of getting ready is necessary but that the most informed planning and decision making for guiding future action will arise from ongoing reflection throughout the implementation process. Just as navigating a plane or sailboat involves a process of continual read-justments to stay on course, so, too, does leading school renewal.

Research on change in schools reveals general patterns and tendencies, but not absolute ones. Why? Because of the plentiful local variables that are not uniform across all practice contexts and that cannot be controlled, such as people, resources, and politics. To be successful, application of change models always involves thoughtful design and ongoing reflection, in, on, and for action. Local application of such models necessarily invokes ongoing refinements and accommodations (Fullan, 2001b). Schön's conception of high, hard ground knowledge (theory and research) versus swamp knowledge (contextual knowledge from practice) is again helpful.

Similarly, Etienne Wenger (1998) explains that as living systems, communities of practice "cannot be legislated into existence or defined by decree. They can be recognized, supported, encouraged, and nurtured, but they are not reified, designable units" (p. 229). Further, he provides the following explanations:

- "One can design systems of accountability and policies for Communities of Practice to live by, but one cannot design the practices that will emerge in response to such institutional systems."
- "One can design roles, but one cannot design the identities that will be constructed through these roles."
- "One can design visions, but one cannot design the allegiance necessary to align energies behind those visions."
- "One can produce affordances for the negotiation of meaning, but not meaning itself."
- "One can design work processes, but not work practices."
- "One can design a curriculum, but not learning."
- "One can attempt to institutionalize a Community of Practice, but the Community of Practice itself will slip through the cracks and remain distinct from its institutionalization." (p. 229)

These words capture well the essence of work in living systems, perhaps especially those occupied by complex inhabitants, such as human beings. The work is design work—ongoing creative design work informed by reflection and intended to spark learning. In these words we also understand the great promise of working in human systems: adaptability and limitless potential. Living systems can evolve into more efficient and effective ways of being. They are capable of renewal because they are alive.

An example of the living and evolving nature of learning work was illustrated in the reflections of McLeskey and Waldron (2002) on their many years of partnerships with educators focused on developing inclusive schools. They argue that professional development must be individually tailored to each school, stating, "the content and format for professional development is best determined by teachers and other stakeholders in the local school, as part of a schoolwide process of school improvement" (p. 163). By way of example, they share that prior to implementing inclusive practices, teachers in one school perceived no need for professional development focused on collaboration. Three months into the implementation process, however, several teachers identified collaboration training as a need and wondered why such professional development had not been built into the change process. The point is that those involved cannot really know what they need to learn until they begin to experience the change. Then the learner is ready and wanting to learn.

McLeskey and Waldron (2002) also point out the ripple effect, which suggests that any change in practice (such as instruction, assessment, grading, curriculum, scheduling) affects every other element in the system of practices. Each element exists in relationship to every other element, making change a multidimensional, complex undertaking. This concept supports, in part, their assertion that when creating inclusive schools, the needs of all students, not just those with disabilities, must be addressed. In effect, efforts to foster inclusivity become school improvement focused on everyone. Many students benefit from differentiation and personalization in the context of general education. Finally, they emphasize that in their work with many schools, professional development is the most effective strategy for ensuring continuous improvement instead of stagnation or decline to more traditional models.

In the following section we describe three significant considerations to guide the development of schoolwide reflective practices. First, we offer an overview of professional learning communities. Second, we share several models for thinking about facilitating change in schools. Third, we argue that leadership for reflective practices be shared and suggest strategies for fostering leadership that is shared among principals and teachers. In addition, most of the considerations for reflective practice in small groups or teams presented in Chapter 5 apply to schoolwide reflective practices, as well. "Schoolwide" is usually operationalized by means of participation in both small-group and whole-school interactions.

Professionals Learning in Community

> Why do palm trees survive hurricanes? They have strong root systems. They are flexible. They live in communities.
>
> —Attributed to Peter Russell

Over the past decade, there has been an increasing emphasis on schoolwide, as opposed to smaller-scale, improvement efforts. Smaller, often isolated, efforts, such as initiatives taken on by individual teachers, teachers at a grade level, or subject-area teachers, typically result in only isolated improvements, with few cumulative or longitudinal gains realized once students move on from those experiences. Spread of effects to other groups of students is unlikely without intentional efforts to design and support implementation of new practices with those students. This is one of the major reasons for the emergence of efforts intended to re-create schools as professional learning communities in which all members actively participate in ongoing improvement work. Fullan (2000b) explains,

> the existence of collaborative work cultures (or professional learning communities) makes a difference in how well students do in schools . . . we now have a much better idea of what is going on inside the black box of collaborative schools. (p. 581)

In successful schools, researchers have found that when educators are engaged in collective learning with an intentional focus on student learning, improvements in instructional practice result (Hord, 2004; Newmann & Wehlage, 1995). The factor to be underscored is the intentional focus on student learning. Schmoker (2004) makes it clear that when teachers meet, it cannot be assumed that conversations will focus on teaching and learning practices. Recall from the previous chapter that Supovitz (2002) found that teaming resulted in a more positive school culture but did not result in instructional improvement, except in the case of teaming that intentionally incorporated group instructional practices. In a major national study in Australia, Ingvarson, Meiers, and Beavis (2005) found a strong positive correlation between professional community and the reported positive impact on teacher knowledge and practice. In this study, professional community was operationalized as opportunities for teachers to talk about teaching practice and student learning and opportunities to share ideas and support each other in attempts to implement new practices. Again, the focus is on instructional level practice and students. Wenger (1998) asserts that the "real work" in organizations happens in communities of practice. Practice communities are closest to the real work, which, in the case of schools, is the relational and instructional interactions among teachers and with students.

Hord (1997) summarized the findings from numerous studies to identify outcomes for students and staff when schools organized themselves as professional learning communities. Students had lower rates of absenteeism and a reduced dropout rate, and they cut fewer classes. In some cases, larger academic gains were noted in math, science, history, and reading. In smaller high schools, increases in learning were also shown to be more equitably distributed throughout the school, with smaller achievement gaps among students. For staff, outcomes were documented related to improved practice and professional conditions for teaching. Also reported for teachers were higher levels of satisfaction and morale and, like the students, lower rates of absenteeism.

Based on a comprehensive review of research and related literature, Kruse, Louis, and Bryk (1995) proposed a framework for analyzing professional community in schools (Figure 6.2). This framework identifies potential benefits, defining characteristics, and organizational supports of professional learning communities in schools. The framework can be used to design, troubleshoot, and reflect on progress being made toward creating professional learning communities, and the authors suggest three potential benefits resulting from their establishment: increased teacher efficacy and empowerment, increased satisfaction that emerges from the dignity of being treated as respected and valued professionals, and collective responsibility for student learning. Also identified are five characteristics that define the presence of a school-based professional community: shared norms and values, reflective dialogue, deprivatization of practice (more openness and sharing about practices), a focus on student learning, and collaboration. Again, high in importance among these characteristics is a focus on student learning.

> Public conversations concerning practice within schools need to focus on four topics: academic content, the intelligent use of generic teaching strategies, the development of students, and the social conditions of schooling and issues of equity and justice. (Kruse, Louis, & Bryk, p. 30)

The structure and social resources identified in the framework are required to support the development of school-based professional communities. Among these supports are specific and important considerations for the design of schoolwide reflective practices, such as times to meet and talk, communication structures, and supportive leadership. These supports will be evident in the examples from practice described later in this chapter.

The professional-community framework (Kruse et al., 1995) has guided our thinking about the design and evaluation of various school improvement initiatives, including those that involve reflective practices. One modification that has proved useful is to reverse the direction of the arrows so that they point up, instead of down. This inversion emphasizes the foundational nature of the support (lower) level in the framework. Without the structural, social, and human-resource supports, the characteristics and benefits of professional learning communities will not emerge. These supports suggest a starting place from which to build the capacity for professional learning communities. They also prompt specific questions on which to reflect in the process of planning for improvement: Is there time to meet and talk? Do teachers work in proximity to others, thereby allowing access to each other? Is interdependence in teaching roles structured? Are channels and mechanisms for communication embedded in daily school functioning? Are teachers and schools empowered to engage fully and direct the progress of improvement? Is there openness,

Figure 6.2   School-Based Professional Community Framework

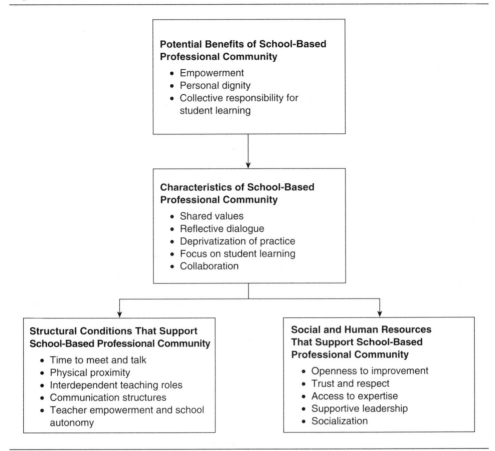

SOURCE: Kruse, S. D., Louis, K. S., & Bryk, A. (1995). "An Emerging Framework for Analyzing School-Based Professional Community." In K. S. Louis & S. D. Kruse (Eds.), *Professionalism and Community: Perspectives on Reforming Urban Schools* (p. 25). Copyright © by Corwin Press. Reprinted by permission of Corwin Press, Inc.

trust, and respect among educators? Is there sufficient access to the expertise needed to advance practices?

Before leaving this discussion on professional learning communities, we pass along to you some words of caution offered by two recognized experts on the topic. First, reflecting on the current state of professional learning communities, Rick DuFour (2004) recently wrote,

> [We are at a] critical juncture. . . . In this all too familiar cycle, initial enthusiasm gives way to confusion about the fundamental concepts driving the initiative, followed by inevitable implementation problems, the conclusion that the reform has failed to bring about the desired results, abandonment of the reform, and the launch of a new search for the next promising initiative. (p. 6)

Bruce Joyce (2004), reflecting on 40 years of research and experience, offers some important lessons of which to be mindful as we venture forward in a quest for learning communities. He notes the formidable force of school culture, specifically professional norms of isolation. Recollecting early forays into team teaching in the 1950s and 1960s, he describes "mass rebellion" by teachers resulting from a "collision with norms and structures of the workplace" (p. 78). Another of his lessons, and one that has been reiterated throughout this book, is that structures are a necessary but insufficient condition for collaborative learning. Further, he emphasizes the need to deeply involve both teachers (the people who make the changes in practice that directly impacts students) and administrators (the people who create structural and resource supports). Finally, Joyce references one of the findings from the work of Miles and Huberman: "commitment follows competence." This finding suggests that teachers must experience success with changes if they are to continue to engage and extend new practices.

We, too, worry that PLCs will become another here today, gone tomorrow initiative of small consequence unless the focus is unequivocally on learning by the grown-ups such that meaningful and substantial improvements result for students. The challenge becomes one of how to have the words *professional learning community* truly reflect meaningful learning that happens among professionals who are in some way intentionally committed to learning together.

Change at the Organizational Level

Fostering schoolwide reflective practices requires an understanding of how individual staff members respond to change and of how to design and support change efforts from an organizational perspective. Before describing several change models, we return to the preeminence of trust, this time as an organizational resource for improvement. Recall that in Chapter 2 we introduced Bryk and Schneider's (2002) concept of relational trust. The focus there was the significance of trust as a dynamic that influences the willingness of individuals to be open about their practices and reflect with others. Here we turn our attention to their assertions about the significance of trust at the organizational level:

Specifically, we see relational trust operating as a resource for school improvement in four broad ways. First, organizational change entails major risks for all participants. . . . Second, the transaction costs associated with decision-making are reduced in environments where individual are predisposed to trust one another. . . . Third, contexts with strong relational trust benefit from clear understandings about role obligations that are routinely reinforced in day-to-day behavior. . . . Finally, relational trust sustains an ethical imperative among organizational members to advance the best interests of children. Participants in schools with high relational trust enact an interrelated set of mutual obligations with one another. (Bryk & Schneider, 2002, p. 33)

As trust among individual members is reinforced and expands over time, the cumulative effects are much greater than just the sum of trust between individuals. Bryk and Schneider's excerpt suggests an exponential effect that positions organizations for substantial growth. Essentially, trust, as an organizational phenomenon, serves as a powerful if not essential point of leverage for directing the collective human potential in schools to unite around shared purpose: teaching all students well. This serves as a reminder to continue explicitly fostering trusting relationships as we venture into orchestrating the development of schoolwide reflective practices.

Next, we introduce several ways of thinking about the dynamics and progressions of facilitating change in schools to consider in your design work of schoolwide reflective practices. Michael Fullan (2001b) explains, "Educational change depends on what teachers do and think, . . . it's as simple and as complex as that" (p. 115). As this quote suggests, individual change is at the heart of organizational change. One way of understanding individual change is the Stages of Concern component of the Concerns-Based Adoption Model (CBAM) (Hall & Hord, 2001). We described this in Chapter 4 (see Table 4.2) as a framework for guiding reflective practices between partners. Recall that the model suggests that individuals are concerned first with how the change will affect them personally: "How will my practices have to change? What will be expected of me?" Next, concerns emerge about managing all the tasks involved in successfully implementing a new program: "How will I get everything prepared? How can I manage all the pieces? Which tasks should come first?" Finally, concerns shift to considering the impact of the change: "What is happening for students as a result of this change? How can I improve implementation? I wonder how others are working with this program?" This model recognizes that the individual is central to the change process and that support for teachers should align with their concerns. Task concerns should be supported with specific information and examples about how to manage and implement the new practice. Impact concerns might be supported by encouraging teachers who have begun experimenting with implementation to talk together about what they are learning and how to refine, extend, and share their practices.

Fullan (2001b) offers a 40-year historical perspective on change in education, explaining how early efforts that were largely narrowly focused, prescriptive, linear, and top-down failed, although they served to inform future change efforts. Of all the lessons described by Fullan, several stand out as particularly pertinent here. First, to achieve substantial and sustainable change, a systems perspective must be adopted. Such a perspective recognizes the interconnectedness of all the dimensions of educational practice and that adjustments in one dimension will influence all others. Second, school change, Fullan explains, can be considered a process of "development in use" (probably similar to Schön's *reflection-in-action*), meaning that through use of new practices, educators learn what works and what doesn't in their particular contexts of practice and make refinements or seek assistance accordingly. Third, school change is more aptly conceived as cultural change. Culture defines typical and expected ways of doing and being. Culture shapes and is shaped by daily practices in schools. For changes in practice to be sustained, existing patterns ultimately must reshape around new practices. All three of these phenomena were articulated in the example of developing inclusive schools (McLeskey & Waldron, 2002) presented earlier in this chapter.

John Goodlad also offers some important insights about facilitating change in schools (Ferrace, 2002). He explains that schools rarely go beyond first-order changes, which are more superficial and involve addressing issues that are obviously in need of attention but do not touch deeper assumptions and structures. First-order changes might include things such as updating curriculum, revising attendance and discipline policies, changing the schedule, or paying teachers for additional responsibilities. Goodlad suggests that second-order changes, those of a more substantial nature, occur only in schools "where the faculty questions everything; nothing is taken for granted" (p. 33). Such change involves questioning assumptions and reexamining beliefs about students, learning, and other elements of educational practice. Further, he contrasts traditional, linear models of change to newer and more effective models which more actively and centrally involve faculty. In most schools, embedding reflective practices as a schoolwide phenomenon will require second-order change. It is the inside-out work of reculturing.

Now we briefly summarize two models of organizational change that illuminate more specifically the facets involved in and influencing this work. We strongly encourage you to seek the original sources to learn more about these models to guide your development work. The Leading Complex Change Model developed by Mary Lippitt (2003) is a deceptively simple framework that clearly identifies key elements of a successful change process and, perhaps more important, the outcomes that can be expected when each element is not addressed. The elements are vision, capabilities, incentives, resources, and action plan. *Without vision*, an initiative is not meaningfully grounded in a desirable future state or purpose, which leads to confusion. What is this supposed to look like? Why are we doing this anyway? *Without capabilities,* anxiety grows as staff members are asked to perform in new ways without the opportunity to learn new behavior and understanding. *Without incentives,* such as engagement being recognized and the educational value being specified, change is adopted gradually, if at all. *Without resources*, such as time for learning and money for materials or training (if appropriate), the system has insufficient capacity to support change, and frustration results. *Without a plan* that is thoughtfully crafted and continually modified in response to feedback about progress, false starts occur. False starts eventually zap the energy of even the most well-intentioned and enthusiastic educators. The team of individuals who assume responsibility for planning and oversight of schoolwide reflection and learning opportunities can use the Leading Complex Change model as a framework for ongoing reflection and problem solving as the professional learning community develops.

Perhaps the change model most well known to educators is the "Triple I" model, described by Michael Fullan (2001b). It consists of three stages: initiation, implementation, and continuation (previously referred to as *institutionalization*). *Initiation* refers to the activity involved in preparing for a strong, well-supported launch for implementation of new practices. This stage involves being sure the innovation aligns with current pressing needs and is of sufficient quality to warrant the personnel, fiscal, and other resources required. Initiation also requires advocacy by teachers and administrators, along with a well-articulated design for implementation.

The second stage, *implementation*, is when changes in practice begin. Both pressure and support are required. Pressure can arise from clearly communicated, jointly held expectations, as well as from compelling student data. Support involves some type of ongoing assistance or follow-up, such as teachers meeting regularly to reflect on the implementation, sharing problems and successes, and collaborating in other ways to create their own meaning and to learn and refine practices as implementation continues. Important to note is the "implementation dip" early in the implementation phase. This refers to the time during which practitioners feel inefficient and ineffective as they learn how to implement new practices. There is a "dip" in performance, so to speak, because learning is occurring. Recall the shape of the learning curve; in early stages of learning, performance is slower and there are more errors. With repeated practice and corrected action, new skills are established and performance is more fluent. Fullan makes the point that it is during the "dip" that implementers will often want to retreat, because it seems as if no progress is being made. Instead of a retreat, this is the point at which encouragement, support, and continuing efforts at implementation are needed to bolster an advance.

The final phase, *continuation*, refers to the point at which new practices become routine. Use is widespread and the effectiveness has been well established, which further reinforces use. In effect, previous expectations, norms, and practices have been replaced, refined, or expanded such that a new culture has formed around or is inclusive of the innovation. In the case of reflective practices, evidence of continuation would be reflected in a new culture in which asking questions, reexamining assumptions, coming up with new ways of thinking that lead to improved practices, and student learning are commonplace.

Another way of thinking about organizational change is offered by two New York City principals, Nancy Mohr and Alan Dichter. Mohr and Dichter (2001) present a practice-level version of organizational change based on their experiences leading variations of site-based management initiatives in the 1990s. In their view, the question at the core of this work was, "How do you develop site-based management to the point where it promotes rigor in teaching and learning?" Their observations serve as an organization-level corollary of Tuckman's stages of group development, presented in Chapter 5. They identify six stages of building a learning organization. We paraphrase their description of each stage as follows:

- *Honeymoon stage: A sense of community emerges.* Participants feel good being part of decision-making or leadership groups and having a voice. The designated leader has to assume primary responsibility for articulating purpose and structuring initial interactions. Others participate by voicing opinions and ideas. They are not yet sharing in leadership functions. The authors state that you cannot just proclaim, "This is your school, so it's up to you to tell me what you want to do" (Mohr & Dichter, 2001, p. 745). Capacity needs to be built in the group.
- *Conflict stage: The honeymoon is over.* This is when inevitable conflicts emerge. It is important that conflicts not be glossed over and that excessive compromise not become a pattern. The leader serves as teacher to support group learning in how to resolve conflicts.
- *Confusion stage: What's the role of the leader?* At this point, group members may question why there is a leader and how it is decided who gets to make which decisions. There is lack of clarity about the roles of the formal leader and other group participants.
- *Messy stage: Now things are even less clear.* At this point, groups learn about the messiness and inefficiency involved in dealing with complex issues. Many members are not comfortable with ambiguity and the risk-taking required to come up with ideas and possible future actions. The leader continues to teach by putting in place processes that support collaboration, collective decision making, and shared responsibility.
- *Scary stage: Where are the authority and accountability?* Being part of a decision-making group involves assuming responsibility for what happens as a result of decisions. This is more responsibility than some people want to assume. The authors stress the need to build an accountability system in which the reasons for making decisions are well documented, as are the multiple perspectives and sources of data considered.

- *Mature-group stage: A learning community is born.* The authors describe this final stage from the perspective of group members:

> We are proactive and make our own agendas rather than react- ing to those of others. We've also learned to be inclusive; we avoid us/them scenarios. We rarely make decisions before we have enough knowledge, and we make better decisions because they include more points of view. Giving up some of our own prefer- ences allow[s] us to see the bigger picture and to work on the common good. Our meetings are now professional development opportunities instead of battlegrounds over details. We're talk- ing about teaching, and we're learning about raising standards and not merely setting them. And we're all taking responsibility for making sure that happens; we've stopped pointing the mental finger at one another. (Mohr & Dichter, 2001, p. 747)

Clearly this final stage reflects a mature stage, not only in terms of group functioning but also for its members as professionals. The progres- sion, overall, points to some common issues in the development of school- wide reflective practices. Leadership is necessary and eventually must be shared, but has to be developed. Leadership is much more than demon- strating effective interpersonal and group-process skills. It involves being grounded in purpose, being explicit about values that underlie decisions, being relentless about seeking sufficient perspectives and knowledge to inform decisions, and being transparent about the deliberations and sub- stantiations for decisions. As the authors point out, giving away respon- sibility before groups have developed their capacity to assume full responsibility can be perilous to the organization, and especially to students. Mohr and Dichter (2001) again remind us of the inevitability of conflict and struggle in the process of *learning* to reflect and learn and function well in a group with others. Quinn (1996) has likened this phenomenon to building a bridge as you walk on it, simultaneously creat- ing the structures and scaffolds for change and traversing the territory. When facilitating change, we serve as architects, engineers, constructors, and pedestrians all at once and on the go.

Leadership Shared by Principals and Teachers

> Leadership is second only to classroom instruction among all school factors that contribute to what students learn at school.
>
> —Leithwood, Seashore, Anderson, & Wahlstrom
> (2004, p. 3), *How Leadership Influences Student Learning*

Recent conceptions of leadership as participative (Leithwood & Duke, 1999), distributed (Spillane, Halverson, & Diamond, 2001), parallel

(Crowther, Kaagan, Ferguson, & Hann, 2002), and broad-based (Lambert, 1998, 2003) connote a sense of shared responsibility for school leadership. Ogawa and Bossert (1995) view leadership as an organizational variable and explain,

> Leadership is not confined to certain roles in organizations. It flows through the networks of roles that comprise organizations. Moreover, leadership is based on the deployment of resources that are distributed throughout the network of roles, with different roles having access to different levels and types of resources. (p. 238)

Leadership that is shared among principals and teachers is increasingly recognized as a core feature of successful school renewal and improvement initiatives (Bryk, Camburn, & Louis, 1999; Camburn, Rowan, & Taylor, 2003; Lambert, 2005; Leithwood et al., 2004; Marks & Louis, 1999).

Fostering leadership among informal leaders in schools, such as teachers, is a primary responsibility of formal leaders. John Goodlad states, "Leadership is developing abilities of others—the entire faculty—to engage in a renewal process. . . . It is a job of deliberately cultivating a culture of change" (Ferrace, 2002, p. 32). Similarly, Michael Fullan (2005) contends that "The main mark of an effective principal is not just his or her impact on the bottom line of student achievement, but also on *how many leaders he or she leaves behind who can go even further*" (emphasis added, p. 31). So, how do principals and teachers go about sharing leadership in schools?

In a review of leadership studies in collaborative school settings, Crow (1998) found that leadership did indeed extend beyond the principal. He also found that figuring out specific ways in which leadership roles were shared between principals and teachers was difficult. Lambert (1998) concurs that asserting that the role of the principal is more important and more complex in this regard. "Among the more important tasks for the principal is to establish collegial relationships in an environment that may previously have fostered dependency relationships" (pp. 24–25). This is difficult, in part, because it involves intentionally redirecting teacher requests for permission and for answers. It can be more difficult to build leadership than to tell colleagues what to do.

Since the first edition of this book, published research has guided us in moving beyond theories and beliefs about the value of shared leadership to what it actually looks like in practice and how it is advanced. Some clearer ideas are forming around differentiation between principal and teacher leadership roles in the process of instructional improvement. In the next section, we share findings about leadership role differentiation between principals and teachers. We also summarize some of what is known about how teachers and principals effectively serve as leaders of school improvement, including how principals can foster leadership capacity in teachers.

In a study of distributed leadership in Chicago's Comprehensive School Reforms (CSR) schools, Camburn et al. (2003) found that of all the formally designated leadership roles, the role of CSR coach (essentially, an instructional coach) had a stronger influence on instruction than did any other formal leadership roles, including the role of principal (although the principal also had influence). This makes sense when it is understood that the CSR coach focuses exclusively and directly on developing instructional capacity by working with teachers, specifically targeting teaching and learning practices. The authors suggest that this finding offers one way to think about resolving the inevitable dilemmas that arise when principals serve both as developers and evaluators of instructional personnel. When teachers serve as instructional coaches, they have the freedom to work directly with teachers at the level of classroom practice without conflicted responsibilities for teacher evaluation. In our view, this also allows teachers to lead from their strength, which often is pedagogical practice.

Similarly, in an extensive study of "extraordinary teachers" in Australia, Crowther et al. (2002) discerned useful distinctions between principal and teacher roles for school improvement. Although principals and teachers were mutually engaged in building and sustaining the knowledge-generating capacities of schools, principals assumed primary responsibility for "strategic leadership" functions and teachers primarily for "pedagogical leadership" functions. Strategic functions included visioning, aligning resources, networking, and other organizational level dimensions of leadership practice. Pedagogical functions included curricular, instructional, and other classroom-level dimensions of instructional practice. Crowther et al. referred to this collective but distributed means of leadership as *parallel leadership,* adding that mutualism, a sense of shared purpose, and allowance for individual expression are essential characteristics of such engagement.

Both these studies demonstrated ways in which teachers and principals can differentially share in leadership functions while moving collectively toward shared aims. Both studies also independently reinforced the central role of teachers in the leadership of instructional improvement at the level of classroom practice. Feiler, Heritage, and Gallimore (2000) also reinforce the benefits of on-site expertise and leadership, suggesting further that "creating internal resources for reform increases the likelihood that curriculum and teaching improvements, from both internal and external sources, will become integrated, sustained qualities of a school's functioning" (p. 66). We see two additional advantages of positioning teachers to lead at the level of classroom practice. First, they continue to be viewed as credible by teacher colleagues, which allows them to continue to have influence on these colleagues. Second, they continue to have opportunities to work directly with children and to reflect and learn together with other teachers, which allows them to continue expanding and refining their pedagogical practices.

Although teachers play an essential role as leaders in successful school improvement efforts, the role of the principal cannot be overemphasized. Many studies point to the role of the principal in successful efforts to improve teaching and learning and to develop leadership capacity. Increasingly, research is explicating the ways in which this happens. Here we report on three studies, emphasizing the specific practices in which principals engaged.

Pursuing complementary interests in leadership capacity and sustainability, Lambert (2005) studied 15 schools, mostly high-poverty and urban schools, from across the United States. The identified schools were known to have been successful in developing high leadership capacity, defined as "broad-based, skillful participation in the work of leadership" (p. 63). One of the common findings across schools was principals who assumed a major role in intentionally developing a culture of shared leadership. The principals in these schools varied in terms of personality and management style but shared similar leadership characteristics, described by Lambert as follows:

> an understanding of self and clarity of values; a strong belief in equity and the democratic process; strategic thought about the evolution of school improvement; a vulnerable persona; knowledge of the work of teaching and learning; and the ability to develop capacity in colleagues and in the organization (p. 63).

This study also revealed three phases of development toward high leadership capacity: instructive, transitional, and high-capacity. Each of the phases involved different leadership practices on the part of principals. During the *instructive phase,* the role of the principal was to be clear about the direction, at the same time rallying participation and gaining momentum. Specific principal practices were to "insist on attention to results, start conversation, solve difficult problems, challenge assumptions, confront incompetence, focus work, establish structures and processes that engage colleagues, teach about new practices, and articulate beliefs that eventually get woven into the fabric of the school" (Lambert, 2005, p. 63). During the *transitional phase,* the role of the principal was to gradually "let go" while continuing to actively support the process "by continuing the conversations, keeping a hand in the process, coaching, and problem-solving" (p. 64). This was identified as a stage in which teachers had a tendency to drop out as the complexity, difficulty, and responsibility of the work increased. It was interesting to note that as principals began to show their own vulnerability (meaning that they did not always know what to do), many teachers were inspired to assume greater responsibility. Lambert also noted that breaking teacher dependence on principals was one of the most challenging aspects of the transitional phase. She observed that "during the transitional phase, principals need[ed] to hand decisions and problem solving back to the teachers, coaching and leading for teacher efficacy while refusing to hold tight to authority and power" (p. 65) Finally, in the *high-capacity phase*, "teachers begin to initiate actions, take responsibility, discover time for joint efforts, and identify crucial questions about student learning" (p. 65). As teachers assumed a higher profile, principals assumed a lower and more facilitative profile.

In a second study of principals identified as effective leaders, Blase and Blase (1999) found that such principals intentionally promoted reflection and collegial interaction among teachers, focused on teaching and learning. The principals actively promoted professional growth by making suggestions, providing feedback, modeling practices, using inquiry, soliciting advice and opinions, giving praise, emphasizing the study of teaching and learning, supporting collaboration and coaching relationships among teachers, supporting program redesign, applying the principles of adult learning to staff-development opportunities, and implementing action research to inform instructional decision making. The authors concluded by stating,

> Our data suggest that principals who are effective instructional leaders use a broad-based approach; they integrate reflection and growth to build a school culture of individual and shared critical examination for improvement. In doing so, they appear to embrace the challenges of growing and changing. . . . Above all, [they] talk openly and frequently with teachers about instruction. (1999, p. 371)

In a third study focused on the instructional leadership role of principals, Ronneberg (2000) identified specific practices used by each of the principals, related to six leadership domains: inspiring a shared vision, creating a positive culture with high expectations for staff and students, challenging existing practices, and promoting relationships with and among staff members. These principals intentionally fostered reflection and learning by means of dialogue. Examples of specific principal practices included keeping the focus of staff learning on student achievement; aligning all staff members' learning activities on the shared vision of the school; scheduling time for collaborative team planning and dialogue, sometimes on a daily basis and intermittently for half- or full days; promoting study groups; conducting weekly brown-bag lunches focused on teaching and learning; encouraging group attendance at conferences to promote sharing and follow-up with colleagues; and establishing a professional library.

Yukl (1994) suggests that leadership is broadly construed as an organizational resource involving "a social influence process whereby intentional influence is exerted by one person [or group] over other people [or groups] to structure the activities and relationships in a group or organization" (Yukl, 1994, p. 3). If this is so, then leadership as influence can be everywhere, at any time, in schools. For sure, the most powerful influence exerted by any leader—formal or informal, principal or teacher, teacher or student—is modeling desired dispositions and practices. It's walking the talk. It's making one's espoused actions authentic ones. Authenticity has the potential to compel even the most reluctant organizational member to consider engaging in reflective practices. Go ahead. Stay committed to your own growth as an educator, as a professional, as a leader. And invite others to join you. You will lead who you are.

SCHOOLWIDE REFLECTIVE PRACTICE: EXAMPLES FROM PRACTICE

As you begin to engage in this work, long before clear indicators of increased professional and student learning are readily discerned, how do you know progress is being made? In truth, progress is often difficult to assess in the early, more vulnerable stages of implementation, when messiness, uncertainty, and conflict are likely. Recall the implementation dip (Fullan, 2001a), described earlier in this chapter, which reminds us that early implementation is much like the acquisition stage of learning: slow, deliberate, conscious, stilted, inefficient, and sometimes fumbling. Early indicators of progress are often subtle, if not microscopic, as depicted in the following example.

At the first gathering of one of several "mandated PLCs," evidence of progress was observed as a shift in body language. Schoolwide PLCs had been mandated in an attempt to engage teachers in a learning process that would increase test scores and shed the school's newly acquired Adequate Yearly Progress (AYP) label. An outside facilitator was employed to get the process off on a strong footing. When the first meeting started, most group members were seated around the table leaning back in their chairs as far as possible, with arms tightly crossed at chest height and without making eye contact with others in the group. Everything about these positions communicated distance and disinterest.

The facilitator initiated the group by asking participants to introduce themselves (teachers were placed in newly configured groups with colleagues from outside their typical associations) and to share their experiences and views regarding the curriculum. A round-robin process was used. The first two people responded to this request as efficiently as possible. One articulated a distinct dislike of the curriculum. The facilitator calmly and sincerely paraphrased each participant's contribution and thanked them. No judgment, no interpretation, no challenge or question— all of which were intentional responses to develop safety and trust. The third person began by looking around at his new group members and introducing himself. He then said that he didn't know much about the curriculum but he was happy to be included and hoped he would learn ways he could better support the students when they were with him in media. As he spoke, the postures around the table relaxed, the eyes softened, and the bodies began leaning in toward the center of the circle instead of angling back away from the circle. You could see the shift happening and feel the tension dissipating. His comments had a magical effect on the group. The learning space had opened up.

We have learned to pay attention to even small suggestions of engagement as noted in this previous example, as well as these other clues of engagement: Continuing to show up. Paying attention. Attempting to figure out applications. Staying enthused about purpose, despite the messiness. Responding to questions and problems with idea generation instead of naysaying. Inviting and affirming participation. Showing up with food. Maintaining a sense of humor. Using metaphor to capture how it feels to be "in process." Choosing to persist.

As you read the examples below, think about what you would consider to be indicators of progress on the way toward more clearly discernable engagement, learning, action, and outcomes. Some of the examples resulted from policy decisions and mandated improvement initiatives. Others were voluntary and emergent, teacher-led and -approved. Regardless of the leverage point, in all the examples, individual and collective reflection and learning were established as the core capacities for improvement. Three of the examples describe a multiyear, evolving process. These examples provide a glimpse of the messiness involved in navigating schoolwide change and the need for a team of persistent, reflective educators to assume the role of facilitator of staff learning. These examples also show how establishing schoolwide reflective practice is not a short-term endeavor but a long-term shift in culture. The other examples describe just a single year's effort, but many have continued in subsequent years.

Inquiring Minds: A Teacher-Led
Reflective Practice Initiative at Urban High School

Urban High School (pseudonym) enrolls 2,000 students in a windowless building designed for 1,500 students. It has over 165 staff members, in 16 departments. There have been six principals in the past 10 years. The teacher-led Inquiring Minds initiative began with a partnership between two teachers at Urban and two colleagues from a nearby university. This foursome shared an interest in creating a more collaborative work culture so that students with various learning challenges would be more successful, academically and socially, in this large urban school. They also shared a set of beliefs that for a meaningful change to take hold at Urban, the process should be voluntary and emergent. This meant that staff would be learning together about how to increase collaboration for student success.

There were no other administrative or external pressures for Urban or its staff to participate. The available resources included a university partner (10 to 20 hours a month of combined onsite and offsite time) and modest funding to pay for substitutes (used only during the first year). Described below is a sketch of the process, outcomes, and learning that spanned this five-year development effort, results of which are still evident today. (Readers interested in a full account are referred to the case study by Montie, York-Barr, Stevenson, & Vallejo, 1997.)

Year 1: Reflect, Explore, and Focus

A series of meetings were held with staff members at Urban to explain the general purpose (increased collaboration for student success) and open-ended process (reflection and learning together to figure out what makes sense for moving forward) of the proposed initiative. The meetings were open to all staff members, and key teachers were specifically invited to attend. These key teachers included individuals who were respected as excellent student-centered teachers representing a variety of content and program areas in the school. Fourteen teachers stepped forward to participate.

During the first year, this group met eight times (two to five hours each time) to share views about current realities at Urban, to study literature about collaboration and organizational learning, and to converse about how they might advance collaboration. Through the interactions, participants became aware of how little the Urban staff knew about staff members throughout the building, and how this lack of connection resulted in fragmentation for students. The idea began to take hold that more intentional connections among teachers throughout the building could create a better learning environment for students. This idea took on personal meaning for participants, served as a source of inspiration, and resulted in continued commitments.

With firm commitments to the ideas and outcomes, Inquiring Minds participants had to figure out specifically how to advance meaningful communication and collaboration among teachers throughout the school in order to increase coherence, support, and learning for students. This proved to be a frustrating task. The enormity of the task, the uncertainty of what might be successful, and a history of failed attempts at meaningful reform contributed to the sense of unease: Will anyone else join in? Who has time to organize and lead this effort? What could we do that might work? How do we know better communication will improve student learning?

One morning, while muddled in the mess of figuring out what to do, one of the teachers suggested they learn more about reflective practice. After further deliberation, participants eagerly decided to launch an invitational schoolwide initiative during the next school year, focused on learning about reflective practice as a way to improve teaching and learning. Expanding the reflective capacities of teachers and providing opportunities for teachers to learn together about their instructional practices was viewed as one way to leverage the school's internal capacities to better serve students by building relationships and instructional knowledge.

All staff members were invited to informal informational sessions held during several lunch periods in the spring. Cake was served. The atmosphere was festive and energizing. The Inquiring Minds initiative was taking shape in the hearts and minds of teachers at Urban. Plans were made to launch the reflective practice learning process during a full-day retreat in August.

Year 2: Learning by Doing and Reflecting

A week before school started in the fall, about 25 Urban educators, including the recently hired principal, attended the Inquiring Minds kickoff at the lakeside center of a nearby city park. The kickoff had four purposes: (a) to get to know one another and articulate desired outcomes of the schoolwide Inquiring Minds initiative; (b) to engage in conversation about the meanings of reflective practice; (c) to introduce specific reflection strategies; and (d) to finalize a structure for learning together through a process of reflection. The structures designed to support reflection and learning were individual journaling, weekly reflection on instructional practice in dyads or triads (self-organized), and monthly gatherings of the whole group at the lakeside meeting center (Figure 6.3). The shared, desired outcomes were expressed as making a difference for kids, promoting capacities for learning within Urban, and creating a sense of community and connectedness among staff members.

Figure 6.3   Inquiring Minds Initiative: Supporting Structures and Desired Outcomes

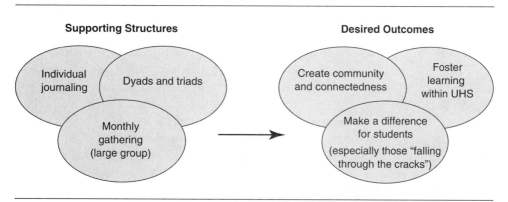

Of the three reflection structures, dyads/triads and monthly gatherings were the two in which participants most consistently engaged. Individual journaling was dropped by most. An additional reflection structure, mailbox prompts, was introduced (described in Chapter 4). These written prompts were placed in participant mailboxes every couple of weeks. They contained humorous or contemplative passages, followed by questions to prompt reflection about the passages or about participants' instructional practices. The lead team of two Urban teachers and two university partners designed and facilitated the monthly sessions, although all participants took turns leading group icebreaking activities and bringing refreshments or flowers. A major boost during the second year was a two-day workshop that formally introduced strategies for effective collaborative learning and work. Because of the relationships that had formed within the group and the reflection skills that were developing, Inquiring Minds participants quickly adopted the collaborative learning and work strategies presented in the workshop.

At the end of the year, a half-day gathering was held to reflect on the year, celebrate, and consider the future of the Inquiring Minds group. Collegial relationships and reflective capacities among participants had increased. The group had taken on both personal and professional value for its members. Excited to continue its schoolwide work, the group decided to resume the dyads/triads and monthly gatherings during the following year. They also decided to expand efforts to continually invite others to participate. The potential of reflection to improve practice was experienced by the Inquiring Minds participants, and they were eager to include others. They also knew greater participation would bolster their desired outcomes for students.

Year 3: Inquiring Minds Sustains Through Transition

The third year was filled with unanticipated transitions and increased demands. A new team of administrators was assigned to Urban. Numerous school-improvement committees were mandated and pressing deadlines imposed. Many Inquiring Minds participants assumed leadership roles in these committees (usually in pairs) and vowed to make the committee processes meaningful. They viewed it as an opportunity to practice the reflection and collaborative group strategies learned the previous year. Their success in this regard was uneven. Participation in monthly gatherings fluctuated but served as a safe and supportive environment for reflecting on and planning for the imposed committee work. Reflective practice in dyads/triads also continued for many of the participants.

By the end of the year, several of the Inquiring Minds participants had been successful in shaping the work of their committees to include reflection and learning. Examples included the Space Committee and Readings Reflection Group examples described in Chapter 5. Further, the Staff Development Committee had garnered support to pay for a two-day, schoolwide Inquiring Minds kickoff for the following August. More than

50 staff members participated in this two-day session that focused on collaboration, emphasizing the critical role of reflection for staff learning and school improvement. This turnout indicated widespread interest in the topic and resulted in significant follow-through in a variety of staff-learning and school-improvement efforts.

Years 4 and 5: Embedding Reflection and Collaborative Norms Schoolwide

In the capable and determined hands of key teacher leaders at Urban, the Inquiring Minds initiative expanded and extended its influence during years 4 and 5. More teachers participated in dyads and triads as a way to reflect on their individual practices. More people participated in the monthly gatherings, which were relocated back to the high school for ease of access. Inquiring Minds extended its reach into more than 12 work groups, with Inquiring Minds participants embedding reflection and collaboration strategies into the work of the groups. Recognizing the success of these groups, the principal asked Inquiring Minds participants to lead some of the more challenging (e.g., Space Committee) and important (e.g., Mentoring) work groups at Urban High. Shown in Figure 6.4 is a web depicting specific groups into which reflective practices were embedded through the teacher leadership and facilitation of Inquiring Minds participants.

Staff and Student Outcomes

What outcomes were realized from this multiyear reflective-practice initiative? Feedback from teachers throughout the Inquiring Minds initiative provided evidence of professional learning, improvement, and connection. The dyad/triad interactions were viewed as a safe and effective way to reflect on practice. Participants described feeling both supported and challenged in the presence of respected and caring colleagues. Furthermore, many of the teachers stepped forward to effectively serve in leadership roles, usually in pairs, for various school-improvement and committee efforts. When they served as leaders in these situations, a major objective was to reframe group work as opportunities for meaningful learning and development. In regard to effects on students, many teachers identified specific improvements in practice that benefited students. They also felt that the strengthened and expanded relationships that had formed among teachers throughout the building created a safety net for students, especially for those students who were the initial focus of the Inquiring Minds initiative: students who tend to fall through the cracks. In the words of one teacher, "If I do not know where to go for a student, I know someone who will know, or someone who will know someone who knows."

Learning From Inquiring Minds

Resulting from the Inquiring Minds initiative are 10 lessons to serve as guidelines for the design and facilitation of school renewal and improvement

Figure 6.4   Inquiring Minds: Spread of Reflective Practices Four Years Later

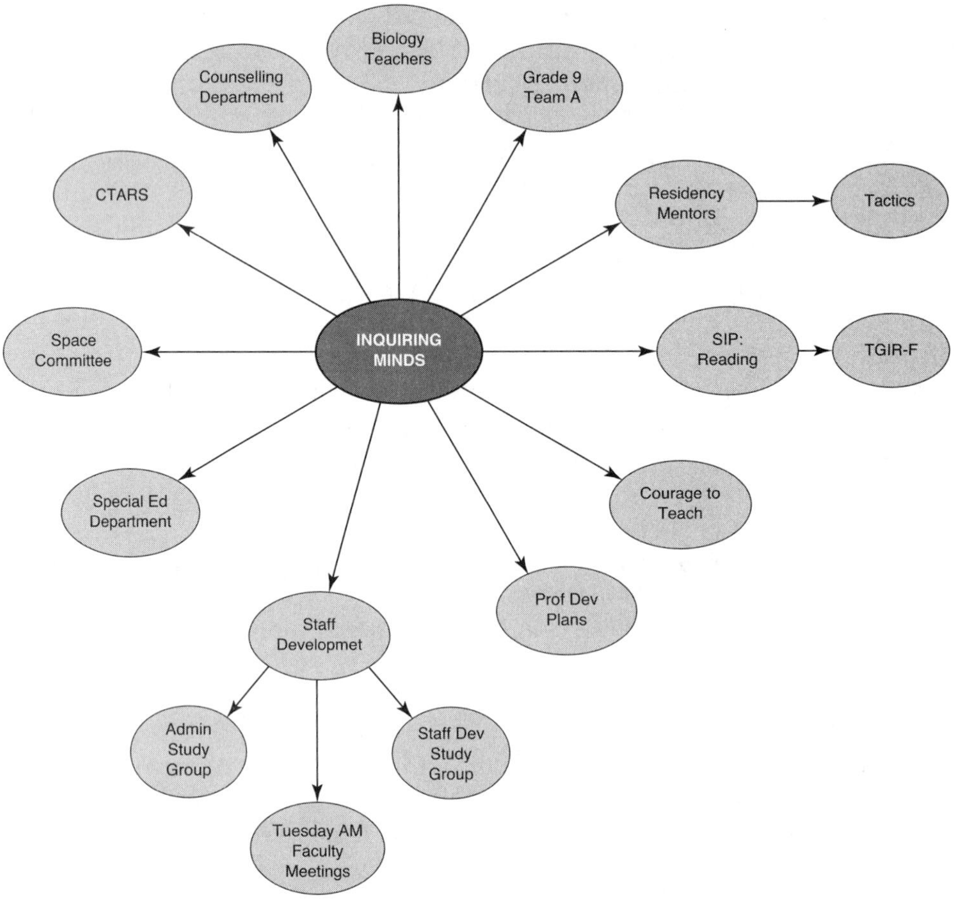

efforts in which reflection and learning are core elements (Montie et al., 1997):

- Leadership that is shared and supported by teachers is a powerful force for improvement.
- External partnerships help to keep the initiative "on the table" and offer valuable outsider perspectives and questions to assist in the ongoing design work.
- The value of time to reflect and talk with colleagues cannot be overemphasized.
- Signs of hope and encouragement are needed to balance the inevitable ambiguities, uncertainties, and energy drains in the design and learning process.
- Relationships serve as both a means and an end of collaborative reflection and learning.

- Intentional efforts to continually invite newcomers into the process enlarge the circle of participation and send a powerful message about inclusivity and openness in the school.
- Reflective practices are fostered by intentional design and by creating open spaces to allow direction and meaning to emerge from within the group.
- Purpose should be revisited regularly, especially when learning gets messy.
- Internal rewards of relevant growth and learning go a long way to sustain participation.
- There is no one right way to start or proceed. Design a reasonable set of initial steps, then expect to continually reflect and adjust as you proceed.

The variables considered most significant in sustaining Inquiring Minds over time were the relationships that formed among participants (teachers throughout the school), the reflective practice skills that developed, and, ultimately, the improvements in practice. These relationships, skills, and improvements were the source of energy that expanded and embedded reflection into numerous and varied teaching, learning, and group practices throughout Urban High School.

PLCs Get Started at Westview High School

Here we describe how Westview High School (pseudonym) got started with forming professional learning communities (PLCs). This involved rethinking how time was typically spent in staff meetings and for staff development days. The underpinnings of the process reflected the views of the principal: "As I reflect back on my 35 years of experience, I do not know any other way to change school culture than having conversations. Conversations become the relationships with people." With this grounding, the principal and the staff development chairpersons decided that getting staff to talk together was a most important initial thing to do.

The principal first met with the president of the teachers' union to explore possibilities for using the monthly faculty meeting time and the March staff-development day in a different manner to be more supportive of professional learning. They decided to dramatically shorten the length of monthly staff meetings from 60 minutes to between 15 and 30 minutes and to also address as many issues as possible via the intranet instead of in face-to-face meetings. The time "saved" by shortening meetings could be used to allow staff to get together in small groups (PLCs). In addition, it was proposed that the one full day of staff development be restructured into one-hour segments spread throughout the year. This resulted in approximately one extra hour each month for staff learning. Essentially, a one-shot form of staff development was replaced with a more embedded set of opportunities for learning throughout the year. We know that ongoing conversations are critical to changing practice.

Before presenting this proposal to the staff, the principal shared the idea with the superintendent to garner her support. He felt that support from both the superintendent and the union's president was critical for the proposal to move forward. With their support, the principal then presented the proposal to the faculty, clearly communicating an expectation that the change would occur only if at least 70 percent of the staff voted to participate. The staff voted with 71 percent in agreement, from a total of more than 250 certified teachers.

Once the decision was made to move forward, staff began forming PLCs. This process was guided by two adult-learning principles: adults support what they help create, and adults want some responsibility in what they decide or what they are directed to do or learn. Multiple groups formed around topics of interest, including English-language learners, assessment, and math instruction. Staff members were encouraged to keep the group size to less than eight people. When all PLCs were organized, there were only two staff members who did not want to participate. In March, then, the two nonparticipants spent a day in staff development, because this had been the expectation for anyone choosing to not join in the extended learning times.

The small-group PLCs met five times during the year, for at least an hour, at their convenience. Many of the PLCs chose to meet right after a faculty meeting, especially if it was a shorter faculty meeting. In addition, the faculty meetings shifted to more time spent on professional learning and less time spent on business. For example, at one meeting a learning segment focused on a particular conversation technique. At another, a learning focus was on conflict. At another, the principal and a colleague modeled a coaching session for the faculty.

At the end of the year, there was a unanimous vote to continue the PLC model rather than go back to the day of staff development. Staff members reported that this was the first time in 25 years there was unanimous agreement on anything.

Tapping the Community of Experts Within

A rural high school teacher, who also served as the staff development coordinator, started a program called Community of Experts. He had noticed that many staff members attended external workshops to improve their skills. He wondered, Why not use the expertise already in the school and district? Although he recognized that outside experts sometimes were appropriately sought, he also knew there were a lot of internal experts whose knowledge and skills could be better utilized and more widely applied locally.

To begin tapping this internal capacity, he started by identifying specific areas of knowledge and expertise held by educators in the schools in his district. Next, he asked these staff members if they would be willing to share their knowledge and skills with colleagues in the district. Having secured their willingness, he published a list of the internal expertise within the district and disseminated it to all district employees. Then he organized a staff development day and scheduled the internal experts to share their knowledge and skills. At the end of the staff development day, he asked all the participants to identify what was needed next. Responses to this question produced ideas for the next staff development day.

This coordinator honored the gifts and talents of those already in the system. In doing so, he strengthened a network of connections and resources among educators in his school and district.

Schoolwide Math PLCs at Eastview Elementary School

Eastview Elementary (pseudonym) is a K–6 public magnet school of 640 students located in a quiet urban neighborhood. Eastview opened in the early 1990s as an inclusive school, organized in multiage classes with thematically focused curricula and with the intention of fostering high degrees of teacher collaboration. Many of the teachers at Eastview were attracted by these educational philosophies.

Over the past decade, a number of changes have evolved at Eastview. The student population is now more culturally, linguistically, and economically varied. There has been a gradual shift from collaborative teaming and teaching to little or no teacher collaboration within or across grade levels, or with the special services teachers. Although many special education and ELL students continue to be included in regular classrooms, the special services teachers have retreated to their separate classrooms. The multigrade classrooms also have become individual domains of practice. This ultimately led to very little continuity across the K–6 curriculum. Teachers did not necessarily know what students in different classrooms or grades were expected to know or what they did. A subtle sense of competition emerged, which typically occurs in such isolated cultures of practice. The lack of continuity and community was exacerbated by the regular turnover of principals. Finally, Eastview's academic programs, once viewed as stellar, were under increasing scrutiny because of concerns about student achievement.

Spring—Initial Planning

By the end of her first year at Eastview, the principal had a much better understanding about the building, the staff, and issues that were blocking improved student achievement. Although the teachers were highly skilled and invested in their students, the culture of professional isolation, with low levels of trust and collaboration, were blocking Eastview from advancing instructional practice. Clear about the direction but not the path, the principal approached a district staff person and a university professor about designing a process for Eastview staff to move away from its culture of isolation and toward a culture of professional learning. The design team grew to include a recently retired elementary teacher, widely known for her curricular and staff development expertise, a graduate student and former teacher mentor, and an Eastview teacher leader interested in staff collaboration.

Conversations among the design team members resulted in several decisions about how a professional learning initiative would be designed. First, a decision was made that the initiative must be schoolwide. To shift culture, everyone had to be involved. Second, the process was to be grounded in authentic teacher learning focused on student learning. Collaborative examination of student work (ESW) was specifically chosen as the learning design so that conversations about what and how students were learning would be fostered. Further, it was intended that conversations about student work would create a foray into schoolwide discussions of standards, curriculum, instruction, and assessment. Third, ESW groups would be small, heterogeneous groups of six to eight teachers to foster both trust and communication. Classroom teachers would be assigned vertically (across grades) to be in groups with teachers whom they did not typically work with or know very well. Groups would also include special services (e.g., special education, ELL) and specialist (e.g., music, art, media) teachers. Fourth, the groups would meet across the entire school year so that learning and relationships could develop over time. Fifth, the groups would meet during the school day to assure a high level of involvement. Sixth, the retired teacher from the design team would serve as an external facilitator for the groups, in an effort to get the groups started well in the dual focus of learning and relationship building. This person was highly skilled and would be viewed as credible by the experienced Eastview teaching staff. Seventh, given various student and staff considerations, writing was identified as the initial target for improvement, specifically narrative, problem-solving, descriptive, and clarification methods.

The principal allocated Eastview's staff development budget (and additional funds) to fund the facilitator and a cadre of substitute teachers employed to free the teachers to meet. At the final staff meeting of the year in June, the principal and the design team formally introduced the professional learning purpose and process. Given the initial ESW focus of writing, teachers were invited to indicate preferences for the type of writing on which they would like to focus. In the summer, an internal team assigned teachers to groups, using their preferences as a guide.

August Through September

In August, Eastview was designated as a school whose students were not making Adequate Yearly Progress (AYP) in math. Staff, understandably, were upset. The principal talked with them about changing the focus of the ESW initiative from writing to math. Most teachers agreed that the purpose of

ESW was not a quick fix to raise test scores, but using significant amounts of professional learning time to focus on the most pressing issue was viewed as appropriate and desirable. A related change was a new district requirement that all teachers were required to use a specific math curriculum. Previously, only some of the teachers used this curriculum. The design team decided to maintain the group heterogeneity despite the change in focus to math.

In late August, initial sessions were scheduled with each of the six ESW groups to introduce more specifically the processes and expectations for professional learning in the groups. The agenda included presenting research on professional learning communities, introducing norms of collaborative work, and practicing use of the protocol that would be used to foster collaborative examination of student work. In addition, baseline evaluation data were gathered on individual and team use of collaborative skills and on existence of specific characteristics of professional learning communities at Eastview Elementary School.

October Through March

During the course of the school year, five two-and-a-half-hour sessions were held with each ESW group. The general format of the sessions was (a) reviewing the previous session and previewing the current session; (b) teachers sharing new ideas or insights about their students learning math; (c) articulating how Eastview's math curriculum and the student work of the day aligned with grade-level state standards; (d) following the ESW protocol to examine, then dialogue about the student work that the teachers brought to share; and (e) identifying the type of math work to be brought the next session. Often, the facilitator shared research, methods, and tools relevant to the math topics. Throughout the year, observational data and teacher feedback were collected. At the end of the year, data were collected again on individual and team use of collaborative skills and characteristics of professional learning communities at Eastview.

June

At the end-of-the-year faculty meeting in June, results of the ESW initiative evaluation were shared with the Eastview staff. Findings indicated that teachers felt strongly they had increased their knowledge of the math curriculum both within and across grade levels, their understanding of the importance of metacognition in students' understanding of math concepts, and their recognition that fidelity to the curriculum was central to coherence in math learning for students—meaning that in order to be successful in later grades, students must learn what is intended in the early grades. Most teachers reported valuing the collegial dialogue. They also indicated more evidence of professional learning community characteristics at Eastview. Most important, student achievement in math, as measured on both the state and district standardized tests, showed significant improvement.

Eastview was removed from the state list for needing improvement after only one year. Finally, staff valued the ESW group process enough to continue it in other content areas the following year.

Coaching Decreases Discipline Referrals at Jane Addams Junior High

At Jane Addams Junior High (pseudonym), a goal for the year was to reduce conflict, discipline referrals, and suspensions. As one way to support this goal, 25 percent of the certified staff was trained in coaching over the summer. This started conversations about questions, such as, How do we deal with students now? How do we want to deal with students? How can we solve discipline problems with the resources available? How could we work as a team? In the fall of the year, another 25 percent of the staff was trained in coaching. In addition, the whole staff was offered a course on conflict and on classroom management, which was taught by the principal.

After the administrators, certified staff members, and noncertified staff members completed coaching courses, conversations about students became more inquiry-oriented and focused on problem solving rather than on complaining and consequences. By the end of the year, data showed a reduction of discipline referrals by 30 percent and suspensions by 25 percent. Staff members also reported a reduction in conflicts with students and among staff members. To have achieved these outcomes required teamwork, conversations, and trust.

SCHOOLWIDE REFLECTIVE PRACTICE: MORE IDEAS TO CONSIDER

Described below are numerous ideas and strategies for fostering school-wide reflective practices that have been excerpted from the literature. These examples suggest a variety of ways to use both internal and external sources of knowledge in reflective processes aimed at advancing instructional and school renewal practices. The initial five examples succinctly describe various learning structures (e.g., philosophy club, study groups) in relationship to a particular focus for learning. The final three examples offer some specific reflection questions that could be adapted and used within various PLC settings.

Schoolwide Study Groups

When a schoolwide focus for improvement has been identified, study groups are a common way to begin the learning and development process. Murphy and Lick (1998) define a study group as "a small number of individuals joining together to increase their capacities through new learning for the benefit of students" (p. 4). A schoolwide study process, for example, might be launched to examine the nature and incidence of discipline referrals, to explore literacy strategies to embed in content-area classes, to develop classroom-based performance assessments that inform instructional decision making, or to consider best practices for professional learning that impacts student achievement. "The power in the whole faculty study group process rests in the promise that teachers will become more knowledgeable and skillful at doing what will result in higher levels of student learning" (p. 5). Murphy and Lick (1988) offer a set of comprehensive strategies for developing whole-faculty study groups.

Francis, Hirsh, and Rowland (1994) describe how a school under pressure to reduce a gap in achievement between student groups used whole-faculty study groups. During the first year, 10 study groups of six to eight teachers each were formed. Participation was mandated. All the groups read the same articles. During the second year, study groups were still mandated, but teachers could select their own group and topical focus of study. In the third year, mixed groups were once again intentionally formed, and the entire staff agreed on common topics. From this multiyear process, the authors concluded that vertical groups (e.g., heterogeneous groups of educators across grade levels) and common readings facilitated more connections and conversations throughout the school. Within groups, facilitators and ongoing communication and feedback were also important. Outcomes included increases in the knowledge base of teaching, professional dialogue, trust, and improvements in classroom instruction and staff morale. A professional code of conduct and a shared vision for the school also developed. Finally, conflict emerged and was viewed as positive and productive evidence that real change was happening.

Implementing an Inquiry-Based Science Curriculum

A significant amount of literature about reflective practice and professional learning emerges from science education, probably as a result of extensive national funding for such efforts. Beerer and Bodzin (2004) describe a districtwide initiative used to implement an elementary inquiry-based science curriculum. After the curriculum was selected and the teachers engaged in a hands-on, inquiry-based science instruction workshop, grade-level study groups were formed to provide ongoing support for learning about the curriculum and for design and using inquiry-based science lessons. The study groups met once or twice a month for six months. The district lead team for this initiative created the Science Teacher Inquiry Rubric (STIR), an observation tool for determining how well teachers implemented inquiry-based lessons. The group was organized around six statements, with each identifying an essential feature of implementing inquiry-based science standards. As articulated by Beerer and Bodzin (2004, pp. 44–45), those statements were as follows:

- Teacher provides an opportunity for learners to engage with a scientifically oriented question.
- Teacher engages learners in planning investigations to gather evidence in response to questions.
- Teacher helps learners give priority to evidence, which allows them to draw conclusions and/or develop and evaluate explanations that address scientifically oriented questions.
- Learners formulate conclusions and/or explanations from evidence to address scientifically oriented questions.
- Learners evaluate their conclusions and/or explanations in light of alternative conclusions/explanations, particularly those reflecting scientific understanding.
- Learners communicate and justify their proposed explanations.

For each statement, there were four descriptive indicators along a continuum ranging from learner-centered to teacher-centered. Although the authors do not view the rubric as offering a full explanation of each feature, they felt it was a useful starting place for teachers to anchor their reflections for and on practice. Findings from postobservations administering STIR indicated that the professional learning process resulted in teachers implementing more of the features of inquiry-based science, as well as more student-centered practices. The authors conclude,

> Standards-based inquiry instruction demands a significant shift in what teachers typically do. . . . Teachers must think about what it means to learn different kinds of science material for different purposes and be able to use different teaching strategies, particularly inquiry-based instruction. . . . Study groups, strong curricular materials, and tools like the STIR can positively affect teachers' implementation of standards-based science and, ultimately, develop in students the necessary skills to achieve scientific literacy. (Beerer & Bodzin, 2004, p. 47)

Teaching Portfolios to Foster Job-Embedded Professional Learning

Xu (2003) describes a study in which teaching portfolios were used as a job-embedded means of promoting reflection, collegial sharing and collaboration, and professional learning in an urban elementary school. Initially only a few teachers participated. Within two years' time, almost all the teachers in the school participated. To participate, teachers identified one area of particular interest related to their own teaching practice to examine more deeply. Each portfolio included three sections: a statement of teaching philosophy; a description of the teacher's primary area of interest and related practice suggestions to be shared with colleagues; and supplementary materials to support their work and to enhance the professional learning of others. As the portfolio project evolved, teachers also included work samples from students with varied abilities. The portfolios grounded conversations about teaching and learning among colleagues.

Interviews with participating teachers and review of portfolios indicated a strong positive impact on professional learning and collaboration. Teachers reported approaching their work more carefully and purposefully, frequently asking themselves about lesson objectives and means by which to reach objectives. They felt these deliberations resulted in better understanding of students and how best to support learning needs. Teachers viewed themselves as taking more risks and learning continuously, given the job-embedded nature of the process. Collaboration among colleagues was fostered, because portfolios provided a specific vehicle for sharing and learning together. Conversations between the principal and individual teachers were enriched, because the portfolios provided more insight about teacher thinking. The portfolio process empowered some teachers to network educators outside their own building and district.

The most salient supporting conditions for the portfolio project were identified as trust, a model of supervision in which the administrator and teachers reflected together on practice, shared control of professional learning by the administrator and teachers, and intentional fostering of a collaborative social climate. Teachers were subtly reinforced for sharing ideas and practices that could be used by other teachers instead of keeping such practices to themselves.

Philosophy Club

A principal in a middle school started a Philosophy Club. Once a month, staff members were invited to join him at a local restaurant. He bought snacks, and staff members purchased their own beverages. The only requirement was that conversation had to be about learning, teaching, instruction, or anything else that would increase thinking and learning about educational practice. It was not permissible to complain, be negative, or talk about issues such as inadequate resources, unsupportive individuals, or excessive demands. Most of the time, conversation centered on an article about teaching and learning, a book someone was reading, a new strategy from a workshop, or a staff-development opportunity.

The number of staff members who showed up was very small at first, five or fewer. By the third month, the number was over five, and by the sixth month, the group had grown to between 10 and 15 of the 35 staff members at the school. The principal shared that as a result of the Philosophy Club, staff members continued conversations at school that had started at the restaurant. In addition, conversations in the school became more focused on learning.

Learning in Faculty Meetings

It is not uncommon for educators to log about 50 hours a year in large-group faculty meetings. Over the course of a career, thousands of hours are captured in this forum. Recognizing that face-to-face time is one of the most valuable assets for staff learning, educators have increasingly turned their attention toward capturing at least some of this time for collaborative learning. Killion (2000), for example, suggests how studying research about instructional strategies could be built into faculty meetings. To accommodate this shift in emphasis during staff meetings, schools use alternative ways to communicate information that must be shared with all staff members. Suggestions offered, Richardson (1999), include departmental, grade-level meetings; round-robin memos; electronic communication (e.g., e-mail, voice mail); newsletters and weekly bulletins; brown-bag lunches; copies of pertinent meeting minutes or reports; and bulletin board messages in high-traffic areas.

Even when faculty meetings persist in their more traditional forms, learning still can be embedded in modest ways. Meetings can begin and end with quick learning connections. For example, invite staff members to locate one person they do not typically work with and share stories from practice about student or staff learning. Intentionally review collaborative group norms, such as those presented in Chapter 5, and ask participants to identify strengths and areas for improvement.

PLCs Examine Student Data

Professional learning communities (PLCs) in K–12 schools are characterized by a focus on student learning, a culture of collaboration, and a dedication to continual improvement and achievement of results (DuFour, 2005). They are ideal structures for examining student data, given the focused structure for educators that is centered squarely on student learning outcomes.

Educators interested in creating a PLC focused on student data must address several key challenges. First, teachers and administrators must work together to create a climate of *data safety* in which educators are willing to face the realities that emerge from analysis of student data. If teachers or principals are reluctant to accept that there are areas in which they could improve, or are hesitant to openly and honestly address these needs with colleagues, then the learning community will fail because of insufficient trust. Members of a PLC must be able to discuss deficiencies and collaboratively strategize to identify appropriate interventions for students.

A second challenge in most schools, as mentioned earlier in this chapter and also in Chapter 5, is finding the necessary *time* for PLCs to meet. Schmoker (1999) recommends that teachers come together to discuss student learning outcomes a minimum of six times a year and preferably every two to four weeks. These meetings should be dedicated to analysis of student learning data and discussion of possible interventions. Each meeting should conclude with a collaborative commitment to implementing the intervention(s) over the next time period.

Perhaps the biggest challenge for PLCs is that most educators do not have access to good *formative data* on student performance. Frequent, formative assessments have been shown to be the primary engine of school and student improvement (Black & Wiliam, 1998), yet most teachers do not engage in high-quality, formal, ongoing assessment of student learning. Formative assessments can take many forms, including selected-response, constructed-response, performance, portfolio, or affective assessments (Popham, 2005; Stiggins, Arter, Chappuis, & Chappuis, 2004). The PLC concept is rooted in the idea that educators have new student learning data to discuss each time they meet. Most teachers and principals will need additional training to implement effective formative assessment practices.

When meeting together to discuss student data, PLC members should be focused and task-oriented. The dedicated purposes of the meeting are to identify student learning needs and effective strategies for meeting those needs. Guiding questions to assist with focus include the following:

- What do the formative data tell us? What student learning needs emerge from our data analysis?
- Are we seeing particular patterns or trends? Which student learning needs are persisting despite our interventions to date? What successes are we seeing?
- Which student learning needs should we focus on for the next time period?
- In addition to (or instead of) what we're already doing, what two or three strategic interventions should we implement to address our students' ongoing learning needs?
- What outside resources or supports will we need to implement our interventions? (adapted from Schmoker, 1999, pp. 119–120)

Meetings should conclude with a shared commitment to implementing the identified strategies and confirmation of the next meeting time. Between each meeting, PLC members should collect another round of formative data to judge the success of the new interventions. *Contributed by Dr. Scott McLeod, University of Minnesota, Department of Educational Policy and Administration.*

Sharing School History

As expressed by O'Neill (2000), "Organizations, like families, have historical memory, and historical memory is a part of an organization's culture" (p. 63). The stories that staff members store and tell about their school have a powerful influence on beliefs, culture, and actions therein. As with individuals, understanding the history of an organization can assist in predicting and planning for the future. A shared understanding of the past can also assist with the induction of new members. For example, one school begins the annual back-to-school staff retreat by passing a wand among teacher-elders, who share stories about the beginnings of the school and significant changes that have occurred throughout its history.

O'Neill (2000) describes a historygram process that provides an opportunity for staff members to review a school's past. A long sheet of shelf paper is mounted along the length of a wall, with a timeline running along the edge. The group is introduced to Neuhauser's (1988) tribal theory. Members are invited to depict specific eras of the school's history. They may also line up around the room, forming a human historygram. Members then write, and are invited to post, responses to the following questions (O'Neill, 2000, p. 64):

- What was the name of your era (for example, "the Crisis Years")?
- What was the culture like? What tribal stories circulated? What symbols and ceremonies were important?
- What were the major initiatives?
- What were the goals of each initiative?
- How was the success of the initiatives measured? How did you know you were making progress? What was the basis for shifting direction?
- What values from the past do you want to bring into the future?

Shared responses offer an opportunity for reflection, analysis, and sense making. The historygram process can be used as a way of "orienting new members, reevaluating the group's purpose, creating a shared vision for the future, and helping members build commitment for a present initiative" (p. 64).

School Self-Review

Sutton (1995) describes a process by which schools can conduct a self-review of teaching and learning. Questions with specific indicators to elicit conversation and reflection about purpose, instruction, and effectiveness are posed. The questions are as follows:

- Is teaching purposeful?
- Does our teaching create and sustain motivation?

- Does our teaching cater to the abilities and needs of all the pupils in the school or group?
- Are our lessons managed in ways that ensure an efficient and orderly approach to teaching and learning?
- Is there effective interaction between teacher and pupils?
- Is evaluation of pupils' progress used to support and encourage them and to extend and challenge them appropriately?

By comparing faculty responses and preestablished indicators for each question, gaps between the current and desired state of practice are identified. This creates tension or dissonance that drives planning and action for movement toward a more desirable future state.

GETTING STARTED WITH SCHOOLWIDE REFLECTIVE PRACTICE

> As one tugs at a single thing in nature, he finds it is attached to the rest of the world.
>
> —Attributed to John Muir, noted conservationist

Getting started with reflective practices on a schoolwide basis is both inspiring and courageous work. It is inspiring because of all the challenges of creating and sustaining significant, meaningful changes in school cultures and practices. To make such a commitment reflects an optimistic view of educators, of schools, and of the potential for successful change. Moving toward reflective practice at the schoolwide level is courageous because the territory is vast and the specific pathways largely uncharted. Additionally, this work is about shifting culture—the established ways of doing and being in a school. Cultures are not easily shifted. Both the challenges and the potential for embedding reflection and learning into daily life in schools are great. To bolster your energy as you go, hold on to the vision of ongoing, meaningful professional learning that energizes staff to continually advance practices that result in higher levels of student learning.

The greater the number and variety of people who will be learning about reflective practices and how to embed such practices in their daily work in schools, the greater the need for intentional design and ongoing support. Schoolwide initiatives require a team of people to guide and support the development process. Who will join you in this leadership work? Colleagues who strive to continually refine and expand their reflective practices serve as authentic models in this work and are likely partners. Authenticity is a powerful attractor. High levels of trust and commitment are also needed—commitment to the shared leadership work of the team, to the growth and development of colleagues and of the school, and to the desired learning outcomes for students. Such shared and worthy commitments help to keep proactive and countercultural initiatives, such as reflective practice, on the front burner. In the "hot action" (Eraut, 1985) of school, it is especially easy for proactive work to fall by the wayside as urgent issues create pressure in the system and on people. A committed team emboldens proactivity.

What's our plan for getting started? The general design and approach? The key individuals who will be involved? The skills or capacities that need to be developed or connected? The structures that allow reflection and learning together? To guide your thinking about advancing schoolwide reflective practice, we offer the reflective practice framework shown in Figure 6.5 (also available as Resource 6.A). In it we identify key elements of a learning system, all of which interact to support learning and renewal. The elements are purpose, people, design and structure, resources, and results, all of which are embedded in your specific local context. Below we offer descriptions of each element and pose related questions to support reflection and planning (questions are also formatted for use in Resource 6.B). The questions are not ordered in a linear sequence. They prompt a potpourri of ideas for reflective planning conversations in your school. Given that much of schoolwide reflective practice occurs in the context of small groups and teams, we again encourage you to review the extensive set design considerations in Chapter 5.

Purpose . . . What and Why?

Purpose is the foundation on which effective schoolwide initiatives are built. The purpose is the reason for getting started in the first place. It is what gives meaning for participants. It is what drives motivation and effort. A primary motivator for educators is student growth. Also motivating for educators are opportunities to learn and grow in their own professional practice and effectiveness. Purpose is operationalized by articulating compelling outcomes or goals which inspire engagement and, ultimately, action. Too often, participants are not clear about or connected to the purpose or hoped-for outcomes of various improvement or renewal initiatives. This results in drag instead of momentum. To consider the purpose element of the reflection-planning framework, we offer the following questions:

- What do students in our school identify as some of the greatest challenges or frustrations? Why? What are their most meaningful experiences in school? How do their perspectives inform our decision making about professional-learning priorities?
- If student data were disaggregated by age, gender, race, or primary language, what would we learn about our effectiveness? What might be some of the actionable implications of these findings?

Figure 6.5   Reflective Practice Planning Framework

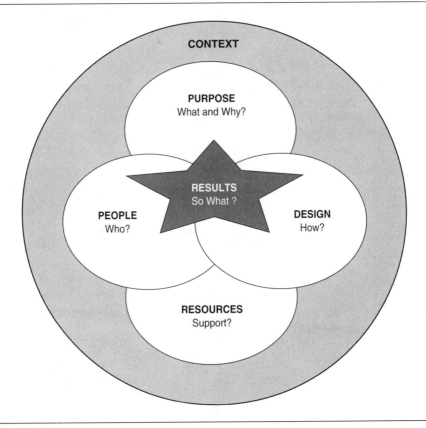

SOURCE: Adapted by permission from J. York-Barr, G. Ghere, & J. Sommerness (2003). What's working and what's not for your team? In T. Vandercook, J. York-Barr, & V. Gaylord (Eds.), IMPACT: Feature issue on revisiting inclusive education. University of Minnesota, Institute on Community Integration, pp. 14-15.

- Looking schoolwide, what do we see as our major strengths related to student learning? In what areas are students experiencing the greatest challenges? What is the range of evidence we use to substantiate and explore these claims? Where does this lead us in terms of targeting improvements in teaching and learning?
- Are there current or pressing schoolwide goals or issues that present an opportunity to embed and advance our capacities for reflective practice and professional learning?
- In what ways do department or grade-level meetings and committee work impact teaching practices and student learning? How are the efforts of departments and committees throughout the school related to improving practice and student learning? How can we support a focus on staff and student learning as central to team conversations, planning, and action?

People . . . Who?

People are the central resource for realizing positive results for any initiative. The greatest resource for learning is within and among the individuals who reflect, create, and work together. Involvement increases ownership and a sense of responsibility for outcomes. Joined by common purpose, strong relationships and complementary strengths, participants leverage the capacity to accomplish great works. In reflecting on the people element of the reflective planning framework, consider the following questions:

- Who would be centrally involved in the design, leadership, and facilitation of a schoolwide initiative? Who would be supporting players? Who and how many among the entire staff would be participants?
- In what ways will we be sure to foster trust, relationships, and learning?
- Who are the highly respected teachers that could serve as instructional leaders? How might their capacities be tapped? What conversations would inspire and support their central involvement in a schoolwide development initiative?
- How will we continually model and foster the value of inclusivity? In what ways will we continually invite and encourage authentic participation by all members so that collective contributions are leveraged?

Design: Structures and Strategies . . . How?

Design encompasses the specific orchestration of structures and strategies intended to support participant engagement. Structures include designated time for professional learning and specific determinations of group composition. Strategies include more specific procedures and skills for guiding interactions, reflection, and learning by participants. The knowledge, skills, and dispositions of participants will influence the design. Highly knowledgeable and skilled participants often need a lesser degree of design than those who are less knowledgeable or skilled. Design work is complex, interesting, and critically important. Reflect on the following questions as you consider the design element of the reflective planning framework:

- How well are opportunities for professional learning embedded into the daily and weekly schedules and the annual calendar?
- What the level of inquiry in our building? How skilled are our staff members with reflective practices? Are there sufficient numbers of people skilled in facilitation, communication, and group process skills to ensure productive use of group time?

- What would be effective ways for staff members to learn together? Vertically? Horizontally? New and experienced mixed? Same- or cross-subject areas?
- Would assigning or rotating specific group roles result in more productive interactions? Are external facilitators needed to get learning groups off to a strong and successful start or to build the confidence and competence of internal facilitators?
- In what ways can we support continuity and accountability within and between groups?

Resources . . . Support?

As used here, *resources* are viewed as the tangible supports, other than people, for initiating and moving the process forward. Such resources include space, time, equipment, materials, and refreshments. Questions for considering resource needs for schoolwide efforts to develop reflective practices are listed here.

- How much time will be allocated for engaging in reflective practices and professional learning? In what ways can we support embedding opportunities into existing schedules and activities?
- Can group members easily access one another at times other than face-to-face meetings, by means of physical proximity, voice mail, or e-mail, for example?
- Are equipment or materials (e.g., books, handouts, media, refreshments) needed to support the development of reflective practices? Is there a budget to support this work?

Context . . . Where?

Context refers to the surrounding conditions in which the reflective practices and professional learning take place. It includes things such as school culture, supportive and shared leadership, power, and politics. Too often, context is overlooked because it is viewed as existing outside the boundaries of core work and learning of educators. To the contrary, surrounding context deeply affects the accomplishments and sustainability of professional learning. The context as depicted in Figure 6.5 surrounds the more operational or core elements of the framework. This is because it can either constrain the core work, squeezing and constricting the development efforts, or it can enlarge and undergird the core work. Even highly effective learning groups can hit a ceiling if their work is not supported in the larger school context. Here are some questions for considering the context in which reflective practices and professional learning are being fostered and its potential influence on this work:

- Does the work align or conflict with high-profile school or district agendas or goals?
- Are administrators and informal school leaders supportive of the goals and proposed means of accomplishing the goals? How is this support communicated?
- How might key individuals who oppose or block the work of the team be engaged?
- Is there a history of failed improvement attempts or of punishing initiation? Such a culture dissuades participation. How can inviting, nurturing conditions be put in place?
- How can our school become a place where innovation and creativity are valued, modeled, and actively encouraged?
- What stories do people tell about our school? What kind of culture is reflected in these stories? What kind of stories reinforce the positive and hopeful views?

Results . . . So What?

Results are the products and outcomes of reflective practices and professional learning. Results are what sustain the interest and energy of participants. Results are both intrinsic and extrinsic, including student, educator, group, and school-level outcomes. Reflecting on the following questions can assist in gauging progress toward results:

- How have students and student learning been affected by our reflective practices? Have we learned to think more creatively and optimistically about influencing the learning and lives of our students, all of them? Are we making progress toward these outcomes? How do we account for progress being made or not?
- Do students notice the effects of our work? Has our professional growth re-created the learning atmosphere for students in positive ways? What might they say about how we learn and work together? Why might this matter?
- Have our groups grown in their capacities for learning and working effectively? Have working relationships improved? What have we noticed as indicators of progress?
- Have individual participants grown and been renewed by their participation? Have dispositions and practices been enhanced?
- How will we know whether reflection, learning, and improvement are taking hold? What evidence would we expect to observe, hear, or collect? How will we obtain and examine feedback about the progress we are making?
- Are more people choosing to engage in and support reflective practices? Is there more interest and confidence in our work by colleagues, administrators, and board members?

The absence of any one of the six elements in the reflection planning framework inhibits effectiveness. We invite you to use the Chapter Reflection Page (Figure 6.6) to write down your thoughts in response to these questions. You may also wish to skim through earlier chapters to be reminded of other ideas and strategies you view as significant. In the next and final chapter, we present lessons learned from our work of embedding reflective practices in the work of individual and school improvement and renewal. These lessons concisely capture a vision for reflective practice and may provide additional insight for the design and ongoing support of schoolwide reflective practice initiatives and efforts. And in this final chapter we offer some personal reflections on hope, possibility, and renewal in our work as educators.

As educators join together to learn and advance practice, their sense of professional efficacy and collegial support seems to increase. This is a critical capacity in the development of schoolwide reflective practices. Teachers must believe that positive and significant change is possible. As they join together, they begin to realize that others, like themselves, are interested in and committed to significant and positive improvements in the teaching and learning process. Together, improvement seems possible. Alone, it seems unlikely.

Figure 6.6   Chapter Reflection Page

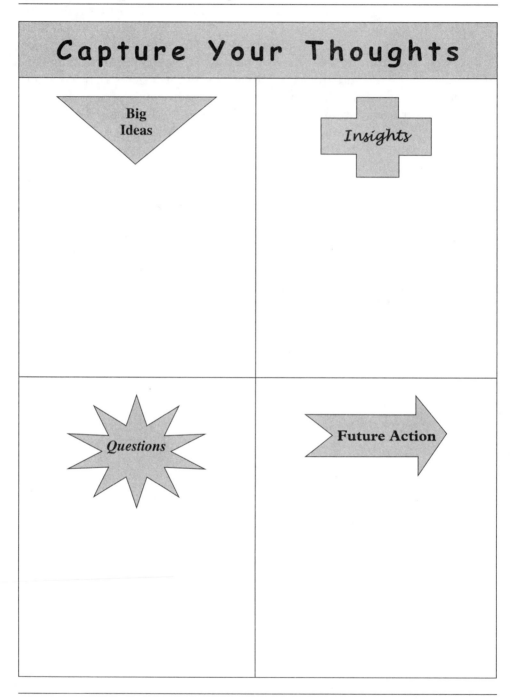

7

Moving Forward With Reflective Practice— in Hope and Possibility

You must become the change you want to see in the world.

—Attributed to Mohandas Gandhi

To become the change you want to see in your world of teaching and leading means making a commitment to continuously learn and improve your practice. It means being a reflective professional. Beginning with yourself, you become a fractal of the larger organization. Then, with others, expand reflective practices toward the outer level of the Reflective Practice Spiral. Modeling is still the best teacher. "Organizations ultimately learn via their individual members" (Kim, 1993, p. 37). It is the collective reflection and learning, the establishment of a professional learning community, that holds the greatest potential for positively affecting student learning and lifelong learning capacities.

Wenger (1998) describes the rich learning opportunities available when individuals come together in a community of practice. He specifically emphasizes the strengths of a community in which members with varied degrees of experience intentionally choose to learn together across levels and areas of the organization. New members learn from and contribute to the culture of practice as they participate more fully in the community. Three key features in Wenger's depiction of communities of practice are mutual engagement, negotiated meaning through dialogue, and a shared repertoire to enhance the system—in other words, joining together, learning together, and then acting together.

As human beings, we have an internal drive for learning and growth. We are also social beings who naturally seek connections to others: to be and to be connected, not just to do. Establishing communities of practice focused on learning is one way to satisfy these growth and social needs in addition to the central purpose of improving educational practice. A desirable future for our schools would be a program of attraction that draws in community members because of opportunities to learn, to connect with others, and to make a difference in the lives of children and families. Creating a program of attraction requires intentionally developing both the intellectual and pathic capacity of the school by promoting inquiry, seeking multiple perspectives on issues of practice, examining both internal and external knowledge, and nurturing connectedness and care. It is likely that the school communities that are most successful in establishing norms of reflection and continuous learning will be rewarded with long-term, enthusiastic commitments by their staff. A teacher, who participated in seasonal retreats focused on what it means to be a teacher and facilitated by Parker Palmer, remarked about the power of "being treated like a plant to grow, instead of a machine to be fixed." Reflective educators who are committed to lifelong learning and improvement will be looking for communities of practice that encourage their values and commitments, that engage their intellectual and social capacities, and that support their growth.

As stated in the preface to this book, we believe strongly in the positive intentions and commitments of today's educators. We also view educators as having knowledge and expertise that are largely untapped and underused. We know that well-designed and -implemented opportunities for reflection and learning together result in new insights about practice and renewed energy for teaching and learning. A question to keep foremost in our minds is, How do we create schools that are communities in which all members—students and adults—continue the journey of learning and continuous renewal? How do we feed and grow a schoolwide culture that supports meaningful learning in genuine community?

In this final chapter, we once again share our Reflective Practice Theory of Action but expand considerations related to application. Possibilities and questions about this particular model are put forward, with an emphasis on applied use as educators. Then we offer some additional lessons learned about establishing reflective practices to promote learning and improvement in schools. Our R-E-F-L-E-C-T-I-O-N mnemonic synthesizes and clarifies some of our learning during the past five-plus years. Then we highlight some of the paradoxes inherent in the ongoing design, implementation, and evolution of reflective practices. The last section of the chapter includes a story and strategies on hope, possibility, and renewal for our work as educators. In this final section we reflect on how hope and possibility are critical dispositions for work in schools and communities. We offer this chapter as inspiration and encouragement in your journey of becoming a more reflective educator who in turn inspires and encourages others.

REVISITING THE REFLECTIVE PRACTICE THEORY OF ACTION

> The growth of understanding follows an ascending spiral rather than a straight line.
>
> —Joanna Field (1934), *A Life of One's Own*
> (quoted in Maggio, 1992, p. 331)

As our reflective practice team gathered to consider how we might bring this second edition of our book to a close, we spent a lot of time in dialogue about the Reflective Practice Theory of Action presented throughout the book. We revisit this theory in this last chapter to share some of our book writing team's reflections on reflective practice. As depicted in Figure 7.1, our Theory of Action for Reflective Practice doesn't stand alone. It is embedded in a messy context which represents the world of practice (Schön's "swamp"), and it can be used to guide reflective practice within each level of the Reflective Practice Spiral, as represented by the individual, partner, small-group and team, and schoolwide symbols.

Theory as a Reframing Tool

Our team reflected upon the Theory of Action for Reflective Practice (Figure 7.1) knowing it was just one way to think about reflective practice and that its clear, linear presentation is deceptively simple. Like Joanna Field (quoted at the beginning of this section), we know that learning does not follow a straight line and that an ascending spiral image may better represent the learning process. One member of our team suggested that the progression of the elements be oriented downward instead of upward to reinforce the idea of moving deeper into the complexities and understandings of practice. Another member thought we should rearrange the geometric shapes in a more random order to illustrate that the elements do

Figure 7.1   Theory of Action for Reflective Practice Embedded in the Messy
Context of Practice

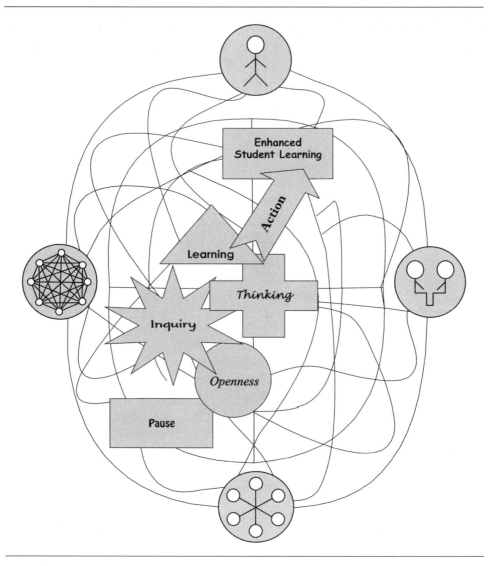

not necessarily occur in the order presented. We all agreed, however, that
regardless of position or orientation, each of the elements indicates an
important dimension of reflective practice. This point, perhaps, is made
more sharply if one considers what happens when any one of the elements
is absent.

Without *pausing,* there is no creation of space in which to engage in
reflection;

Without *openness,* there is no entertainment of divergent viewpoints;

Without *inquiry,* there is no predisposition for questioning practice;

Without *thinking,* there is no potential for expanded understandings;

Without *learning,* there is no generation of new knowledge to guide practice;

Without *action,* there is no change in practice and no possibility of impact on students;

Without *enhanced student learning and growth,* what does it matter?

One purpose of a theory or framework is to assist in understanding or explaining something about the world. In our case, this theory grew out of our need to put some order and structure around many important—and at times unwieldy—ideas, hoping to in some way support more effective learning and reflective action. So, does looking at this theory help you to better attend to various ideas of reflective practice? In what ways might this theory help you to reframe and better understand elements of your learning and design work? For example, consider the following questions: Am I creating enough of a pause (time, space) for effectively examining our science instruction? In what ways are we attending to safety, trust, and active listening to support openness? How might our study-group design attend to inquiry? What questions would expand inquiry in our meeting structure? What practice or action am I hoping to change to the benefit of students? How will I assess my effectiveness?

Theory as a Catalyst for Asking More Questions

For the authors, the theory, along with other ideas and experiences contained within this book, has also been a catalyst for raising further questions. For example, in our team's dialogue we deliberated about the role of choice in the reflective practice process: *choosing* to be open and to ask questions of ourselves; *choosing* to take the risks involved in examining our thinking, our practices, and the effects of our practices; *choosing* to take action. We have observed that many who begin the process of reflection and learning together never move to action—neither individual nor collective action. We know this is sometimes true of ourselves, as well. One member posited that because school culture typically fosters isolation, educators are starved for connection. When they actually have the opportunity to engage with colleagues, that is fulfilling in itself. To move beyond this early stage of group development in which everyone revels in the sense of connection and seems to get along (i.e., the forming stage, as described in Chapter 5, p. 149) involves more risk and discomfort that becomes evident in the storming stage. Moving beyond congeniality and thinking together to implementation and action has the potential to expose oneself to judgment, questioning, and possibly disapproval by peers.

Moving more deeply into reflective practice can be risky and lead to vulnerability and may often require active choice and intention to move into the tension and the less familiar: *choosing* to move through the conflict and tensions.

Our theory prompts us to raise new questions about intention and choice making in the reflective practice learning process and also leads us to pose numerous other questions as we think about the theory in relationship to our experiences. How and why do we move beyond connection and insight to action? What conditions can we create such that action is an expected and anticipated part of the process? Without action there is no authentic feedback from which to determine effectiveness. Is it reflective practice if there is no action? What compels us and what deters us from action? To count, does action need to occur in temporal proximity to thinking and learning? Might there be important changes happening even when evidence of change in behavior is not readily apparent? Do we sometimes act without knowing that our actions have in fact been influenced by the thinking and learning that arise from a reflective process?

These are just some of the many questions about reflective practice that remain elusive. We encourage you to create your own theory of action in conversation with colleagues and to raise your own questions. Take out a pencil and make additions or subtractions to Figure 7.1. We believe the laws of physics hold true equally well in the context of professional practice. Bodies at rest tend to stay at rest; bodies in motion tend to stay in motion. It may seem ironic that we urge action, given our emphasis throughout the book on taking time out from daily doings to engage in reflection and learning. We presume, however, the purpose of reflection and learning is to in some way take action that improves teaching and learning for the ultimate benefit of students. We urge you to continue your growth as a reflective practitioner by creating momentum around combining reflection *and* action. Move forward with this dual focus.

LESSONS LEARNED ABOUT REFLECTIVE PRACTICE

A Mnemonic Strategy to Synthesize Key Learning

Having just muddied the waters, we now shift gears to offer lessons learned through our experiences and study of reflective practice. We developed a R-E-F-L-E-C-T-I-O-N mnemonic (see Figure 7.2 or Resource 7.A) as the way to share these lessons. These lessons grew from reflecting on experiences and evolved over time and through many conversations. So, another part of the learning represented within our sharing of these lessons is that, to learn from experience, it is important to create rest stops with others along the way.

Figure 7.2   R-E-F-L-E-C-T-I-O-N Mnemonic: Lessons Learned About Reflective Practice

---

Relationships are first

Expand options through dialogue

Focus on learning

Leadership accelerates reflective practice

Energy is required for any system to grow

Courage is needed to reflect and act

Trust takes time

Inside-out

Outside-in

Nurture people and ideas

R: Relationships Are First

Establishing positive working relationships focused on student learning is an essential foundation for reflective practice. Relationships are the means by which information is communicated within a system. Relationships are the means for exploring who we are, what we believe, and how we might act. Relationships are the building blocks for any system (Wheatley, 1992). Webber (1993) advises that when you want to understand how an organization works, map the relationship flow, not the formal organizational structure. Wheatley (1992) writes, "The time I formerly spent on detailed planning and analyses, I now spend looking at the structures that might facilitate relationships" (p. 36). How can a web of interconnected relationships among staff members be woven throughout our school?

E: Expand Options Through Dialogue

Much knowledge about practice is inside the minds and hearts of educators. Conversations and dialogue are a way to "discover what they know, share it with their colleagues, and in the process create new knowledge for the organization" (Webber, 1993, p. 28). The value of time to reflect together cannot be overemphasized. Through dialogue, understanding is increased, assumptions are made explicit, possibilities are explored, and options are expanded. Creative and divergent thoughts emerge as colleagues inquire and share their perspectives and interpretations about events, circumstances, and experiences. Creativity is one of our most valuable resources as education moves forward in the new millennium. An open exchange through dialogue allows community members to participate in the creative process of shaping future directions and moving forward with important work. Ownership, responsibility, and commitment increase. In what ways might educators gather together to know one another, to remain open to other points of view, and to engage in dialogue that results in greater insights and expanded options for practice?

F: Focus on Learning

The purpose of reflective practice is to improve staff and student learning. If educators are not focused on learning, it is hard to imagine why students would be. At the core of reflective practice are the desire and commitment to continuously learn so that practices improve and students learn at higher levels. A focus on learning requires a certain amount of humility. We must acknowledge that we do not know everything. We have to give up needing to be right. Ultimately, "enlightened trial and error outperforms the planning of flawless intellects" (Kelley, as cited in Webber, 2000, p. 178). Reflection on practice involves learning through planning and reflective trial and error. Such learning transforms events, experiences, and information into the tacit knowledge and wisdom of distinguished educators. Opportunities for learning are limitless. How can learning become an explicit focus of staff conversations?

L: Leadership Accelerates Reflective Practice

Leadership by the formal and informal leaders in schools is an essential organizational resource for reflective practice and improvement. Leadership is influence and action, not position. Leadership must be shared by administrators and teachers. Without the principal, commitment—of resources and by people—wavers. The values and actions of the principal strongly influence the engagement of staff. Without teacher leaders, the relationships that are essential for successful change will not be activated. The learning that emerges from the firsthand knowledge of students in the classroom context will not be part of the conversation. Teacher leaders understand the inner workings and relationships within a school and can access those relationships as resources to positively influence student learning. To support educators' learning, schools must be structured to encourage the intellectual stimulation that fosters continuous development (Stewart, 1997). It is the job of the leadership team to create the conditions necessary for fruitful conversations about practice to happen (Webber, 1993). How do formal and informal leaders work together to create an environment that promotes conversations about learning?

E: Energy Is Required for Any System to Grow

Living systems require energy to grow. Energy in schools emerges from people who are meaningfully engaged in teaching, leading, and learning processes. Reflection creates energy by leading to new discoveries and insights about practice. Reflection with others creates even more energy as discoveries and insights are shared and channeled through relationships among educators throughout the school. Without positive energy that is productively channeled, systems die. Living systems cease to function when they do not have, or cannot make use of, the critical ingredients that create energy for life. Without supportive leaders and cultures, reflection and learning will not be defining elements in schools. Without educators reflecting and learning, schools will die. How do we harness and multiply the positive energy that already exists in our school? Learning is a renewable source of energy.

C: Courage Is Needed to Reflect and Act

Courage is the internal capacity that supports taking action, despite knowing the inherent risks. Making a commitment to reflective practice on a personal basis is a courageous act because it means opening ourselves up to considering multiple perspectives and ways of doing things. It means critically examining our assumptions and our behaviors. It means taking responsibility for our own learning and growth as professional educators and modeling this valued way of practice among our peers. Making a commitment to support reflective practice in groups or teams and throughout the school is a courageous act because it means going public with our commitments. It means being part of something that runs counterculture to the strong norms in schools of constantly doing rather than learning and doing. It means trying to walk the talk of reflective practitioners, holding ourselves accountable. How do we develop, demonstrate, and sustain the courage it takes to critically examine our practice and to make our learning public?

T: Trust Takes Time

Trusting relationships are the foundation for learning together. In a trusting relationship, we allow ourselves to be vulnerable—a requisite for learning. We can be open to exploring our assumptions. We choose to take risks, confident that we will not be punished or embarrassed if we make mistakes. "Learning requires tolerating people who make mistakes. Learning requires inefficiency. Learning requires tolerating failure. Learning requires letting people try things that they've never done before, things that they probably won't be very good at the first time around" (Webber, 2000, p. 176). Fear, which is the opposite of trust, is way too prevalent in some schools today. Webber (2000) points out that everyone seems interested in organizational learning, but no one is much interested in allowing individuals to learn. Mistakes and inefficiencies are inevitably part of the learning process but too often are not gracefully accepted. Educators will not choose to learn, at least not publicly, unless they are in a reasonably safe environment. Trust is difficult to build and easy to destroy. How do we foster a high-trust culture of learning in schools? How might each of us increase our own trustworthiness?

I: Inside-Out

Becoming a reflective educator is a process of inside-out change. Reflection is an internal capacity that is tapped by a genuine desire to learn and grow, not by external mandates. In the words of Michael Fullan (1993), "You can't mandate what matters" (p. 125). What matters most for teaching and learning is what is in the minds and hearts of educators. It is this inner capacity that connects educators with children, and children with learning. Becoming a reflective educator involves figuring out our own identity—who we are as people, as teachers, and as learners. We can teach only who we are (Palmer, 1998). And, by extension, we can lead only who we are. As we become more reflective, we can inspire an interest in others to become more reflective and to take the risks involved in continuously learning from and improving practice. Actions reflect beliefs and values. As Oliver Wendell Holmes reportedly said, "What you do speaks so loudly no one can hear what you are saying." What spaces can we create in our own lives to begin or to expand our commitment to reflective practice and personal change?

O: Outside-In

Becoming a reflective educator also requires being open to outside influences, such as colleagues with different views, findings from research, experiences of other schools and systems, and concerns expressed by the public and by policymakers. We must be willing to ask for input as well as to receive it. None of us is an island. None of our schools are islands in the community. We are influenced individually and organizationally by our surrounding context and must pay attention to it. Sometimes, change happens only when forces from the outside press in. Everything is connected to everything else. Open systems that engage with the environment grow and evolve (Wheatley, 1992). If we ignore external influences, we do so at our own peril. Closed systems eventually devolve. This principle holds whether the system is a person, a partnership, a team, a school, a district, or a community. Reflection is a process for making sense of both internal and external influences and for determining priorities for action. What helps us to remain continually aware of and open to our surrounding environments?

N: Nurture People and Ideas

Be inclusive; be caring. Create a culture of attraction in which educators are drawn into a school community because their needs to learn, to create, and to make a difference in the lives of children are met. Nurture their creativity and their spirit. Allow them to bring their unique contributions and gifts to the teaching and learning process. Teaching and learning are highly interpersonal. Effective educators vary greatly in their approaches and styles. For educators to bring their best to their work with children, they must be in places that nurture their growth, support their creativity, and offer feedback in the context of a trusting, professional learning community. Continue to invite people into the community of reflective educators. It is the collective energy that emerges from reflection and learning by many people that has the greatest potential for sustained and widespread improvement in educational practice. How might we be more inclusive and nurturing of the many, varied individuals in our school communities?

Paradox of Reflective Practice: More Lessons Learned

To light a candle is to cast a shadow.

—Ursula K. Le Guin (1968),
A Wizard of Earthsea (quoted in Maggio, 1992, p. 237)

Pathways to school renewal and improvement are less specific and more ambiguous than was once thought. The dynamic interplay among internal factors, combined with the influence of external factors, does not lend itself well to prescriptions for improvement. The best we can do is to be guided by principles, not specific steps. Only the direction and design can be controlled, not the outcomes. And even the design must constantly evolve in response to feedback that emerges with implementation, changing context variables, and new insights. Experimenting with reflective practice as one means of supporting school renewal has raised as many questions as answers about how to do this kind of work. Our work has heightened our understanding about paradox within reflective practice. Paradox can be thought of as tension that exists around ideas that seem both contradictory and true at the same time. This is the nature of our world as a whole and also of education today. Both the light and shadow are a part of the experience of a lit candle. The universe is one of randomness as well as pattern. Reflective practice requires both clarifying one's own voice and being open to other viewpoints. Schoolwide renewal may be fed by both inside-out and outside-in energy. Areas of paradox that become evident in our reflection and analyses are shown in Figure 7.3.

For reflective practices to be initiated, there must be enough vision and direction for participants to know where the initiative is headed and why, as well as enough flexibility to allow participants to shape the initiative to make it personally meaningful and contextually relevant. There must be enough design and structure for the process to get underway, as well as enough flexibility and creativity to allow ongoing adjustments that support an emergent learning process. There must be enough support and encouragement for participants to feel safe, as well as enough pressure and challenge to promote divergent thinking and action. At a personal level, individual teachers must attend well to their own wholeness first (remember the "oxygen mask" image from Chapter 3), and teachers and schools also must be focused on the well-being of all members of the community; both care of self and care about others are needed. There must be acknowledgment of the uncertainty, ambiguity, and value of practice in the swamp, as well as consideration of the clarity found in "high hard ground" knowledge reported in research literature. There must be enough focus on individual learning and growth needs, as well as attention to the learning and growth needs of the organization. There must be sustained attention around student needs, because this is ultimately why we are teaching, and there must be persistent attention toward the adult-learning needs within a community, because when the adults stop growing, student learning becomes vulnerable, as well.

Again, we offer our Paradox of Reflective Practice visual (Figure 7.3) to become another seed for further inquiry. How much is enough planning and yet still open enough? How do we discover the balance between the points of tension? It's hard to tell until you get underway. What's important is to know that these areas of apparent contradiction are actually inherent tensions. Imagine launching a reflective practice initiative without any direction or aim. Why would anyone be compelled to participate? Imagine only the presence of support and encouragement, without pressure and challenge. How would new thinking emerge? Imagine a commitment to reflective practice without a design or structure to support it. How would you start? The nature of paradox is the coexistence of multiple and seemingly contradictory truths. The work of reflective practice rests solidly within both/and thinking instead of either/or thinking. And noticing the presence of paradox is an invitation for more learning, not something to be feared or run away from.

Figure 7.3   Paradox of Reflective Practice

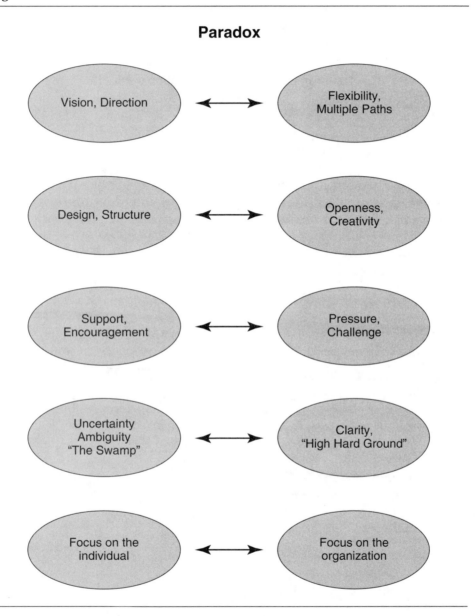

FOSTERING HOPE AND RENEWAL

In this final section of the book, we focus on hope and renewal. What is hope? In Scott Sanders's book (1998) *Hunting for Hope*, he shares, "I have discovered that the words *hope* and *hop* come from the same root, one that means to leap up in expectation" (p. 20). Further, he adds, "Memory grips the past; hope grips the future" (p. 22). Hope involves expectations. In *The*

Impossible Will Take a Little While: A Citizen's Guide to Hope in a Time of Fear (2004), editor Paul Loeb suggests that believing we have options, as well as seeing abundance in our world, is a way to move toward hope and not descend into despair. Loeb writes,

> Whether the challenge is political or personal, effective remedies differ from individual to individual. But solutions always involve altering perspective, replacing tunnel vision with an expanded view that lets in more light, more possibility. And possibility is the oxygen upon which hope thrives. (p. 19)

Although Sanders and Loeb do not use the term *reflective practice,* these ideas of expectation, options, possibilities, and abundance resonate with the work of reflective practice and connect this work to a broader context. Consider the six strategies identified in Figure 7.4 and described below to nourish your spirit of hope, possibility, and renewal on your reflective practice journey.

Ask Questions and Listen Well

A dual focus on both inquiry and listening is key to reflective practice in schools and to an overall orientation of fostering hope. Questions bring in new perspectives and possibilities. Questions can help create a "crack" that can let the light in, replacing tunnel vision with expanded view. Listening—deep listening—suggests deepened understanding and new insights that can grow from considering new possibilities. Listening requires a deliberate pause, a slowing down, a focus on seeking to understand one's own voice and other voices. To feed hope, ask questions and listen well. In other words, be reflective.

Acknowledge the Despair and Fear

Many educators feel pulled and squeezed. Many experience a narrowing of the curriculum and are concerned about movement toward less relevant and lifeless school experiences. There are changes that we fear. There are students and families with difficult lives. The budget cuts and loss of staff positions are painful. There can be points of despair in our work. We believe that part of nourishing hope involves finding ways to understand and constructively address despair and fear, not pretending that fears and concerns don't exist. Both Parker Palmer, a renowned educator, and Pema Chödrön (1994), a renowned Western Buddhist nun, describe moving into and through fear instead of following an instinct or tendency to run from it. Administrators and teacher leaders can be role models for dealing with fear and despair in constructive ways. We think that it can be hard for teachers to move on to hopeful actions if fears and moments of despair are never validated. Both you and this book hold insight and strategies for naming and learning from fears and concerns.

Shift to an Abundance Mindset

An abundance paradigm feeds hope and possibility. Abundance is reflected in beliefs such as *Everything that we need is right here. . . . We have enough. . . . The*

Figure 7.4   Strategies for Hope, Possibility, and Renewal

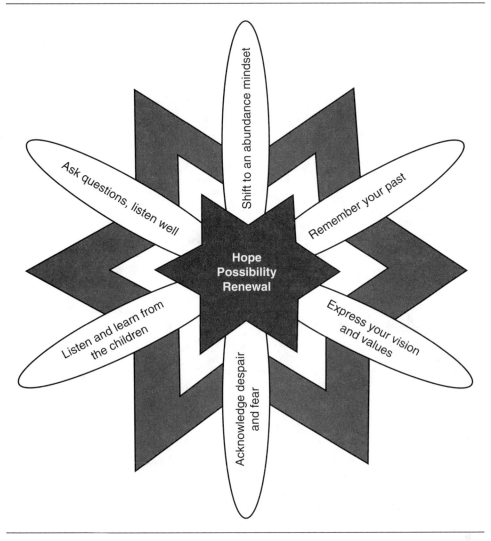

answers exist within; we just have to find them. Abundance is sometimes contrasted with a paradigm of scarcity: *We don't have enough. . . . You have what I need. . . . I won't be okay until I get _____.* We acknowledge the genuine scarcity of resources such as staff, chairs, reading books, paper, computers, and assistive technology for students with disabilities. This is real. We also challenge ourselves to focus on a paradigm of abundance: abundance of ideas, creativity, and capacities within for growth and renewal. This is also real. An abundance lens looks to name the progress; notices what *is* and not just what is not; celebrates the movement forward even when it seems like baby steps; says, "Wow . . . look at that"; nurtures and renews the garden instead of doing a complete overhaul; and celebrates the points of light. A friend of one of the authors says: "There's a crack in everything—that's how the light gets in." The paradigm of possibility, of abundance, is "the oxygen upon which hope thrives" (Loeb, 2004, p. 19).

Remember Your Past

Consider historian Howard Zinn's words: "What we choose to emphasize in this complex history will determine our lives. If we see only the worst, it destroys our capacity to do something. If we remember those times and places—and there are many—where people have behaved magnificently, this gives us the energy to act, and at least the possibility of sending this spinning top of a world in a different direction." (Loeb, 2004, p. 71). So we ask ourselves: Who has inspired my development as an educator and as a person, and how? What magnificent people do I want to remember in my journey as an educator and human being? And, in looking at our history as reflective practitioners, we savor the present voices of knowledge and inspiration from Dewey, Schon, van Manen, Sparks, Langer-Colton, Chödron, Palmer and _____ (fill in the blank). And then we stretch back to Dewey. And then we stretch much farther back in time to Socrates, Buddha, Lao-tzu. We are not the first and we will not be the last in this quest to create reflection in our work and in our lives. This instills hope, knowing that we are a part of an important, sustainable idea: that of reflective thought.

Listen to and Learn From the Children and Youth

Ultimately, what may give many of us the most hope is in continuing to find ways to listen and learn with and from our children and youth. Why are we teaching? The children. Why are we trying to improve ourselves as teachers? The children. Who can hold deep insights and excellent questions about learning and life? The children. The power and possibilities that emerge from our youth are astounding.

Express Your Vision and Values

A final strategy for building hope and renewal involves keeping vision and values alive in our daily work: naming, showing, asking, drawing, telling a story, expressing our beliefs as educators through our daily actions. What are the non-negotiables for me as a teacher when it comes to how to teach and what I teach? What feelings and experiences do I want each child to have when entering this learning community? What matters most in our school, and how do we express this? *Vision* as a verb brings hope to our work by inspiring us to reach to our ideals.

Located in Table 7.1 is a Masai story from Walter Olsen and Bill Sommers's (2004) book *A Trainer's Companion: Stories to Stimulate Reflection, Conversation, and Action.* We invite you to consider the hope and possibilities within such a story. We believe that this story challenges us with a vision that many educators and citizens would like to see permeate all communities. Many agree that we are not doing enough for the children in the world.

Table 7.1   A Story of Hope and Possibility

A Masai Story: How Are the Children?

Among the most accomplished and fabled tribes of Africa, no tribe was considered to have warriors more fearsome or more intelligent than the mighty Masai. It is perhaps surprising then to learn the traditional greeting that passed between Masai warriors. "Kasserian ingera," one would always say to another. It means, "And how are the children?"

It is still the traditional greeting among the Masai, acknowledging the high value that the Masai always place on their children's well-being. Even warriors with no children of their own would always give the traditional answer, "All the children are well." This meant, of course, that peace and safety prevail, that the priorities of protecting the young, the powerless are in place, that Masai people have not forgotten its reason for being, its proper function and responsibilities. "All the children are well" means that life is good. It means that the daily struggles of existence, even among a poor people, do not preclude proper caring for its young.

I wonder how it might affect our consciousness or our own children's welfare if, in our own culture, we took to greeting each other with the same daily question. "And how are the children?" I wonder if we heard that question and passed it along to each other a dozen times a day, if it would begin to make a difference in the reality of how children are thought of or cared for in this country?

I wonder if every adult among us, parent and non-parent alike, felt an equal weight for the daily care and protection of all children in our town, in our state, in our country. I wonder if we could truly say without hesitation, "The children are well, yes, all the children are well."

What would it be like? If the president began every press conference, every public appearance, by answering the question, "And how are the children, Mr. President?" If every governor of every state had to answer the same question at every press conference. "And how are the children, Governor? Are they well?" Wouldn't it be interesting to hear their answers?

SOURCE: Reprinted by permission from W. Olsen & W. A. Sommers (2004). *A trainer's companion: Stories to stimulate reflection, conversation, and action.* Baytown, TX: AhaProcess.

CLOSING

> The world is round and the place which may seem like the end may also be only the beginning.
>
> —Ivy Baker Priest, in *Parade* (1958)
> (quoted in Maggio, 1992, p. 28)

In coming to the end of the book, we acknowledge the blur between beginnings and endings, and our belief in wholeness, cycles, and connections. Our wish is for you, the reader, to "end" the book with not only a greater understanding of reflective practice concepts, skills, and strategies, but also a sense of renewal, new beginnings, and recommitment to possibility that exists in our work with children in our schools. We also realize that some readers may never "end" the book, because perhaps you are the type that skims and pokes through various parts of the book that look the most relevant and you're always starting new or continuing on.

Embedding reflective practice in education is about creating significant cultural change in schools. It is messy. It is complicated. There are no certain paths. The outcomes, however, can significantly and positively affect both educators and the students they serve. As you move through a process of becoming more reflective as an individual and with your colleagues, reflection-in-action, reflection-on-action, and reflection-for-action will provide the feedback needed to make ongoing adjustments. The "Capturing Your Thoughts" Chapter Reflection Page (Figure 7.5) can be used to write down ideas from this chapter that you may find useful for future reference as you continue your work in this area. Future practice and study about reflective practices for professional development and school renewal will increase our understanding about how to move forward. For now, congratulate yourself on beginning the process, or on this new beginning of sorts!

Feel confident that your choice to reflect on your practice will result in changes and thought and action that positively influence learning and development by you, your students, and your community. Remember that the objective is progress, not perfection. Keep the following clearly in mind:

> To reflect on action is to be a lifelong learner. To be reflective is a choice that is made against the background of beliefs and values. To be a constantly developing performer or to remain an expert performer requires the constant input of energy to do the work of reflection and learning with commitments to action. This energy source is inside the self; it is released by enabling understandings within a worldview. Quality performance is the outcome of a belief in quality. (Butler, 1996, p. 280)

What do you think you might do first as a result of reading this book? In what ways could you use this information tomorrow? Who else might work with you to expand reflection and learning in your school? If your school were a place in which students and staff continuously learn and have fun doing so, what would that look like? What would a desirable future school be like for you? How might you be part of that vision? How might you be part of making that vision a reality?

Figure 7.5   Chapter Reflection Page

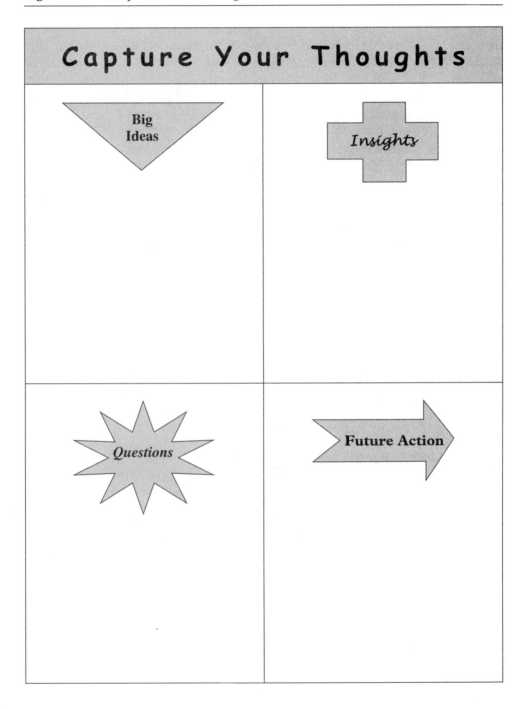

We leave you here to begin. We leave you in the spirit of hope and possibility. What better time than now to leap up in expectation of a future in which the importance of teaching and learning is transparent to students, is appreciated by our communities, and is validated through the continued goodwill and good works of educators? Such a future is possible as individual educators join together, join with students and families, and join with their communities to create places in which reflection, learning, growth, and action are anticipated, honored, and valued. Our collective futures are in our hands. The children and young adults whom we serve today will be serving the world tomorrow. We must do what we can to teach them well, to help them realize their potential, to instill in them a sense of connection, curiosity, and a drive for learning that will be so very needed in tomorrow's world, the world they will lead.

> *Leap up in expectation.*
>
> *Grip the future.*
>
> *Be reflective.*
>
> *Nurture relationships, nurture the garden.*
>
> *Choose to learn. Choose to pause. Choose to act.*
>
> *Take risks. Be daring. Be human.*
>
> *Find a crack to let the light in.*
>
> *Be aware. Be kind. Be human.*
>
> *Leap up in expectation. Hope. Hope.*

Resources

Resource 1.A Theory of Action for Reflective Practice

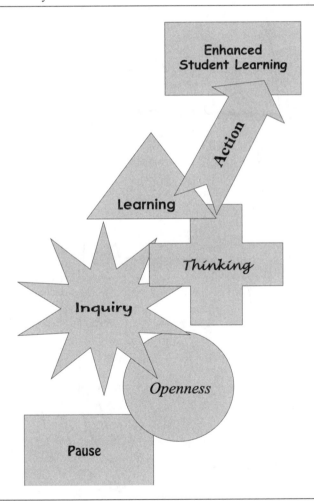

Resource 1.B Reflective Practice Spiral

Resource 1.C Schoolwide Web of Relationships

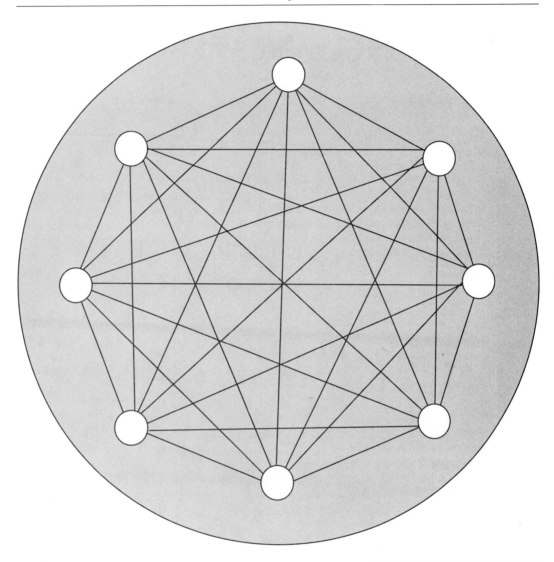

Resource 1.D   Framework for Closing Reflections

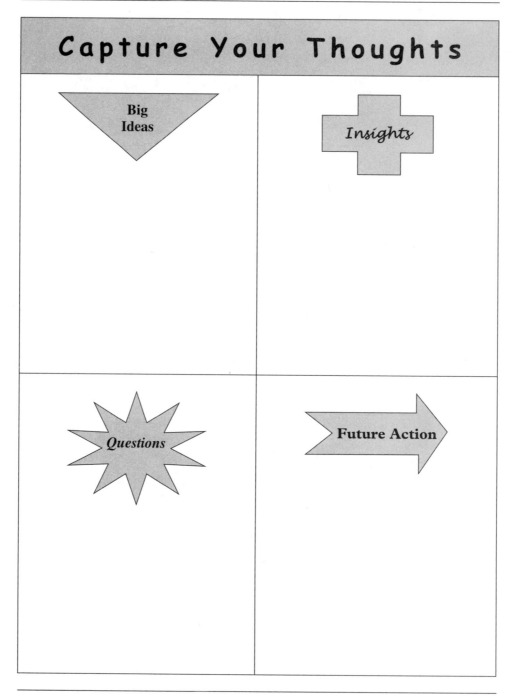

Resource 2.A Questions to Support Reframing

Tightly held views block us from considering different explanations and from learning new ways of thinking and practice. For learning to occur, firmly entrenched views must be let go. As Butler (1996) explains, "Learning is and should be, on some occasions, a disturbing and unsettling process . . . deep learning involves frame breaking and discomfort" (pp. 275–76). Listed here is a menu of questions that can assist with reframing and understanding circumstances, events, or behavior from a different point of view.

- *How might I think about this situation differently?*

- *What am I not considering?*

- *What judgments and assumptions are blocking alternative ways of seeing this situation?*

- *Why do I hold so strongly to this one view? What function does this serve? Is there something that I am protecting or defending?*

- *Has this always been the case, or have there been times when something different has happened? Why?*

- *What influences on my thinking and behaving have I not considered? What influences on another person's thinking and behaving have I not considered, including contextual and personal circumstances?*

- *How might understanding the life experiences of another person help me to see things in a new way? How do my own life experiences block me from seeing things in a new way?*

- *How do my values and beliefs guide me to think this way? How might other values and beliefs alter my thinking?*

- *If I trusted people's intentions, would I interpret their responses differently?*

- *Are there other people who could help me see this differently?*

- *What would happen if I were to think of this as an opportunity to learn instead of a threat to defend or a fear to protect against?*

- *What are some other ways I could go about addressing this goal?*

Resource 3.A Framework for Personal Reflection on Professional Purpose and
Practice

Level	Reflection Questions	Personal Response
Mission or Overarching Purpose	What am I working toward? What are we creating or aiming to achieve?	
Identity	Who am I in this work? How do I hope to contribute?	
Values and Beliefs	What do I believe about or value in this work? Why should we proceed in this way?	
Capabilities, Strategies, Mental Maps	How do I or will I accomplish this work? What strategies will guide my actions?	
Behaviors and Skills	What do I do to advance this work?	
Environment and Structure	What structures and surroundings support this work?	

(Framework adapted from Dilts, 1996, and Garmston & Wellman, 1998).

Resource 3.B Personal Inventory of Reflective Practices

Reflective Educator ... Take Inventory

	CURRENT REALITIES In what specific situations do you find yourself....	REFLECTION PROMPT How much reflection and learning is going on?	POSSIBILITIES How might reflection and learning be advanced?
	... on your own?		
	... in dyads or triads?		
	... in small groups or teams?		
	... in large groups (e.g., school or organizational level)?		

271

Resource 3.C A 4-Step Reflection Process

Think about a significant event, interaction, or lesson that occurred in your classroom or school, with students or adults, that you feel is worth further reflection. You might choose a positive and encouraging experience, or you might choose a more unsettling and challenging experience.

Now consider the following series of questions to prompt your thinking about the experience. You may wish to write down your thoughts. You may even want to share your thoughts aloud with another person.

1. *What happened?* (Description)

2. *Why?* (Analysis, interpretation)

3. *So what?* (Overall meaning and application)

4. *Now what?* (Implications for action)

Resource 3.D   Questions to Reflect on Meaning in Life

Amid the busyness of everyday life, there are times we find ourselves deep in thought about who we are, how we contribute or would like to, what is important to us, and to whom we are especially grateful. There are times we are out of balance and must claim space to consider these life-meaning perspectives. Are we human doings, or human beings? In what ways are we both doings and beings? Select from among the following questions to prompt your personal reflection.

1. *What is it that I want to do with my most precious thing—my life?*

2. *If 80 percent of what I do has little noticeable impact and 20 percent provides me with the best results, what things in the 80 percent am I going to stop doing?*

3. *Is my self-worth stronger than my self-critic, and how do I know? Is my self-critic preventing me from moving toward my most valued life pursuits?*

4. *How do I use my gifts and talents to foster caring, commitment, and interdependence in my work?*

5. *What am I willing to get fired for?*

6. *What words of wisdom would my parents or grandparents offer as I sort through what matters most and how I can contribute?*

7. *How do my children think of me, not only as a parent, but as a person? A citizen? What lessons do I hope to have taught them through modeling?*

8. *Who are the people that bring joy to my life? And to whose life do I bring joy?*

9. *Who have been the most important mentors in my life? Have I thanked them lately? What is stopping me?*

10. *If I had one week to live, what would I do?*

11. *In one sentence, what would I want written in my obituary?*

Resource 3.E   Questions for Getting Started With Individual Reflective Practice

The longest relationship that you have is with yourself. May as well make the best of it! Becoming more reflective is a way to learn more about who you are as a person and educator, what is important to you, how you think, and what you say and do. Choosing reflection supports your desire for excellence and effectiveness in your work. To guide thinking about your reflection capacities and your preferred means of reflection, contemplate the following questions.

1. *Thinking about your own development as an educator, what are you most interested in learning more about? Why does this seem important to you?*

2. *What about the considerations of identity, ethics, courage, care, and voice? Which of these areas seem most important to ponder further right now, and why? What thoughts do you have about how you might step into examining such an area of your identity and/or beliefs and values?*

3. *As you reflect on your teaching and learning practices with students, what are your big interests and questions? What parts of the curriculum are students missing? How can you maximize the learning strengths of all your students?*

4. *What would be the best way to go about addressing these interests and questions? What ways of reflection are best aligned with your learning styles (e.g., journaling, exercising, reading, mapping)?*

5. *How might you create space in your life to reflect and learn on a regular basis?*

6. *Are there additional people you want to include in your process of reflection?*

Resource 4.A   Questions to Prompt Questions for Instruction

Most of the time, educators are either planning for a future event or reflecting back on something that has already occurred. Following are some questions that may be helpful in promoting reflective thinking about a lesson and about professional goals and resources for achieving those goals.

1. *How do you think the lesson went? What happened that caused it to go that way?*

2. *When you think about what you had planned and what actually happened, what were the similarities, and what were the differences?*

3. *As you think about the results you got, what were some of the ways you designed the lesson to cause that to happen?*

4. *When you reflect back, what would you do differently next time you teach this lesson?*

5. *As you consider this lesson, what outcomes do you want to have happen again?*

6. *What are some of the professional goals that you are working on in your practice?*

7. *What resources are available as you work toward your professional goals?*

Resource 4.B   Questions to Prepare for Being Coached
(From Jim Roussin, Big Lake, Minnesota)

Cognitive Coaching: Preconference Form

Staff member _____

Administrator _____   Coach _____

Grade/subject to be observed _____

Preconference date/time _____

Observation date/time _____

Postobservation date/time _____

Please complete this form and send a copy to the building principal who will be observing your lesson in the Cognitive Coaching cycle. The questions below will be the focus of the preconference session with your coach.

- What are the ***learning goals you are targeting*** for the lesson/event that will be observed?

- What ***indicators or evidence will you collect*** to know that you were successful in reaching your targeted learning goals?

- What are the ***strategies or learning activities*** you will be implementing to engage and guide your students toward the identified learning goals?

- What is a ***personal learning focus*** you have for this particular lesson?

- What ***data would you like the coach to collect*** for you that could be helpful in supporting your own learning or success in reaching your targeted professional learning goals?

- Is there anything in particular that you want the principal and coach to know prior to the lesson?

Resource 4.C   Questions for Getting Started With Partner Reflective Practice

Reflection with a partner is a gift you can give to yourself and to a partner. Most of us are driven to learn and improve. A trusted partner can support our growth. In addition to the benefit of improvements in practice, a relationship is formed that is a valuable resource and support in many aspects of your work life. As you walk down the hallways, into a faculty meeting, or through the work room, you carry with you the assurance that at least one person knows and cares about you, your practice, and your desire to continuously improve. You are not alone. By reflecting with partners you can move from a congenial level of interaction to a more substantial and collaborative interaction, in which commitments to improvement are shared. To guide your thinking in moving forward with partner reflective practice, contemplate the following questions.

1. *What are my biggest questions about my teaching or leadership practice? What do I want to learn more about? How do I hope such learning would improve my practice?*

2. *Why am I drawn to reflecting with a partner or two? Who can support and enrich my learning? Who would bring a different perspective that would enrich my learning? Who would be interested in contributing to my growth as an educator?*

3. *What type of environment is conducive to listening, exploring, and thinking?*

4. *How often would I like to, or would it be reasonable to, get together?*

5. *What would make our reflection time a real treat (e.g., coffee and good food)?*

6. *What type of reflection framework, strategy, or protocol would support our learning together?*

Resource 5.A   Selected Quotes About Reflective Practice

Selected quotes about reflective practice. Which are meaningful to you?

The main objective of reflective practice is to ensure a more accurate and relevant understanding of a situation . . . to produce effective, relevant action which will facilitate the occurrence of more desired and effective outcomes. Barry Bright, 1996.

The ultimate guardians of excellence are not external forces, but internal professional responsibilities. Paul Ramsden, 1992.

Reflective practice is as much a state of mind as it is a specific set of activities. Joseph Vaughan, 1990.

Trust is perhaps the essential condition needed to foster reflective practice in any environment. If the reflective process is going to flourish in an organizational setting, the participants must be confident that the information they disclose will not be used against them—in subtle or not so subtle ways. Osterman & Kottkamp, 1993.

To suspend is to change direction, to stop, step back, and see things with new eyes. This is perhaps one of the deepest challenges humans face—especially once they have staked out a position. William Isaacs, 1999.

Empathic relationships generally confer the greatest opportunity for personal, and thus professional, growth in educational settings. Carl Rogers, 1986.

Thinking together implies that you no longer take your own position as final. You relax your grip on certainty and listen to the possibilities that simply result from being in relationship with others—possibilities that might not otherwise have occurred. Isaacs, 1999.

Awareness of one's own intuitive thinking usually grows out of practice in articulating it to others. Donald Schön, 1983.

The student cannot be taught what he needs to know, but he can be coached. . . . Nobody else can see it for him, and he can't see just by being told. Donald Schön, 1987.

Resource 5.B   Tabletop Collaborative Group Norms
(Content from Garmston & Wellman, 1998)

Dialogue

Discussion

Suspension

Pause

Paraphrase

Presume positive intentions

Probe for specificity

Pursue balance inquiry/advocacy

Put ideas on the table

Pay attention to self and others

Resource 5.C   Protocol for Meeting or Learning-Group Design

Meeting/Learning Group Agenda	
Overall Purpose: Meeting Purpose:	Schedule of Meetings:
Outcomes:	

CONTENT		PROCESS
	O P E N I N G	
	C O R E	
	C L O S I N G	

Resource 5.D   Protocol for Planning Differentiated Instruction
(Adapted from Kronberg & York-Barr, 1998)

Step 1: Identify key concepts, standards, guiding principles or essential questions, and desired outcomes.

Step 2: Differentiate levels of student understanding.

Step 3: Determine which skills are important for the students to learn, review, and apply.

Step 4: If relevant to your particular context, identify which district objectives and/or state standards might interface with the unit or topical area.

Step 5: Given the range of student needs, abilities, strengths, and experiences, determine how students can best learn about the identified concepts, principles, or essential questions.

Step 6: Select product options that will encourage students to apply their learning from the unit, as well as integrate the knowledge and skills from the unit with previous knowledge and experiences.

Step 7: Select formative and summative assessment approaches that can be used throughout the unit to provide helpful feedback to both students and staff.

Note: Questions to guide reflection on each of the steps are located in Chapter 5, Table 5.5.

Resource 5.E   Protocol for Collaborative Examination of Student Work

---

1. Get started and study the student work (15 minutes)
   - *Group members identify the learning goal correlated with the student work.*
   - *Group members individually look at student work and make notes about the strengths and weaknesses evident in the work.*

2. Describe the work: What do you see? (20 minutes)
   - *Group members describe what they see in the work.*
     (a) What are the specific skills and understandings evident in the work?
     (b) What don't students know, as evidenced in or missing from the work?

3. Identify next steps for instruction (20 minutes)
   - *Everyone is invited to share ideas for the next instructional steps to improve achievement toward and beyond lesson objective:*
     (a) How has the group approached these skills and concepts in the past? What instructional strategies did they focus on since last session?
     (b) How can the group build on the skills/concepts evidenced in the work?
     (c) What will each member of the group do within his or her instructional setting to improve learning in this area?
     (d) What ideas does this generate for the group or school?

4. Reflect on the experience and identify next steps for staff development. (5 minutes)
   - *Group discusses how the protocol process is working.*
   - *Group identifies any needed professional development or resources.*
   - *Group schedules next review of student work and determines the learning goal on which to focus and the type of work to bring.*

SOURCE: Developed by Nancy Nutting, consultant from Richfield, Minnesota, and Cindy Stevenson of the Lakeville Public Schools, Minnesota.

Resource 5.F Questions for Getting Started with Reflective Practice in Small Groups or Teams

When reflecting in groups or teams, the potential emerges to influence more broadly the educational practices within and throughout the school. This potential significantly increases when multiple groups and teams embed reflective practices in their work and when efforts expand to include the vast majority of individuals and groups in a school. The sustainability of groups depends on four factors: a meaningful and continuing purpose; positive and productive working relationships; the opportunity for learning, growth, and contribution; and the outcomes realized by students. The highest priority for educators spending time together should be reflection and learning focused on students and instruction. Consider the following questions in the design of collaborative reflective practice in small groups and teams:

1. *What is the purpose of the group? What is the focus for learning? What are the desired outcomes? How will students benefit from the learning that occurs within this group?*

2. *How structured will the group process need to be to address the given purpose? Is there a specific time frame that must be honored? What kind of design will best promote participation, learning, and positive outcomes?*

3. *Should an existing group or team of individuals convene? Should additional individuals be included? Does a new group need to be configured?*

4. *Who should be part of the group? Who has an important perspective to share? Who will be expected to follow through with the outcomes?*

5. *How big should the group be? If a large number of people are involved, how will full participation be fostered? How might selective breaking into smaller groups be useful?*

6. *Do we need to assign specific group roles? Should they be rotated? Who will assume lead roles in the group? Might two teachers share responsibility for organizing, communicating, and preparing? Is a facilitator needed? If so, who might that be?*

7. *Do the group members know one another well? If they do not, how should we explicitly focus on developing relationships and trust?*

8. *What experiences do group members have with reflection and learning? How intentional do we need to be about developing individual and group capacities for reflection, learning, and working together?*

9. *How will we determine the effectiveness of the group process? What content and process reflection strategies might we use?*

10. *Are there specific elements in Chapter 5 that would support our development work?*

Resource 6.A Framework for Reflective Practice Planning and Design

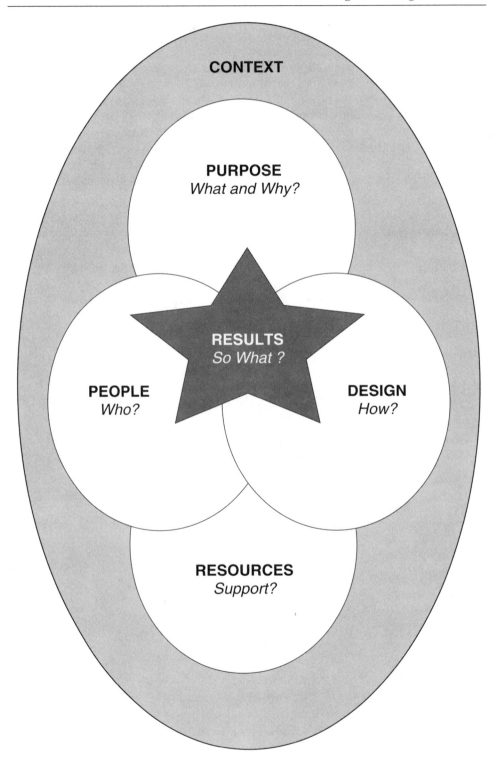

Resource 6.B   Questions for Getting Started with Schoolwide Reflective Practice

Getting started with schoolwide reflective practices is both inspiring and courageous work. Both the challenges and potential for embedding reflection and learning into daily life in schools are great. The greater the number and variety of people, the greater the need for intentional design and ongoing support. To guide planning for advancing schoolwide reflective practice, consider the following questions, organized by the elements of the Reflective Planning Framework.

Purpose . . . What and why?

1. *What do students in our school identify as some of the greatest challenges or frustrations? And why? What are their most meaningful experiences in school? How do their perspectives inform our decision making about professional learning priorities?*

2. *Looking schoolwide, what do we see as our major strengths related to student learning? In what areas are students experiencing the challenges? What is the range of evidence we use to substantiate and explore these claims? If student data were disaggregated by age, gender, race, or primary language, what might we learn about our effectiveness? Where might this lead us in terms of targeting improvements in teaching and learning?*

3. *Are there current or pressing schoolwide goals or issues that present an opportunity to embed and advance our capacities for reflective practice and professional learning?*

4. *In what ways do department or grade-level meetings and committee work impact teaching practices and student learning? How can we better support a focus on staff and student learning as central to team conversations, planning, and action?*

People . . . Who?

1. *Who should be centrally involved in the design, leadership, and facilitation of a schoolwide initiative? Who would be supporting players? How will the entire staff participate?*

2. *In what ways will we be sure to foster trust, relationships, and learning?*

3. *Who are the highly respected teachers that could serve as instructional leaders? How might their capacities be tapped? What conversations would inspire and support their central involvement in a schoolwide development initiative?*

4. *In what ways will we foster the value of inclusivity? How can we continually invite and encourage authentic participation by all so that collective contributions are leveraged?*

Design: Structures and Strategies . . . How?

1. *How well are opportunities for professional learning embedded into the daily and weekly schedules and the annual calendar?*

2. *What is the level of inquiry in our building? How skilled are our staff members with reflective practices? Are there sufficient numbers of people skilled in facilitation, communication, and group process skills to ensure productive use of group time?*

3. *What would be effective ways for staff members to learn together? Vertically? Horizontally? New and experienced mixed? Same or cross subject areas?*

4. *Would assigning or rotating specific group roles result in more productive interactions? Are external facilitators needed to get learning groups off to a strong and successful start or to build the confidence and competence of internal facilitators?*

5. *In what ways can we support continuity and accountability within and between groups?*

Resources . . . Support?

1. *How much time will be allocated for reflective practice and professional learning? In what ways can we embed opportunities into existing schedules and activities?*

2. *Are there equipment or materials (e.g., books, handouts, media, refreshments) needed to support the development of reflective practices? Is there a budget to support this work?*

Context . . . Where?

1. *Does the work align or conflict with high-profile school or district agendas or goals?*

2. *Are administrators and informal school leaders supportive of the goals and proposed means of accomplishing the goals? How is this support communicated?*

3. *How might key individuals who oppose or block the work of the team be engaged?*

4. *Is there a history of failed improvement attempts or of punishing initiation? Such a culture dissuades participation. How can inviting, nurturing conditions be put in place?*

5. *How can our school become a place where innovation and creativity are valued, modeled, and actively encouraged?*

6. *What stories do people tell about our school? What kind of culture is reflected in these stories? What kinds of stories reinforce the positive and hopeful views?*

Results . . . So what?

1. *How have students and student learning been affected by our reflective practices? Have we learned to think more creatively and optimistically about influencing the learning and lives of our students, all of them? Are we making progress toward these outcomes? How do we account for progress being made or not?*

2. *Do students notice the effects of our work? Has our professional growth re-created the learning atmosphere for students in positive ways? What might they say about how we learn and work together? Why might this matter?*

3. *Have our groups grown in their capacities for learning and working effectively? Have working relationships improved? What have we noticed as indicators of progress?*

4. *Have individual participants grown and been renewed by their participation? Have dispositions and practices been enhanced?*

5. *How will we know whether reflection, learning, and improvement are taking hold? What evidence would we expect to observe, hear, or collect? How will we obtain and examine feedback about the progress we are making?*

6. *Are more people choosing to engage in and support reflective practices? Is there more interest and confidence in our work by colleagues, administrators, and board members?*

Resource 7.A R-E-F-L-E-C-T-I-O-N Mnemonic: Lessons Learned About
Reflective Practice

Relationships are first

Expand options through dialogue

Focus on learning

Leadership accelerates reflective practice

Energy is required for any system to grow

Courage is needed to reflect and act

Trust takes time

Inside-out

Outside-in

Nurture people and ideas

References

Adelman, N. (1998). Trying to beat the clock: Uses of teacher professional time in three countries. Washington, DC: Policy Studies Associates.

Aleman, A. M. (2003). Waiting for Gabriel: Philosophical literacy and teacher education. *The Teacher Educator, 39*(1), 35–50.

Ambrose, D. (1987). Managing complex change. Pittsburgh, PA: Enterprise Group.

American Psychological Association. (1997). Learner-centered principles: A framework for school redesign and reform. Washington, DC: Author.

Argyris, C. (1977, September–October). Double loop learning in organizations. *Harvard Business Review,* 115–125.

Argyris, C., & Schön, D. (1974). Theory in practice: Increasing professional effectiveness. San Francisco: Jossey-Bass.

Arnold, G. C. S. (1995). Teacher dialogues: A constructivist model of staff development. *Journal of Staff Development, 16*(4), 34–38.

Arrien, A. (1993). The Four-Fold Way: Walking paths of the warrior, teacher, healer, and visionary. New York: HarperCollins.

Ash, D., & Levitt, K. (2003). Working within the zone of proximal development: Formative assessment as professional development. *Journal of Science Teacher Education, 14*(1), 23–48.

Attwood, P., & Seale-Collago, J. (2002). The toolbox and the mirror: Reflection and practice in "progressive" teacher education. *Radical Teacher, 64,* 14–20.

Bailey, K., Curtis, A., & Nunan, D. (1998). Undeniable insights: The collaborative use of three professional development practices. *TESOL Quarterly, 32*(3), 546–556.

Barnett, C. (1999). Cases. *Journal of Staff Development, 20*(3), 26–27.

Barnett, B., & O'Mahoney, G. (2002). One for the to-do list: Slow down to think. *Journal of Staff Development, 23*(3), 54–58.

Bateson, G. (1972). Steps to an ecology of mind. Chicago: University of Chicago Press.

Beerer, K. M., & Bodzin, A. M. (2004). How to develop inquiring minds: District implements inquiry-based science instruction. *Journal of Staff Development, 25*(4), 43–47.

Berliner, D. C. (1986, August–September). In pursuit of the expert pedagogue. *Educational Researcher,* 5–13.

Bergsgaard, M., & Ellis, M. (2002). Inward: The journey toward authenticity through self-observing. *Journal of Educational Thought, 36*(1), 53–68.

Black, R., Molseed, T., & Sayler, B. (2003). Fresh view from the back of the room: Coaching in their classrooms offers teachers more points of view. *Journal of Staff Development, 24*(2), 61–65.

Black, P., & Wiliam, D. (1998). Inside the black box: Raising standards through classroom assessment. *Phi Delta Kappan, 80*(2), 139–148.

Blase, J., & Blase, J. (1999). Principals' instructional leadership and teacher development: Teachers' perspectives. *Educational Administration Quarterly, 35*(3), 349–378.

Black, R., Molseed, T., & Sayler, B. (2003). Fresh view from the back of the room. *Journal of Staff Development, 24*(2), 61–65.

Block, P. (1987). The empowered manager. San Francisco: Jossey-Bass.

Block, P. (2002). The answer to how is yes: Acting on what matters. San Francisco: Berrett-Koehler.

Bohm, D. (1989). On dialogue. Ojai, CA: David Bohm Seminars.

Bonder, N. (1999). Yiddishe kop: Creative problem solving in Jewish learning, lore, and humor. Boston, MA: Shambhala.

Brandt, R. (1998). Powerful learning. Alexandria, VA: Association for Supervision and Curriculum Development.

Bright, B. (1996). Reflecting on "reflective practice." *Studies in the Education of Adults, 28*(2), 162–184.

Brookfield, S. (1992). Why can't I get this right? Myths and realities in facilitating adult learning. *Adult Learning, 3*(6), 12–15.

Brown, J. D., & Wolfe-Quintero, K. (1997). Teacher portfolios for evaluation: A great idea or a waste of time? *Language Teacher, 21,* 28–30.

Brown, R. (1998). The teacher as a contemplative observer. *Educational Leadership, 56,* 70–75.

Brubacher, J. W., Case, C. W., & Reagan, T. G. (1994). Being a reflective educator: How to build a culture of inquiry in the schools. Thousand Oaks, CA: Corwin.

Bryk, A., Camburn, E., & Louis, K. S. (1999). Professional community in Chicago elementary schools: Facilitating factors and organizational consequences. *Educational Administration Quarterly, 35*(Suppl.), 751–781.

Bryk, A. S., & Schneider, B. (2002). Trust in schools: A core resource for improvement. The American Sociological Association's Rose Series in Sociology. New York: Russell Sage College.

Burley-Allen, M. (1995). Listening: The forgotten skill. New York: Wiley.

Butler, J. (1996). Professional development: Practice as text, reflection as process, and self as locus. *Australian Journal of Education, 40*(3), 265–283.

Caine, R. N., & Caine, G. (1997). Education on the edge of possibility. Alexandria, VA: Association for Supervision and Curriculum Development.

Calhoun, E. (1994). How to use action research in the self-renewing school. Alexandria, VA: Association for Supervision and Curriculum Development.

Camburn, E., Rowan, B., & Taylor, J. E. (2003). Distributed leadership in schools: The case of elementary schools adopting comprehensive school reform models. *Educational Evaluation and Policy Analysis, 25*(4), 347–373.

Canning, C. (1991). What teachers say about reflection. *Educational Leadership 48*(6), 18–21.

Carlson, R. (1997). You can be happy no matter what: Five principles your therapist never told you. Novato, CA: New World Library.

Carlson, R., & Bailey, J. (1997). Slowing down to the speed of life: How to create a more peaceful, simpler life from the inside out. San Francisco: HarperCollins.

Carse, J. P. (1986). Finite and infinite games. New York: Ballantine Books.

Chaleff, I. (1995). *The courageous follower: Standing up to and for our leaders.* San Francisco: Berrett-Kohler.

Chödron, P. (1994). Start where you are: A guide to compassionate living. Boston: Shambhala.

Chrispeel, J. H. (1992). Purposeful restructuring: Creating a culture for learning and achievement in elementary schools. New York: Falmer.

Christensen, L. M., Wilson, E. K., Sunal, C. S., Blalock, D., St. Clair-Shingleton, L., & Warren, E. (2004). Through the looking glass: Reflection or refraction? Do you see what I see? *Journal of Social Studies Research, 28*(1), 33–46.

Clarke, A. (1995). Professional development in practicum settings: Reflective practice under scrutiny. *Teaching and Teacher Education, 11*(3), 243–261.

Colton, A. B., & Sparks-Langer, G. M. (1993). A conceptual framework to guide the development of teacher reflection and decision making. *Journal of Teacher Education, 44*(1), 45–54.

Cooner, D. D., & Tochterman, S. M. (2004). Life inside a professional development school: What experienced teachers learn. *The Teacher Educator, 39*(3), 184–195.

Costa, A. L., & Garmston, R. J. (2002). Cognitive coaching: A foundation for renaissance schools (2nd ed.). Norwood, MA: Christopher-Gordon.

Costa, A. L., & Kallick, B. (2000a). Activating and engaging habits of mind. Alexandria, VA: Association for Supervision and Curriculum Development.

Costa, A. L., & Kallick, B. (2000b). Getting into the habit of reflection. *Educational Leadership, 57*(7), 60–62.

Covey, S. (1989). The seven habits of highly effective people. New York: Fireside.

Cranton, P. (1996). Types of group learning. In S. Imel (Ed.), Learning in groups: Exploring fundamental principles, new uses, and emerging opportunities. New Directions for Adult and Continuing Education, 71. San Francisco: Jossey-Bass.

Crow, G. M. (1998). Implications for leadership in collaborative schools. In D. G. Pounder (Ed.), *Restructuring schools for collaboration: Promises and pitfalls* (pp. 135–153). Albany: State University of New York Press.

Crowther, F., Kaagan, S. S., Ferguson, M., & Hann, L. (2002). Developing teacher leaders. How teacher leadership enhances school success. Thousand Oaks, CA: Corwin.

Danielson, C. (1996). Enhancing professional practice: A framework for teaching. Alexandria, VA: Association for Supervision and Curriculum Development.

Daroszewski, E. B., Kinser, A. G., & Lloyd, S. L. (2004). Online directed journaling in community health advanced practice nursing clinical education. *Educational Innovations, 43*(4), 175–180.

de Bono, E. (1970). Lateral thinking. New York: Harper & Row.

Deci, E. L. (1995). Why we do what we do. New York: Grosset/Putnam.

Delpit, L. (1995). Other people's children: Cultural conflict in the classroom. New York: New Press.

Desouza, J. M. S., & Czeniak, C. M. (2003). Study of science teachers' attitudes toward and beliefs about collaborative reflective practice. *Journal of Science Teacher Education, 14*(2), 75–96.

Dewey, J. (1933). How we think. Boston: D. C. Heath.

Dewey, J. (1938). Experience and education (6th ed.). New York: Macmillan.

Dietz, M. E. (1999). Portfolios. *Journal of Staff Development, 20*(3), 45–46.

Dilts, R. (1983). Applications of neuro-linguistic programming. Cupertino, CA: Meta Publications.

Dilts, R. (1996). The new leadership paradigm. Santa Cruz, CA. Retrieved May 5, 2003, from http://www.nlpu.com/Articles/article8.htm

Dinkelman, T. (2000). An inquiry into the development of critical reflection in secondary student teachers. *Teaching and Teacher Education, 16,* 195–200.

Diss, R. E., Buckley, P. K., & Pfau, N. D. (1992). Interactive reflective teaching: A school-college collaborative model for professional development. *Journal of Staff Development, 13*(2), 28–31.

Donahoe, T. (1993, December). Finding the way: Structure, time, and culture in school improvement. *Phi Delta Kappan, 75*(3), 298–305.

Doyle, M., & Straus, D. (1993). How to make meetings work. New York: Berkley.

Dorsey, D. (December, 2000). Positive deviant. *Fast Company, 41,* 284.

Drath, W. H., & Palus, C. J. (1994). Making common sense: Leadership as meaning-making in a community of practice. Greensboro, NC: Center for Creative Leadership.

DuFour, R. (2005). What is a professional learning community? In R. DuFour, R. Eaker, & R. DuFour (Eds.), On common ground: The power of professional learning communities. Bloomington, IN: National Educational Service.

DuFour, R. (2004, May). What is a Professional Learning Community? *Educational Leadership, 61*(8), 6–11.

DuFour, R., & Eaker, R. (1998). Professional learning communities at work. Alexandria, VA: Association for Supervision and Curriculum Development.

Easton, L. B. (1999). Tuning protocols. *Journal of Staff Development, 20*(3), 54–55.

Easton, L. B. (Ed.) (2004). Powerful designs for professional learning. Oxford, OH: National Staff Development Council.

Elliott, V., & Schiff, S. (2001). A look within: Staff developers use structures, inquiry and reflection to examine feelings about equity. *Journal of Staff Development, 22*(2), 39–42.

Ellinor, L., & Gerard, G. (1998). Dialogue: Rediscovering the transforming power of conversation. New York: Wiley.

Eraut, J. (1985). Knowledge creation and knowledge use in professional contexts. *Studies in Higher Education, 10*(2), 117–133.

Even, M. (1987). Why adults learn in different ways. *Lifelong Learning: An Omnibus of Practice and Research, 10*(8), 22–25, 27.

Feiler, R., Heritage, M., & Gallimore, R. (2000). Teachers leading teachers. *Educational Leadership, 57*(8), 66–69.

Fendler, L. (2003). Teacher reflection in a hall of mirrors: Historical influences and political reverberations. *Educational Researcher, 32*(3), 16–25.

Ferrace, B. (2002). Renewing the teaching profession: A conversation with John Goodlad. *Principal Leadership, 3*(1), 31–34.

Fisher, R. & Ury, W. (1981). Getting to yes: Negotiating agreement without giving in. New York: Penguin Books.

Francis, S., Hirsh, S., & Rowland, C. (1994). Improving school culture through study groups. *Journal of Staff Development, 15*(2), 12–15.

Frankl, V. (1959). Man's search for meaning. Boston: Beacon.

Fullan, M. G. (1993). Why teachers must become change agents. *Educational Leadership, 50*(6), 12–17.

Fullan, M. G. (2000a). The three stories of education reform. *Phi Delta Kappan, 81*(8), 581–584.

Fullan, M. G. (2000b). The return of large scale reform. *Journal of Educational Change, 1,* 5–8.

Fullan, M. G.(2001a). Leading in a culture of change. San Francisco: Jossey-Bass.

Fullan, M. G., (2001b). The new meaning of educational change (3rd ed.). New York: Teachers College Press.

Fullan, M. G. (2005). Leadership and sustainability. Thousand Oaks, CA: Corwin.

Garet, M. S., Porter, A. C. Desimone, L., Birman, B., & Yoon, K. S. (2001). What makes professional development effective? Results from a national sample of teachers. *American Education Research Journal, 38*(4), 915–945.

Garmston, R., & Wellman, B. (1995). Adaptive schools in a quantum universe. *Educational Leadership, 52*(7), 6–12.

Garmston, R., & Wellman, B. (1997). The adaptive school: Developing and facilitating collaborative groups. El Dorado Hills, CA: Four Hats.

Garmston, R., & Wellman, B. (1999). The adaptive school: A sourcebook for developing collaborative groups. Norwood, MA: Christopher-Gordon.

Gitlin, A. (1999). Collaboration and progressive school reform. *Educational Policy, 13*(5), 630–658.

Glanz, J. (1998). Action research: An educational leader's guide to school improvement. Norwood, MA: Christopher-Gordon.

Glanz, J. (1999). Action research. *Journal of Staff Development, 20*(3), 22–23.

Glickman, C. D. (1988). Knowledge and uncertainty in supervision of instruction. In P. P. Grimmet & G. L. Erickson (Eds.), Reflection in teacher education (pp. 57–66). New York: Teachers College Press.

Glickman, C. D. (1995). Action research: Inquiry, reflection, and decision making [Video 4–95037]. Alexandria, VA: Association for Supervision and Curriculum Development.

Goldberg, M. (1998). The art of the question. New York: Wiley.

Goldberg, N. (1993). Long quiet highway: Waking up in America. New York: Bantam.

Goldberg, S. M., & Pesko, E. (2000). The teacher book club. *Educational Leadership, 57*(8), 39–41.

Godstein, J. & Kornfield, J. (1987). Seeking the heart of wisdom: The path of insight meditation. Boston: Shambhala.

Grimmet, P. P., MacKinnon, A. M., Erickson, G. L., & Riecken, T. J. (1990). Reflective practice in teacher education. In R. T. Clift, W. R. Houston, & M. C. Pugach (Eds.), *Encouraging reflective practice in education: An analysis of issues and programs* (pp. 20–38). New York: Teachers College Press.

Grinder, M. (1993). ENVoY: Your personal guide to classroom management. Battle Ground, WA: Michael Grinder & Associates Training.

Haberman, M. (1995). Star teachers of children in poverty. Indianapolis, IN: Kappa Delta Pi.

Hackman, R. J. (1991). Groups that work and those that don't: Creating conditions for effective teamwork. San Francisco: Jossey-Bass.

Haefner, T. (2004). Assessment as magnification of internal, parallel, and external reflection. *Action in Teacher Education, 25*(4), 14–17.

Hagstrom, D., Hubbard, R., Hurtig, C., Mortola, P., Ostrow, J., & White, V. (2000). Teaching is like . . . ? *Educational Leadership, 57*(8), 24–27.

Hall, G. E., & Hord, S. M. (2001). Implementing change: Patterns, principles, and potholes. Boston: Allyn & Bacon.

Hare, A. P. (1994). Small group research: A handbook. Greenwich, CT: Ablex.

Hargreaves, A. (1994). Guilt: Exploring the emotions of teaching. In A. Hargreaves (Ed.), *Changing teachers, changing times* (pp. 141–159). New York: Teachers College Press.

Hargreaves, A. (2001). Learning to change: Teaching beyond subjects and standards. San Francisco: Jossey-Bass.

Harri-Augstein, S., & Thomas, L. (1991). Learning conversations. London: Routledge.

Harste, J., & Leland, C. (1999). Testing the water with mini-inquiry projects. In R. Hubbard & B. Power (Eds.), *Living the questions* (pp. 68–69). Portland, ME: Stenhouse.

Harvey, O. J. (1967). Conceptual systems and attitude change. In W. Sherif and M. Sherif (Eds.), Attitude, ego-involvement, and change (pp. 201–226). New York: Wiley.

Harwell-McKee, K. (1999). Coaching. *Journal of Staff Development, 20*(3), 28–29.

Hatton, N., & Smith, D. (1995). Reflection in teacher education: Towards definition and implementation. *Teaching and Teacher Education, 11*(1), 33–49.

Hashweh, M. A. (2003). Teacher accommodative change. *Teaching and Teacher Education, 19,* 421–434.

Hawkins, M. R. (2004). Researching English language literacy development in schools. *Educational Researcher, 33*(3), 14–25.

Hawley, W. D., & Valli, L. (2000, August). Learner centered professional development. *Phi Delta Kappa Research Bulletin, 27,* 7–10.

Henry, S. K., Scott, J. A., Wells, J., Skobel, B., Jones, A., Cross, S., Butler, C., & Blackstone, T. (1999). Linking university and teacher community: A "think tank" model of professional development. *Teacher Education and Special Education, 22*(4), 251–268.

Hock, D. (1996, October/November). Dee Hock on management. *Fast Company, 79.*

Hord, S. (Ed.). (2004). *Learning together, leading together: Changing schools through professional learning communities.* Austin, TX: Southwest Education Development Laboratory.

Hord, S. (1997). Professional learning communities: Communities of continuous inquiry and improvement. Austin, TX: Southwest Educational Development Laboratory.

Huberman, M. (1992). Critical introduction. In M. Fullan (Ed.), *Successful school improvement.* Milton Keynes: Open University Press.

Huberman, M., & Miles, M. B. (1984). *Innovation up close: How school improvement works.* New York: Plenum.

Hurley, V., Greenblatt, R. B., & Cooper, B. S. (2003). Learning conversations: Transforming supervision. *Principal Leadership, 3*(9), 31–36.

Igoa, C. (1995). The inner world of the immigrant child. Mahwah, NJ: Lawrence Erlbaum.

Ingvarson, L., Meiers, M., & Beavis, A. (2005). Factors affecting the impact of professional development programs on teachers' knowledge, practice, student outcomes and efficacy. *Education Policy Analysis Archives, 13*(10). Retrieved February 12, 2005, from http://epaa.asu.edu/epaa/v13n10/

Isaacs, W. (1999). Dialogue and the art of thinking together. New York: Currency.

Jackson, P. W. (1968). Life in classrooms. New York: Holt, Rinehart & Winston.

Jay, J. K., & Johnson, K. L. (2002). Capturing complexity: A typology of reflective practice for teacher education. *Teaching and Teacher Education, 18,* 73–85.

Johnson, D. W., & Johnson, R. T. (1999). Learning together and alone: Cooperative, competitive, and individualistic learning (5th ed.). Needham Heights, MA: Allyn & Bacon.

Johnston, M. (1994). Contrasts and similarities in case studies of teacher reflection and change. *Curriculum Inquiry, 24*(1), 9–26.

Joyce, B. (2004). How are professional learning communities created? History has a few messages. *Phi Delta Kappan, 86*(1), 76–83.

Joyce, B. & Showers, B. (2002). *Student achievement through staff development* (3rd ed.). Alexandria, VA: Association for Supervision and Curriculum Development.

Kagan, J. (1969). Reflection-impulsivity and reading ability in primary grade children. *Child Development, 36,* 609–628.

Kahn, W. A. (1992). To be fully there: Psychological presence at work. *Human Relations, 45*(4), 321–349.

Kane, R., Sandretto, S., & Heath, C. (2004). An investigation into excellent tertiary teaching: Emphasizing reflective practice. *Higher Education, 47,* 293–310.

Keating, C. N. (1993). Promoting growth through dialogue journals. In G. Wells (Ed.), *Changing schools from within: Creating communities of inquiry* (pp. 217–236). Toronto, Canada: Ontario Institute for Studies in Education.

Killion, J. (1999). Journaling. *Journal of Staff Development, 20*(3), 36–37.

Killion, J. (2000, March). Explore research to identify best instructional strategies. *Results, 3.*

Killion, J., & Todnem, G. (1991). A process of personal theory building. *Educational Leadership, 48*(6), 14–17.

Killion, J. P., & Simmons, L. A. (1992). The Zen of facilitation. *Journal of Staff Development, 13*(3), 2–5.

Kim, D. (1993, Fall). The link between individual and organizational learning. *Sloan Management Review,* 37–50.

Kinchloe, J. L. (2004). The knowledges of teacher education: Developing a critical complex epistemology. *Teacher Education Quarterly, 31*(1), 49–66.

King, M. B., & Newmann, F. M. (2000). Will teaching learning advance school goals? *Phi Delta Kappan, 81*(8), 576–580.

Knoster, T. P., Villa, R. A., & Thousand, J. S. (2000). A framework for thinking about systems change. In R. A. Villa & J. S. Thousand (Eds.), *Restructuring for caring and effective education* (2nd ed., pp. 93–128). Baltimore, MD: Paul H. Brookes.

Kohn, A. (1993). *Punished by rewards: The trouble with gold stars, incentive plans, A's, praise, and other bribes.* New York: Houghton Mifflin.

Kolar, C., & Dickson, S. V. (2002). Preservice general educators' perceptions of structured logs as viable learning tools in a university course on inclusionary practices. *Teacher Education and Special Education, 25*(4), 395–406.

Koszalka, T. A., Grabowski, B. L., & McCarthy, M. (2003). Reflection through the ID-PRISM: A teacher planning tool to transform classrooms into web-enhanced learning environments. *Journal of Technology and Teacher Education, 11*(3), 347–375.

Kroeger, S., Burton, C., Comarata, A., Combs, C., Hamm, C., Hopkins, R., & Kouche, B. (2004). Student voice and critical reflection: Helping students at risk. *Teaching Exceptional Children, 36*(3), 50–57.

Kronberg, R., & York-Barr, J. (Eds.). (1998). *Differentiated teaching and learning in heterogeneous classrooms: Strategies for meeting the needs of all students.* Minneapolis, MN: University of Minnesota, Institute on Community Integration.

Kruse, S. D., Louis, K. S., & Bryk, A. (1995). An emerging framework for analyzing school-based professional community. In K. S. Louis & S. D. Kruse (Eds.), *Professionalism and community: Perspectives on reforming urban schools* (pp. 23–42). Thousand Oaks, CA: Corwin.

Ladson-Billings, G. (2000). The dreamkeepers: Successful teachers of African-American children. San Francisco: Jossey-Bass.

Lambert, L. (1998). Building leadership capacity in schools. Alexandria, VA: Association for Supervision and Curriculum Development.

Lambert, L. (2003). Leadership for lasting school improvement. Alexandria, VA: Association for Supervision and Curriculum Development.

Lambert, L. (2005). Leadership for lasting reform. *Educational Leadership, 62*(5), 62–65.

Lame Deer, J., & Erdoes, R. (1994). Lame Deer, seeker of visions. New York: Washington Square.

Langer, G. M., & Colton, A. B. (1994). Reflective decision-making: The cornerstone of school reform. *Journal of Staff Development, 15*(1), 2–7.

Lasley, T. J. (1992). Promoting teacher reflection. *Journal of Staff Development, 13*(1), 24–29.

Leat, D. (1995). The costs of reflection in initial teacher education. [Cambridge, UK] *Journal of Education, 25*(2), 161–174.

Lee, P. (1995). Creating collaborative work cultures: Effective communication. Drake, CO: Changing Points of View.

Leithwood, K., & Duke, D. L. (1999). A century's quest to understand school leadership. In K. S. Louis & J. Murphy (Eds.), *Handbook of research on educational administration* (2nd ed., pp. 45–72). San Francisco: Jossey-Bass

Leithwood, K., Seashore, K., Anderson, S., & Wahlstrom, K. (2004). How leadership influences student learning. Minneapolis: University of Minnesota, Center for Applied Research and Educational Improvement; and Toronto, Ontario: Ontario Institute for Studies in Education.

Lerner, P. (1997). Collaborative action research: Study guide. Santa Monica, CA: Canter Educational Productions.

Levin, B. B. (1995). Using the case method in teacher education: The role of discussion and experience in teachers' thinking about cases. *Teaching and Teacher Education, 11*(1), 63–79.

Lieberman, A., & Miller, L. (1999). Teachers transforming their world and their work. New York: Teachers College Press.

Lindsey, R. B., Nuri Robins, K., & Terrell, R. D. (2003). Cultural proficiency. A manual for school leaders (2nd ed.). Thousand Oaks, CA: Corwin.

Lippitt, M. (2003). Leading complex change. Potomac, MD: Enterprise Management, Ltd.

Littky, D., & Grabelle, S. (2004). The big picture: Education is everyone's business. Alexandria, VA: Association for Supervision and Curriculum Development.

Loeb, P. (Ed.). (2004). The impossible will take a little while: A citizen's guide to hope in a time of fear. New York: Basic Books.

Loughran, J. J. (2002). Effective reflective practice: In search of meaning in learning about teaching. *Journal of Teacher Education, 53*(1), 33–43.

Louis, K. S. (1992). Restructuring and the problem of teachers' work. In A. Lieberman (Ed.), *The changing contexts of teaching: 91st yearbook of the National Society for the Study of Education, 1,* 138–156. Chicago: University of Chicago Press.

Louis, K. S., & Kruse, S. D. (Eds.). (1995). Professionalism and community: Perspectives on reforming urban schools. Thousand Oaks, CA: Corwin.

Magestro, P. V., & Stanford-Blair, N. (2000). A tool for meaningful staff development. *Educational Leadership, 57*(8), 34–35.

Maggio, R. (1992). The Beacon book of quotations by women. Boston: Beacon Press.

Marks, H., & Louis, K. S. (1999, December). Teacher empowerment and the capacity for organizational learning. *Educational Administration Quarterly, 35*(Suppl.), 707–750.

Marks, H. M., & Louis, K. S. (1997). Does teacher empowerment affect the classroom? The implications of teacher empowerment for instructional practice and student academic performance. *Educational Evaluation and Policy Analysis, 19*(3), 245–275.

Marzano, R., Pickering, D., & Pollock, J. (2001). Classroom instruction that works: Research-based strategies for increasing student achievement. Alexandria, VA: Association for Supervision and Curriculum Development.

McGregor, G., Halvorsen, A., Fisher, D., Pumpian, I., Bhaerman, B., & Salisbury, C. (1998). Professional development for all personnel in inclusive schools. *Consortium on Inclusive Schooling Practices Issue Brief, 3*(3). Retrieved January 10, 2000, from the Allegheny University of the Health Sciences Child and Family Studies Program at www.asri.edu/CFSP/brochure/ prodevib.htm

McLean, J. E. (1995). Improving education through action research: A guide for administrators and teachers. Thousand Oaks, CA: Corwin.

McLeskey, J., & Waldron, N. (2002). Professional development and inclusive schools: Reflections on effective practice. *The Teacher Educator, 37*(3), 159–172.

Merriam, S. B. (1993). An update on adult learning theory. San Francisco: Jossey-Bass.

Milner, H. R. (2003). Teacher reflection and race in cultural context: History, meaning, and methods in teaching. *Theory Into Practice, 42*(3), 173–180.

Mitchell, R. (1999). Examining student work. *Journal of Staff Development, 20*(3), 32–33.

Mohr, N., & Dichter, A. (2001). Building a learning organization. *Phi Delta Kappan, 82*(10), 744–747.

Montie, J., York-Barr, J., Stevenson, J., & Vallejo, B. (1997). Inquiring minds unite at urban high school. In J. Montie, J. York-Barr, & R. Kronberg (Eds.), *Reflective practice: Creating capacities to improve schools* (pp. 49–76). Minneapolis: University of Minnesota, Institute on Community Integration.

Moore, M., & Gergen, P. (1989). Managing risk taking during organizational change. King of Prussia, PA: Organization Design and Development.

Murphy, C., & Lick, D. W. (1998). Whole faculty study groups: A powerful way to change schools and enhance learning. Thousand Oaks, CA: Corwin.

Neuhauser, P. C. (1988). Tribal warfare in organizations. New York: HarperBusiness.

Newmann, F. M., Smith, B., Allensworth, E., & Bryk, A. S. (2001). Instructional program coherence: What it is and why it should guide school improvement policy. *Educational Evaluation and Policy Analysis, 23*(4), 297–321.

Newmann, F. M., & Wehlage, G. (1995). Successful school restructuring. Madison: University of Wisconsin, Center on Organization and Restructuring of Schools.

Nhat Hanh, T. (1993). Interbeing: Fourteen guidelines for engaged Buddhism. Berkeley, CA: Parallax.

Nichol, L. (Ed.). (1996). On dialogue. New York: Routledge.

North Central Regional Educational Laboratory. (1994). Professional development: Changing times. *Policy Briefs, Reports, 4*, 1–6.

Norton, B. (2000). Identity and language learning: Gender, ethnicity, and educational change. Essex, UK: Pearson Education.

Ogawa, R. T., & Bossert, S. T. (1995). Leadership as an organizational quality. *Educational Administration Quarterly, 31*(2), 224–243.

Olsen, W., & Sommers, W. (2004). A trainer's companion: Stories to stimulate reflection, conversation, and action. Baytown, TX: AhaProcess.

O'Neill, J. (2000). Capturing an organization's oral history. *Educational Leadership, 57*(7), 63–65.

Osterman, K. F., & Kottkamp, R. B. (1993). Reflective practice for educators: Improving schooling through professional development. Thousand Oaks, CA: Corwin.

Osterman, K. F., & Kottkamp, R. B. (2004). Reflective practice for educators: Professional development to improve student learning (2nd ed.). Thousand Oaks, CA: Corwin.

Palmer, P. (1998). The courage to teach. San Francisco: Jossey-Bass.

Parades-Scribner, J. (1999). Professional development: Untangling the influence of work context on teacher learning. *Educational Administration Quarterly, 35*(2), 238–266.

Perkins, D. (1992). Smart schools. New York: Free Press.

Perry, C. M., & Power, B. M. (2004). Finding the truths in teacher preparation field experiences. *Teacher Educator Quarterly, 31*(2), 125–136.

Pierce, J. W., & Kalkman, D. L. (2003). Applying learner-centered principles in teacher education. *Theory Into Practice, 42*(2), 127–132.

Popham, W. J. (2005). Classroom assessment: What teachers need to know (4th ed.). Boston, MA: Pearson.

Posner, G. J. (1996). *Field experience: A guide to reflective teaching* (4th ed.). New York: Longman.

Pounder, D. G. (1999). Teacher teams: Exploring job characteristics and work-related outcomes of work group enhancement. *Educational Administration Quarterly, 35*(3), 317–348.

Powerful designs for learning. (1999, Summer). *Journal of Staff Development, 20*(3).

Pugach, M. C., & Johnson, L. J. (1990). Developing reflective practice through structured dialogue. In R. T. Clift, W. R. Houston, & M. C. Pugach (Eds.), *Encouraging reflective practice in education: An analysis of issues and programs* (pp. 186–207). New York: Teachers College Press.

Pugh, S. L., Hicks, J. W., Davis, M., & Venstra, T. (1992). Bridging: A teacher's guide to metaphorical thinking. Urbana, IL: National Council of Teachers of English.

Pultorak, E. G. (1996). Following the developmental process of reflection in novice teachers: Three years of investigation. *Journal of Teacher Education, 47*(4), 283–291.

Quinn, R. E. (1996). Deep change: Discovering the leader within. San Francisco: Jossey-Bass.

Raelin, J. A. (2002). 'I don't have time to think!' versus the art of reflective practice. *Reflections: The SoL Journal, 4*(17), 66–75.

Ramsden, P. (1992). Learning to teach in higher education. London: Routledge.

Rapaport, D. (1999). Cadres. *Journal of Staff Development, 20*(3), 24–25.

Raywid, M. (1993). Finding time for collaboration. *Educational Leadership, 51*, 30–34.

Reiman, A. J. (1999).The evolution of social role-taking and guided reflection framework in teacher education: Recent theory and quantitative synthesis of research. *Teaching and Teacher Education, 15*(6), 597–612.

Rich, S. (1992). Teacher supports groups: Providing a forum for professional development. *Journal of Staff Development, 13*(3), 32–35.

Richards, J. C., & Lockhart, C. (1994). Reflective teaching in second language classrooms. Cambridge, UK: Cambridge University Press.

Richardson, J. (1997). Putting student learning first put these schools ahead. *Journal of Staff Development, 18*(2), 42–47.

Richardson, J. (1998). We're all here to learn. *Journal of Staff Development, 19*(4), 49–55.

Richardson, J. (1999, October–November). Harness the potential of staff meetings. Tools for Schools, 1–3. Oxford, OH: National Staff Development Council.

Richardson, J. (2004). From the inside-out: Learning from positive deviance in your organization. Oxford, OH: National Staff Development Council.

Risko, V. J., Vukelich, C., & Roskos, K. (2002). Preparing teachers for reflective practice: Intentions, contradictions, and possibilities. *Language Arts, 80*(2), 134–144.

Robbins, P. (2004). Peer coaching. In L. B. Easton (Ed.), *Powerful designs for professional learning* (pp. 163–174). Oxford, OH: National Staff Development Council.

Robbins, P. (1999). Mentoring. *Journal of Staff Development, 20*(3), 40–42.

Robins, K. N., Lindsey, R. B., Lindsey, D. B., & Terrell, R. D. (2002). Culturally proficient instruction: A guide for people who teach. Thousand Oaks, CA: Corwin.

Robinson, D. N. (1997). Socrates and the unexamined life. In *The Great Ideas of Philosophy.* Springfield, VA: The Teaching Company.

Rockler, M. J. (2004). Ethics and professional practice in education. *Phi Delta Kappa Fastbacks, 521,* 7–47.

Rodgers, C. (2002). Defining reflection: Another look at John Dewey and reflective thinking. *Teachers College Record, 104*(4), 842–866.

Rogers, C. (1986). Carl Rogers on the development of the person-centered approach. *Person-Centered Review, 1*(3), 257–259.

Ronneberg, J. C. (2000). The urban school leader as change agent: Case studies of three urban school principals. Unpublished doctoral dissertation, University of Minnesota, Minneapolis.

Rosenholtz, S. J. (1989). Teachers' workplace: The social organization of schools. New York: Longman.

Ross, D. D. (1989, March–April). First steps in developing a reflective approach. *Journal of Teacher Education,* 22–30.

Ross, D. D. (1990). Programmatic structures for the preparation of reflective teachers. In R. T. Clift, W. R. Houston, & M. C. Pugach (Eds.), *Encouraging reflective practice in education: An analysis of issues and programs* (pp. 97–118). New York: Teachers College Press.

Sagor, R. (1992). How to conduct collaborative action research. Alexandria, VA: Association for Supervision and Curriculum Development.

Sagor, R. (2000). Guiding school improvement with action research. Alexandria, VA: Association for Supervision and Curriculum Development.

Sagor, R. (2003). Motivating students and teachers in an era of standards. Alexandria, VA: Association for Supervision and Curriculum Development.

Sanders, S. R. (1998). Hunting for hope: A father's journeys. Boston: Beacon.

Sanford, C. (1995, September/October). Myths of organizational effectiveness. *At Work,* 10–12.

Saphier, J., & Gower, R. (1997). The skillful teacher: Building your teaching skills (5th ed.). Acton, MA: Research for Better Teaching, Inc.

Schall, E. (1995). Learning to love the swamp: Reshaping education for public service. *Journal of Policy Analysis and Management, 14*(2), 202–220.

Schein, E. (1992). Organizational culture and leadership. San Francisco: Jossey-Bass.

Schein, E. (2004). Organizational culture and leadership (3rd ed.). San Francisco: Jossey-Bass.

Schmoker, M. (2004). Learning communities at the crossroads. *Educational Leadership, 86*(1), 84–88.

Schmoker, M. (1999). Results: The key to continuous school improvement (2nd ed.). Alexandria, VA: Association for Supervision and Curriculum Development.

Schön, D. A. (1983). The reflective practitioner: How professionals think in action. New York: BasicBooks.

Schön, D. A. (1987). Educating the reflective practitioner: Toward a new design for teaching and learning in the professions. San Francisco: Jossey-Bass.

Schwahn, C. J., & Spady, W. G. (1998). Total leaders. Arlington, VA: American Association for School Administrators.

Scribner, J. P. (1999). Professional development: Untangling the influence of work context on teacher learning. *Educational Administration Quarterly, 35*(2), 238–266.

Seidel, S. (1991). Collaborative assessment conferences for the consideration of project work. Cambridge, MA: Project Zero, Harvard Graduate School of Education.

Senge, P. (1990). The fifth discipline: The art and practice of the learning organization. London: Century.

Senge, P., Cambron-McCabe, N. H., Lucas, T., Smith, B., Dutton, J., & Kleiner, A. (2000). Schools that learn: A fifth discipline fieldbook for educators, parents, and everyone who cares about education. New York: Doubleday.

Sherin, M. G. (2000). Viewing teaching on videotape. *Educational Leadership, 57*(8), 36–38.

Showers, B., & Joyce, B. (1996). The evolution of peer coaching. *Educational Leadership, 53*(6), 12–16.

Smyth, J. (1989). Developing and sustaining critical reflection in teacher education. *Journal of Teacher Education, 40*(2), 2–9.

Spalding, E., & Wilson, A. (2002). Demystifying reflection: A study of pedagogical strategies that encourage reflective journal writing. *Teachers College Record, 104*(7), 1393–1421.

Sparks, D. (2003). The answer to 'when?' is 'now': An interview with Peter Block. *Journal of Staff Development, 24*(2), 52–55.

Sparks-Langer, G. M., & Colton, A. (1991). Synthesis of research on teachers' reflective thinking. *Educational Leadership, 48*(6), 37–44.

Sparks-Langer, G. M., Simmons, J. M., Pasch, M., Colton, A., & Starko, A. (1990). Reflective pedagogical thinking: How can we promote it and measure it? *Journal of Teacher Education, 41*(4), 23–32.

Speck, M. (2002). Balanced and year-round professional development: Time and learning. *Catalyst for Change, 32*(1), 17–19.

Spillane, J. P., Halverson, R., & Diamond, J. B. (2001). Investigating school leadership practice: A distributed perspective. *Educational Researcher, 30*(3), 23–28.

Starkey, K. (1996). How organizations learn. London: International Thomson Business Press.

Steffy, B. E., Wolfe, M. P., Pasch, S. H., & Enz, B. J. (2000). Life cycle of the career teacher. Thousand Oaks, CA: Corwin.

Stewart, T. A. (1997). Intellectual capital: The new wealth of organizations. New York: Doubleday/Currency.

Stiggins, R. J., Arter, J. A., Chappuis, J., & Chappuis, S. (2004). Classroom assessment for student learning: Doing it right—using it well. Portland, OR: Assessment Training Institute.

Straus, D. (2002). How to make collaboration work: Powerful ways to build consensus, solve problems, and make decisions. San Francisco: Berrett-Koehler.

Stringer, E. T. (1996). Action research: A handbook for practitioners. Thousand Oaks, CA: Sage.

Supovitz, J. A. (2002). Developing communities of instructional practice. *Teachers College Record, 104*(8), 1591–1626.

Sutton, R. (1995). School self review. Salford, UK: RS Publications.

Suzuki, S. (1982/1970). Zen mind, beginner's mind: Informal talks on Zen meditation and practice. New York and Tokyo: Weatherhill.

Taggart, G. L., & Wilson, A. P. (1998). Promoting reflective thinking in teachers: 44 Action strategies. Thousand Oaks, CA: Corwin.

Thousand, J. S., & Villa, R. (2000). Collaborative teams: Powerful tools for school restructuring. In R. Villa & J. S. Thousand (Eds.), *Restructuring for caring and effective education* (2nd ed., pp. 254–291). Baltimore, MD: Paul H. Brookes.

Towery, T. (1995). The wisdom of wolves: Nature's way to organizational success. Franklin, TN: Wessex.

Tuckman, B. W. (1965). Developmental sequence in small groups. *Psychological Bulletin, 63*, 384–399.

U.S. Department of Education. (1996). Breaking the tyranny of time: Voices from the Goals 2000 Teacher Forum. Washington, DC: Government Printing Office.

Valiga, T. M. (2003). Teaching thinking: Is it worth the effort? *Journal of Nursing Education, 42*(11), 470–480.

Valli, L. (1997). Listening to other voices: A description of teacher reflection in the United States. *Peabody Journal of Education, 72*(1), 67–88.

van Manen, M. (1977). Linking ways of knowing with ways of being practical. *Curriculum Inquiry, 6*(3), 205–228.

van Manen, M. (2002). The pathic principle of pedagogical language. *Teaching and Teacher Education, 18*, 215–224.

Vaughan, J. C. (1990). Foreword. In R. T. Clift, W. R. Houston, & M. C. Pugach (Eds.), *Encouraging reflective practice in education: An analysis of issues and programs* (pp. vii–xi). New York: Teachers College Press.

Vella, J. (1994). Learning to listen, learning to teach: The power of dialogue in educating adults. San Francisco: Jossey-Bass.

Villa, R. A., & Thousand, J. S. (1992). Restructuring public school systems: Strategies for organizational change and progress. In R. A. Villa, J. S. Thousand, W. Stainback, & S. Stainback (Eds.), Restructuring for caring and effective education: An administrative guide to creating heterogeneous schools (pp. 109–138). Baltimore, MD: Paul H. Brookes.

Wallace, D. (1996). Journey to school reform: Moving from reflection to action through storytelling. Washington, DC: National Education Association Library Publication.

Wallace, M. J. (1979). Microteaching and the teaching of English as a second or foreign language in teacher training institutions. Edinburgh, Scotland: Moray House College of Education, Scottish Centre of Education Overseas.

Wang, C., & Burris, M. A. (1997). Photovoice: Concept, methodology, and use for participatory needs assessment. *Health Education and Behavior, 24*(3), 369–387.

Watts, G. D., & Castle, S. (1993, December). Reform of and as professional development. *Phi Delta Kappan, 75*(3), 306–310.

Webb, G. (1995). Reflective practice, staff development and understanding. *Studies in Continuing Education, 17*(1 & 2), 70–77.

Webber, A. M. (1993, January–February). What's so new about the new economy? *Harvard Business Review*, 24–42.

Webber, A. M. (2000, June). Why can't we get anything done? *Fast Company, 35*, 168–170, 176–180.

Wenger, E. (1998). Communities of practice. Cambridge, UK: Cambridge University Press.

Wesley, P. W., & Buysse, V. (2001). Communities of practice: Expanding professional roles to promote reflection and inquiry. *Topics in Early Childhood Special Education, 21*(2), 114–123.

Wheatley, M. (1992). Leadership and the new science. San Francisco: Berrett-Kohler.

Will, A. M. (1997, Winter). Group learning in workshops. *New Directions for Adult and Continuing Education, 76*, 33–40.

Wilson, B. L., & Corbett, H. D. (1999). Shadowing students. *Journal of Staff Development, 20*(3), 47–48.

Wolfe, P. (1997, December). Brain theory applications to the classroom. Preconference workshop presented at the National Staff Development Council, Nashville, TN.

Wong, J. K., & Wong, R. T. (1998). First day of school. Mountain View, CA: Harry K. Wong.

Xu, J. (2003). Promoting school-centered professional development through teaching portfolios: A case study. *Journal of Teacher Education, 54*(4), 347–361.

York-Barr, J., & Duke, K. (2004). What do we know about teacher leadership? Findings from two decades of scholarship. *Review of Educational Research, 74*(3), 255–316.

York-Barr, J., Kronberg, R., & Doyle, M. B. (1996). Creating inclusive school communities. Module 4: Collaboration: Redefining roles, practices, and structures. Baltimore, MD: Paul H. Brookes.

Yost, D. S., Sentner, S. M. & Forlenza-Bailey, A. (2000). An examination of the construct of critical reflection: Implications for teacher education programming for the 21st Century. *Journal of Teacher Education, 51*(1), 39–49.

Yukl, G. (1994). Leadership in organizations (3rd ed). Englewood Cliffs, NJ: Prentice Hall.

Zeichner, K. M. (1993). Connecting genuine teacher development to the struggle for social justice. *Journal of Education for Teaching, 19*(1), 5–20.

Zeichner, K. M., & Liston, D. P. (1987). Teaching student teachers to reflect. *Harvard Educational Review, 57*, 23–48.

Zeichner, K. M., & Liston, D. P. (1996). Reflective teaching: An introduction. Mahwah, NJ: Lawrence Erlbaum.

Index